My Chicago Activist Life: From Ireland to Palestine 1968-2025

Bill Chambers

ALSO BY BILL CHAMBERS

Poetry

Huwarra Watercolors

Non-Fiction

The Muslim American Fight for Social Justice:
From Civil Rights to Black Lives Matter

My Chicago Activist Life: From Ireland to Palestine 1968-2025

Community Road Publishing LLC

Copyright Bill Chambers
Published 2025
First Edition

ISBN: 9798348587765

LCCN: 2025903675

Publishing, Formatting, and Cover Design by Zoey K.

Cover Photo by Bill Chambers

All photos are by Bill Chambers
unless indicated otherwise.

Paintings by Elaine Fleming

Special thanks to the *Muslim Journal, Electronic Intifada, Fight Back! News, Mondoweiss* for permission to reproduce their articles.

His previous books are *Huwarra Watercolors* (poetry and photos about his trips to Palestine) and *The Muslim American Fight for Social Justice: From Civil Rights to Black Lives Matter*.

*Dedicated to Colin, Sarah, and Devin
so you can know who your dad really was.*

"Do the Right Thing"

- Spike Lee

"I'm a Muslim, but I know it's not in the mosque that we will win: it's in the streets and the cities side by side with those who, whites included, want to rid the country of the racism that is eating it away."

- Malcolm X, Speech at the Oxford Union - 1964 (*Malcolm X at the Oxford Union* 119)

Table of Contents

Introduction 1

High School – People Against Racism (1964-1968) 4

College – Ending the Vietnam War (1968-1972) 11

Irish Republican Years (1990s-2000s) 18

    Becoming an Irish Republican 19

    Irish Northern Aid (INA) 21

Palestine Activist Years (2001-Present) 39

    Becoming a Palestine Activist 39

    Al-Awda Chicago 41

    Palestine Solidarity Group (PSG) - Chicago 44

    Chicago Coalition for Justice in Palestine 78

    Huwarra Watercolors 84

    Palestine Delegations 92

FBI Campaign Against Palestinian Activists and Rasmea Odeh (2010-2017) 141

    USA vs. Rasmea Odeh 148

Becoming a Muslim Activist (2010-2025) 195

    Masjid al-Taqwa and the *Muslim Journal* 198

    CAIR-Chicago and The *Chicago Monitor* 243

    Campaign Against Islamophobia 254

Black Lives Matter and Community Control of the Police (2013-2016) 322

Genocide in Gaza (2024-2025) 340

Resistance to Trump (2025-) 367

    Resistance Tactics 385

Conclusion 389

Appendix 392

    Palestine Support and Solidarity in Chicago: 2000-2016 392

    MuslimARC Releases Guide for White Muslims by White Muslims 400

Acknowledgments 403

About the Author 405

Introduction

This book represents one of the most important traditions in American life, resistance. Resistance to tyranny, oppression, fascism, racism, greed, xenophobia, misogyny, and Islamophobia. American values of treating everyone with respect, dignity, equality, and justice are the core of every social justice movement. The American Revolution, abolition, civil rights, anti-racism, anti-war, Black Power, American Indian Movement, Puerto Rico Independence, immigrant rights, workers' rights, LGBTQ rights, Occupy Wall Street, Black Lives Matter, End Police Brutality, Anti-Apartheid in South Africa, United Ireland, Palestine Solidarity are movements that have made America what it is today (or tried to stop it from what it has become). *My Chicago Activist Life* chronicles the most important social justice movements that took place in Chicago between 1968-2025, some of which will continue far beyond those dates. My memoir reflects the experiences of only one of the millions of people who have been part of these movements. When you read this memoir, don't think of just me. Think of the millions of Americans who have been involved in our great history of resistance.

"Pray for the Viet Cong who have died in Vietnam". Making this statement as an intention during mass at my Catholic high school in Detroit was one of my first public expressions of my politics. This book is a memoir about how this Catholic boy would become an anti-war, anti-racist, Irish Republican, Palestine, and Muslim activist. I won't be telling you every detail of my life. Although they might make interesting stories, they are not related to the theme of this memoir, my life as an activist. I will only be talking about personal details as they relate to my activism as certainly many of them influenced the activist I turned out to be. My parents were not political, and my father was a life-long Republican. But both my parents accepted people for who they were regardless of race, religion, ethnic background, sexual orientation, or how much money they had. That view of always accepting other people no matter who they are, being genuinely interested in them and the life they lead, has always been a key value I inherited from my parents. I have also been exposed to the opposite by my racist, critical grandmother and the block-busting and redlining that drove all the white people out of my neighborhood in Detroit growing up.

Somewhere I got my other major value, 'do the right thing'. No matter what the situation, even if it is difficult, it is important to me to fight against injustice, treat people as individuals with dignity, and always be on the right side of history. Whether it was in my anti-racism, anti-war, Irish Republican, Palestine solidarity, and anti-Islamophobia work so far, I am very confident that history will show that I picked the right side. Many people will say that it is hard to know what the right thing is. I disagree. If you have firm values in treating a person or people with equality, respect, understanding, and justice, there is rarely a situation where you can't apply your values and fight for the right side.

Throughout this memoir, I will be including articles I wrote for the *Chicago Monitor* where I was Editor-in-Chief for four years when I volunteered at CAIR-Chicago. The articles I include describe protests and events I was involved in and will give you more background and context. Some other articles are from *The Electronic Intifada, Palestine in America*, and the *Muslim Journal*, the latter where I have been a contributor for about ten years. For many years, I was an activist/journalist covering many topics that were not written about in the standard media. I decided to include many of these articles as they demonstrate the activities I was involved in and tell an important history of the activism going on in Chicago at that time.

My story starts in high school as that is the first time I really became an activist. There was an earlier time when I was a Barry Goldwater supporter, but that was when I picked up the wrong values to emulate from my dad. I have organized this memoir around my years in high school, college, and then major decades after that time when I became active as an Irish Republican, Palestine solidarity person, and a Muslim. I remain as active as I can in each of those areas, given some physical limitations. If you want to read more about my transition to becoming a Muslim beyond what I talk about in this memoir, you can read my first book, *The Muslim American Fight for Social Justice from Civil Rights to Black Lives Matter*.

High School – People Against Racism (1964-1968)

As I said in my introduction, "Pray for the Viet Cong who have died in Vietnam," as an intention during mass at my Catholic high school in Detroit was one of my first public expressions of my politics. The year was 1967, and I was a Junior in high school. The War in Vietnam was becoming more intense, and the opposition to it was growing too. Eugene McCarthy was the Democrat challenger to President Lyndon Johnson in the primaries, and his entire platform was based on being against the war. I would go on to wear a Gene McCarthy for President button along with my best friend Mike Quinn through my junior and senior years at the University of Detroit High School. Mike had very liberal views on this subject and influenced my thinking.

After my provocative verbal intention during mass, most said nothing to me except for one of my classmates on the football team, who threatened to beat me up. (He would go on to join the Marines.) Given that U of D High was a Jesuit run, all-boys school where rational discourse was highly valued, my comment shocked people (I also was a quiet, shy student), but it was forgotten soon afterward. Being an English major, one of my later intentions was a quote from the Matthew Arnold poem "Dover Beach" when I said, "Let us pray for the ignorant armies who clash in the night." Maybe they appreciated the literary quote, but I never got in trouble for that, either.

During my senior year, we had a religion class called Social Responsibility using a textbook titled "Social Justice" with chapters on different social issues of the time including civil rights and the Vietnam War. Unfortunately, the entire chapter on the Vietnam War was written as a justification of the war according to the Catholic principles of a just war. There was no alternative position entertained. I remember being shocked and angry especially as there was no open discussion about the topic in class. When I complained about it to my teacher, who was also a Jesuit priest I respected, I could tell he was very uncomfortable with the textbook and the position it took. This was the beginning of my rejection of the Catholic Church and my identity as a Catholic.

I also wanted to find a way of being active and doing something other than wearing a button and making intentions during mass. Another student from one of the all-girls Catholic schools and I started an education group called Students for Social Justice with the intention of sponsoring anti-war and civil rights speakers. They would pass the Civil Rights Act the next year, just weeks after the murder of Dr. Martin Luther King Jr. In 1967, the Civil Rights movement had built momentum primarily through faith-based groups. To be a white student in a 99% white high school, if you wanted to join an anti-racism group, you had to create your own. Our first and only speaker we promoted at a local college was Daniel Berrigan, a famous anti-war and civil rights priest who was very active in protests. His brother Phillip Berrigan was also active in this same way. The talk was well-attended as he was a compelling speaker and attractive to a Catholic audience being a Jesuit priest. The Catholic Church itself and his bishop saw him and his brother as troublemakers, but because of their popularity, they were generally left alone. But they were not left alone by the government. Shortly after the speech he gave for our group, Daniel and his brother were arrested for using homemade napalm to destroy draft records at the Catonsville, Maryland, draft board on May 17, 1968. They ended up serving two years in federal prison before being released in 1972.

My Chicago Activist Life

During my senior year of high school and freshman year of college in 1968-1969, I was a member of a group called People Against Racism (PAR). PAR believed the central contradiction in American society was racism, and the job of white people was to organize against racism in their own community. I was very excited to find a group whose views matched my view of the world. The group did anti-racism advocacy work in churches and community centers, plus took part with Black community groups protesting curfews and police occupation of their neighborhoods. It was a national organization started in Detroit with multiple chapters, including Chicago and Ann Arbor, Michigan.

PAR Monthly Newsletter

It has been many years of activism since then, and I still believe that racism is the central contradiction in American institutions, government, laws, and foreign policy. I have always wondered why PAR, an all-white organization that believed in education, advocacy, and protest within the white community against racism, seems to have completely disappeared from even the "Leftist" or "People's" history of America. It looks like a case of history being redacted to take out elements that didn't fit the dominant narrative. If you search for "People Against Racism" or "PAR," this is all you will find.

According to Frank Joyce, who founded the Detroit chapter of NSM [Northern Student Movement],

> Somewhere around 1965, a serious conversation began within NSM about the role of whites in what had always been a multiracial organization. The awareness grew that the more appropriate task of whites was not in helping blacks but in taking the antiracist struggle into the white community." In response to this conclusion, NSM split into two organizations, NSM and Friends of NSM (FNSM). NSM became a black organization, and FNSM became a white organization. Within about a year, FNSM expanded nationally and became People Against Racism (PAR). Often, with faith-based groups, PAR conducted workshops on race and racism, organized campus chapters, and took part in the broader New Left movement. ("The National Civil Rights Movement in Detroit." RiseupDetroit.org)

PAR was a very active group, especially in Detroit, and was likely one of the earliest manifestations of the "white people's role in the civil rights movement" and how to be good allies to Black organizations. There have been many books and leaflets written in the last 2-3 years on how white people can be good allies. [See Appendix: "MuslimARC Releases Anti-Racism Guide for White Muslims by White Muslims."]

My Chicago Activist Life

Here is a document that describes PAR's founding principles.

> **PEOPLE AGAINST RACISM (PAR)**
>
> We are at a point of new departure for the civil rights struggle. As the recent furore over "black power" has brought out, black people in the U.S. are increasingly determined to develop political power and responsibility for themselves and to separate themselves from white initiative and leadership.
>
> What black spokesmen like Carmichael, Strickland, and Harrison are saying makes sense to many black people; but whites who have been identified with the civil rights movement are left feeling offended, baffled, and paralyzed by this new state of affairs—much like rejected parents or defeated political parties.
>
> The question now is, What is the role of whites who genuinely want to be part of the struggle?
>
> A year ago, when the Northern Student Movement (NSM) wrestled through to its present position, the NSM Detroit Project split to form what, so far as we know, is the first white-oriented civil rights organization in the country—People Against Racism (PAR). Of its original objectives, these now have priority:
>
> - To support the black movement in those instances where direct support is possible.
> - To educate ourselves and others to the existence and manifestations of racism and to the analysis, objectives, and struggle of the black movement.
> - To raise the issue of racism in our own communities.
> - To confront institutions on issues which arise both locally and nationally and to take action.
>
> Last winter and spring (1965-66), PAR corporately or members of PAR:
>
> - Secured financial support for, and maintained indirect communication with, its black counterpart (ACME) and other people and organizations in the black community.
> - Launched a project to encourage the more accurate and inclusive teaching of American history in public schools, especially in white suburbs.
> - Supported and participated in the freedom school that resulted from the student revolt at Northern High School. On May 12, PAR held an open meeting with a black and white panel setting forth facts.
>
> PAR will continue to:
>
> - Maintain communication with the black community while leaving it entirely free to pursue its own way to power and responsibility.
> - Support and sponsor meetings to allow Detroiters to hear the truth on issues as they arise.
> - Continue to educate ourselves and others to recognize the racism implicit in our society and to act against it.
>
> CLIP & MAIL TO: P A R / 1101 W. Warren / Detroit 48201   Tel. 832-1890
>
> ☐ Put me on your mailing list & notify me of PAR's first fall meeting.
>
> ☐ Enroll me as a member of PAR. I enclose $_____ and pledge $_____ a month.
>
> NAME_____ ADDRESS_____
>
> PHONE_____

This is how PAR answered the question of, "What is the role of whites who genuinely want to be part of the [Black Power] struggle?" They should directly support Black organizations, when possible, but organize within the white community. PAR also believed that U.S. foreign policy was driven by racism, as was the Vietnam War. It was not a faith-based or socialist group, although it took many "leftist" positions. There is a good reason PAR does not show up in history.

> American history shows that good Christian whites worked with the Black Christian leaders of the Civil Rights movement to bring about equal rights for African Americans, passing the Voting Rights Act in 1967 and the Civil Rights Act in 1968. (Chambers, *The Muslim American Fight for Social Justice* 7)

PAR does not fit this version of American history, and neither do Muslims. There is also no place for anti-racist whites who believe America is a racist state, especially if they are not Christian.

In the summer after high school in 1968, I so wanted to go to the Democratic Convention in Chicago. Many of my friends in PAR were going, but I couldn't come up with a good reason why my parents should let me go, especially given that my father was a Republican. That summer, I had an orderly job at Northville State Mental Hospital in a separate building where they put all the 40 patients who had been institutionalized so long they had little chance of ever leaving. There were only one or two coherent patients. All the orderlies were African-American except me, the college bound summer worker. I watched two of the most important events that year on TV. The moon landing on a TV in the hospital day room covered by mesh so the patients wouldn't break it or try to change the channel. The second was the police riot that was unfolding at the Democratic Convention, that I watched on a TV in my small bedroom. (While I write this in 2024, there is a large protest against the Gaza war planned for August when the Democratic Convention will be in Chicago. The Gaza War, supported by "Genocide Joe Biden," has been going on for ten months with the assistance of the U.S. government. This time, I plan on being there.)

College – Ending the Vietnam War (1968-1972)

When I went to Northwestern University in Evanston, Illinois, in the Fall of 1968, I continued my anti-racism work given that Chicago had an active PAR chapter. One humorous event that occurred was when I covered the door of my freshman dorm room with photos of my heroes at the time, i.e., Malcolm X, Huey Newton, Eldridge Cleaver, and Angela Davis. I remember coming back to my dorm room one time, and the door was open, and several African-American students were standing around looking confused while my very conservative white engineering roommate looked terrified. They also stared at me and asked if those where my photos; I said yes, and they just shook their heads and walked out.

During my first two years, I regularly went to Chicago PAR meetings until the group disbanded because of the white activist focus on ending the Vietnam War. (More on that later.) We supported a lot of the Chicago Black Panther rallies and protests against police brutality. The last action we did as a group was putting up bumper stickers to Free the Chicago Conspiracy 7. (This was the trial of activist leaders of the Democratic Convention protest. The trial lasted from 1969 to 1970.) Our anti-racism was activated during the trial when the judge ordered the binding and gagging of Bobby Seale, a Black Panther leader, who they wanted to stop from disrupting the kangaroo court.

The most important National PAR action took place during and after Nixon's inauguration in January of 1969. I went to the inauguration with my PAR friends; and thousands of protestors attended, but media did not publicize it at the time. We stayed at a church the first night, and on the second day, police raided it, and everyone was detained. The DC police approach at the time was to break up large protests and just arrest people. We just traveled around the city, joining random protest groups. During the inauguration parade, groups of us protested along the route, and I remember yelling at Ronald Reagan driving by. They had the inaugural ball in six different locations with the National Guard lined up on either side of the walkway up to the door of the hotel. Couples in gowns, tuxes, and fur coats looked very nervous, walking the gauntlet of soldiers with guns as they went in.

After the inauguration, PAR members from multiple chapters joined a protest in Wilmington, Delaware. The town seemed to be owned by the Dow Corporation, one of the makers of napalm, as every street seemed to have Dow in the name. At the time, there was a city-wide hysteria over a group called the Black Liberation Army operating there. It reminded me of slaveholders fearing a slave revolt. The city declared martial law and a curfew, mainly in the Black areas of the town, outlawing any type of demonstration. The PAR contingent joined a mixed, mostly Black protest, defying the curfew and walking through the prohibited neighborhoods. There were no arrests, and shortly after that time, the city finally lifted the curfew.

Other activist work I was involved in during college included the anti-Vietnam War, anti-ROTC on campus, and later the women's liberation movement. I never wanted to join groups like Students for a Democratic Society (SDS) since I was already in PAR, but I did go to all their anti-ROTC demonstrations. That campaign culminated in the ROTC graduation protest, where the Chicago Police Department "Red Squad" traveled to Evanston to take photos of the protestors. (It was common during that time for the Chicago Police and the FBI to monitor protests of whatever kind and wherever they were.)

With the Young Socialist Alliance (one of the "New Left" groups), I also did a leaflet twice at Fort Sheridan Army base for a Chicago anti-war protest. We got away the first time, but the second time were stopped by MPs and ended up sitting in the main office while they called the district attorney to see if he wanted to prosecute us. He said no. I attended the "Bring the War Home" Weatherman protest in Chicago, arrived late, and was searched after it was over. The police were looking to see if we had lead pipes, given that we were dressed as Weathermen with blue jean outfits and carrying a motorcycle helmet. Several windows were broken, and police were hurt.

The Weathermen had the most sophisticated analysis at the time, seeing US foreign policy as racist in sending people of color to fight against other people of color, what PAR had been saying all along. The majority of white activists, especially those in college, had given up any focus on anti-racism work and instead became part of the anti-Vietnam War movement. As I indicated above, this was the main reason PAR disbanded, i.e., white activists were not interested in fighting racism in the white community anymore. During this period, like the Weathermen, I continued to support the Black Panther Party at their protests and heard the very powerful Fred Hampton, Jr. speak. He would be later murdered in his bed by law enforcement officials.

The other white activists in SDS and other "New Left" groups were now more interested in "joining the working class" to promote a Marxist revolution, which seemed a failed and hopeless strategy to me. Even then, there were all black unions being set up in Detroit and NYC because of the racism within the standard union organizations. The Coalition of Black Trade Unionists (CBTU) was founded in 1973 by African American union workers displeased with the policies and practices of the American Federation of Labor-Congress of Industrial Organizations (AFL-CIO), the nation's largest federation of trade and labor unions. Another powerful union at the time was the Dodge Revolutionary Union Movement (DRUM) and its associated League of Revolutionary Black Workers.

Daily Northwestern on the First Day of the Strike

In 1970, Northwestern was one of the many universities that went on strike to protest President Nixon's expanding the Vietnam War by invading Cambodia. The strike lasted for about a week, shutting down the university and all classes. My participation involved handing out daily papers put together on the strike, attending teach-ins and some time at the barricade blocking Sheridan Road. Some students had pulled up the iron fencing in front of the English Department building and put it in the road to block all traffic from coming into the university. When the intensity of the strike died down, the police came early in the morning and removed the barricade.

As I write this, students at more than 89 universities across the country, including 12 international universities, are setting up encampments to protest the war on Gaza. They are demanding that the universities divest from companies doing business with Israel. Many of these universities, including Columbia, University of Chicago, and USC, have had their encampments attacked by police. Officials at these universities (and, in one case, the mayor of New York) justified these attacks by saying that these protests were instigated by "outside agitators" and, in some cases, by Iran and Hamas. In the 1960s and 1970s, this approach was often used to justify the attacks on the protesters in the civil rights and anti-war movements. Then, it was Communists who were the "outside agitators." These statements seemed to permit any level of police or FBI violence against protestors. Recently, I spoke in support of the student divestment campaign at the College of DuPage, where my son Devin is a faculty member.

Near the end of 1971, I attended a talk at Loyola University in Chicago that would be prescient of my future Irish Republican activism. The talk was given by Bernadine Devlin, who was representing the Northern Ireland Civil Rights Association, talking about their civil rights work. During the question period, a priest interrupted and said she was only there to raise money for the IRA and his use of misinformation to try to undermine her work was shouted down.

During this time, I attended multiple very large anti-Vietnam war protests in Chicago and one in DC. At the one in DC, I remember hearing my favorite folksinger Phil Ochs play his anti-war songs like "We Aren't Marching Anymore." Sadly, he would go onto commit suicide a few years later in 1976.

Another important movement happening during these years was women's liberation. I was naturally a supporter as I had always believed men and women were equal and did not accept standard gender roles. At that time, women were challenging men in activist groups (like "why do they have to make the coffee and always take care of the kids") and forming their own groups. At the same time, men's liberation groups started. People today would find the need for those groups surprising. I joined a local one in Chicago. These groups reminded me of "sensitivity groups," which were also big at the time, where the participants would share their feelings with the group and get feedback. The men's groups were working on challenging the typical male roles and attitudes toward women by holding meetings and conferences. I was already questioning these typical male and female roles, and this was a place where I could express my feelings and beliefs. And no, there were not any circles where men banged on drums.

Irish Republican Years (1990s-2000s)

After my graduation from college in 1972, I moved to Boston with Marsha Flood (my soon to be wife) to get my MA degree in English from Tufts University. We lived in Boston for a year and moved back to Chicago because there were no jobs in Boston due to the recession. I got a job at Alexian Brothers Medical Center as a psychiatric assistant in their closed mental health unit. Eventually, I was promoted to Adolescent Program Coordinator and completed a two-year professional training program in family therapy at the new Family Institute of Chicago. During this period, Marsha and I divorced amicably; we did our divorce online, picking desertion by me as our reason – no fault divorce didn't exist then – and the judge was very surprised when I accompanied Marsha to court.

I remained at Alexian Brothers until 1979, when I was admitted to the PhD program in English at Northwestern University. My PhD was never completed as the dissertation committee did not accept my topic, i.e., Using Family Systems Theory to Analyze Modern Family Novels. Psychological criticism of literature at the time was all Freudian analysis, which I believed was very outdated and did not reflect modern psychological theories like family systems theory. Unfortunately, the Freudian psychological critic and the department head who hated psychological criticism disagreed. (The one female on the committee, a modern literature professor, thought it was great and publishable, but being a woman, she had the least influence.) During this time, I remarried Marsha, and we had our first child, Colin, in 1983, with the twins Sarah and Devin coming in 1986. While I was married to Marsha, I worked as a project manager in Technical Planning at Continental Bank; Program Manager, Imaging Systems at Ameritech Information Systems; Consulting Services Manager at Avalon Technologies; and finally, a Senior Consultant and Vice President at Doculabs, a consulting company specializing in enterprise content management strategies for Fortune 500 companies and state and local government.

This long introduction to this section is to demonstrate that during this time I was very busy with family and work obligations with the same progressive views but little time to be an activist. Marsha and I would divorce again with me moving out in 1996. This began the longest period when I was an activist.

Becoming an Irish Republican

The first major area where I was an activist was Irish Republicanism. It seemed to me to be an extension of the anti-racism work I had done in high school and college. For many years, I was an Irish Republican activist working toward a united Ireland and supporting, as one book called them, Ulster's White Negroes. As Bernadette McAliskey said in the foreword:

> Indeed, the title of this book, *Ulster's White Negroes* - which might strike the reader as a dated terminology –

refers to the headline of the *London Sunday Observer* in 1968 after a speech made by Finnbarr O'Doherty [book's author] comparing the plight of America's black ghettos, the people of South Africa and the nationalist working class in Northern Ireland. (O'Doherty, *Ulster's White Negroes* xvii)

Derry mural commemorating Bernadette Devlin and the Northern Ireland Civil Rights Association

It is fitting that Bernadette McAliskey (Bernadette Devlin at the time I heard her in college) would write the foreword as she was co-founder of the Northern Ireland Civil Rights Association modeled on the U.S. Civil Rights Movement. This was the movement for Irish Nationalist civil rights that was crushed by the British Army, who shot 26 unarmed protestors, killing 14 of them on Bloody Sunday in January 1972. The Nationalists tried non-violent protest for many years and were met with greater violence. Bloody Sunday was the beginning of the war between the IRA and the British government. (And no, it was not "The Troubles," the term mainly invented by British colonists).

Mural in Belfast

Britain showed their own version of colonial racism by declaring that all those shot and killed on Bloody Sunday were IRA members and the British Paratroopers were only defending themselves. (Currently, the British Government has passed legislation that bans all prosecutions related to the "Troubles," essentially providing amnesty for every British soldier and any other British officials "accused in the murders of more than a thousand innocent Irish civilians." (*Irish Republican News* 2/17/22.) Ireland is the oldest colony in world history, beginning with the English conquest in 1169. For hundreds of years, the British have called the Irish lazy, irresponsible, incapable of governing themselves, and sub-human.

Irish Northern Aid (INA)

For a time, I was a member and then head of Irish Northern Aid (INA) in Chicago. Along with multiple trips to Ireland supporting the Irish Republican movement, INA also worked in the U.S. to support the unification of Ireland by lobbying the U.S. government to pressure the British. The INA also supported Irish Republican ex-prisoners that the U.S. was trying to deport.

During this time, when I talked to Irish Americans, many had their own version of forgetting where they came from. I quickly found most wanted nothing to do with "Irish politics". In fact, they were hostile to it and were often some of the most racist people you could meet. This was coming from people descendent of Irish immigrants who were called "monsters... irrational, subhuman... a drink addicted moron... with his female counterpart sexually promiscuous" and incapable of self-government. (If you are African American, many of these characterizations will sound familiar.) The roots of Irish racism go back as far as the 13th Century in England—the English being the first settlers in the American colonies. (Curtis, *Black Muslim Religion in the Nation of Islam, 1960-1975* 63, 89) The American use of the word "plantation" originates from the English creating "plantations" in Ireland where English and Scottish settlers used the local Irish as tenant laborers. The descendants of these settlers in the North of Ireland consider themselves English to this very day. (Note: I will be referring to "Northern Ireland" as the "North of Ireland" throughout this memoir as I do not recognize it as a valid state or part of the UK and consider it occupied by the British.)

Mural in Belfast

Many of the Irish Americans I spoke to wanted nothing to do with INA, and it was common for us to be kicked out of the Irish American Heritage Center. What is happening here? Many other commentators have described the phenomenon of later generations of Irish Americans being accepted as "white" and their religion not disqualifying them from public life (e.g. election of John F. Kennedy, Joe Biden). They too, could forget about their terrible history of being "welcomed" to America and the ongoing discriminatory treatment of their compatriots in the North of Ireland.

"The Recruit" by Conor McGrady

INA used to have a booth during the Irish Music Festival at the Irish-American Heritage Center where we would have information on the 1981 Hunger Strike, supporting ex-prisoners and a united Ireland. The Irish Americans at the Center were never happy to see us, as I found the vast majority of Irish Americans did not care what went on in the North of Ireland. When the Good Friday Agreement (GFA) was in the news, then they were all over it. But even once that was over, they went back to caring little for a united Ireland or the violence still going on in the North.

One startling example of this negative attitude was the year Gerry Adams came to Chicago and marched in the St. Patrick's Parade. At that time, he was President of one of the largest political parties in all of Ireland, i.e. Sinn Fein. After the parade, a group of us drove him over to the Irish Heritage Center, figuring people there might want to meet him. But that was not how he was treated. He ended up interrupting some Irish dance recital for two minutes to say a few words and was hustled away with no applause or notice. Finally, the Center was even tired of us having a booth and even though some of us were members, they banned us from having a booth during the music festival.

My interest in Irish Republican politics was boosted by my first trip to Ireland with my mother, brother, and sister-in-law in 1997. Before then, I had been reading about the history of Ireland, the Easter Rising, and the War for Independence. Much of my focus was on the battles going on in the North of Ireland. Although I was sympathetic to the Irish struggle for civil rights in the North, I had not yet joined an activist group nor visited Ireland itself. At the time, I knew I was one-quarter Irish on my father's mother's side. (Later I would find out that I was a third Irish, a third English, and a third French.) My grandmother Rose was born in Port Stanley, Canada, the year after her father Bryan Briody, had emigrated from Ireland in 1862. My father and brother were only interested in the English side of the family; my grandfather Henry was born in Devon, England, emigrated to American in 1896, and married Rose in 1904. So, there was a family history of the Chambers family in Devon that my father and brother traced and visited. (One discovery they made was that my grandfather had a mother, Jane Chambers, listed on his birth certificate but no father. His mother died six months after he was born. This discovery was disturbing to my father.)

After I returned from Ireland that first time, I joined Irish Northern Aid (INA), also called Noraid, which was very active in Chicago and had about 15 people who would regularly come to meetings. Some of the members used to march in the St. Patrick's Day parade with a color guard and members dressed in black with black berets, masks covering their faces, and white gloves. After a time, the city didn't allow that anymore, so we just dressed normally, still carrying Irish Tri-Color and the Starry Plough flags. (The Starry Plough was James Connolly's Citizen Army flag.) There was usually a debate about whether to carry the American flag, too. I and others usually opposed that, but the "patriotic" members usually won. I took Sarah and Devin to the St. Patrick's Day parade twice. We always got a positive response from the onlookers. One of the times I took my kids I realized they were chanting "Troops Downtown" instead of the "Troops Out Now" that everyone else said. Whenever I bring it up, it's good for a laugh. We were never happy about St. Patrick's Day as our favorite rebel pubs in Chicago would fill up with drunken teenagers from the suburbs.

Bloody Sunday Commemoration in Derry

INA's activities were usually to protest whenever British officials came to town, celebrate the Easter Rising, and commemorate the 1981 Hunger Strikers. One time, the Black Watch Band came to Rosemont to perform. We set up a protest since the Black Watch were part of the First Paras, who were the ones who murdered 14 people on Bloody Sunday in Derry.

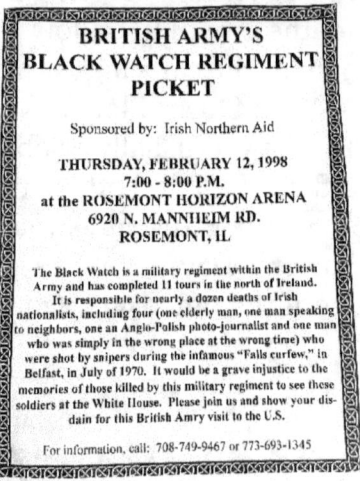

Leaflet for Black Watch Army Protest

I put together a fake program that we handed out to people as they went into the stadium. The front had a photo of the Queen honoring the Black Watch Band. Inside was the list of names of all the Irish civilians, including children that their regiment had murdered in the North of Ireland. Every year, even if there were only five of us, we commemorated Bloody Sunday, January 30, 1972, in front of the Tribune Building on Michigan Avenue in Chicago. We could only take about an hour of the cold handing out leaflets. For the 25th Anniversary of the Hunger Strike, I was co-organizer of the commemoration held at a hotel near O'Hare Airport that included about 500 attendees.

Bill Chambers

Chicago Bloody Sunday Commemoration

As a group, we often sponsored Sinn Fein MLA (Northern Ireland Assembly member), who would come to Chicago as one of their stops on a multi-city tour. One year, we had the Sinn Fein rep from Fermanagh come to town during his first trip to the U.S. I remember when we were showing him around Chicago how astounded he was by how large Lake Michigan was. It looked like the ocean to him. After speaking at a sparsely attended event at an Irish pub on the Southside, I drove him up to Milwaukee for a speaking engagement there. On the way, we were hungry, so I stopped at Culver's for lunch. After ordering a hamburger, fries, and shake and having it brought to him, he said, "Is this all supposed to be for just me?!" It's then I realized how ridiculously large our portion sizes are compared to other countries. No wonder we have such an obesity problem. He was able to eat about half of what he got. (I finished all mine, of course.)

Another major INA activity was supporting former IRA members who had served their time in Ireland, but the U.S. government was trying to deport them. Officially, they were here illegally since the immigration forms ask if you have ever been convicted of a felony (whether you served your time or not).

British Base in Crossmaglen, Armagh

If any of them had said yes, they would not have been let in. Loyalists threatened some and would have been killed if they had remained in Ireland. We held fundraisers for them and lobbied legislators to allow them to stay. Even during the time of the negotiations for the Good Friday Agreement, there were still federal prosecutors who saw them as terrorists and wanted to deport them. All of them were living quiet lives as nurses and tradesmen, and many had American wives and children.

Chicago Benefit for Irish Ex-Prisoners

Bill Chambers

One of the ex-prisoners was a young man in his 20s with an American wife and five-year-old daughter. While I was in Colorado Springs for work, I visited him at the federal prison nearby. The prison was very high security for the worst of the worst. Visiting him meant using telephones on either side of very heavy glass, and our visit was severely time limited. He stayed there for at least a year in isolation and was only able to see his wife and daughter twice, as they lived in the Chicago area. Finally, when it looked like his case could not be appealed, he agreed to be deported back to Belfast. On one of my trips to Belfast, he was having trouble finding a job as employers were not willing to hire any former felons. Most of the employers were Protestant or Unionist, and it was difficult for any Catholic or Nationalists workers to find a job. At least one of the other ex-prisoners we supported also agreed to be deported back home as it was preferable to being in jail or in legal limbo. INA and I personally provided a lot of support and funds for Coiste, the ex-prisoner support organization in Belfast.

Leaflet for Hunger Strike Commemoration

They did great work in providing services, job training, and mental health support. Later in the memoir, I will write about my involvement in establishing a link between Coiste and Addameer, the Palestinian prisoner support organization.

During the early times when I visited Ireland, the IRA, Loyalist groups like the UUF and UVF, and the British Army were all still active. There were still occasional bombings and people being shot by one of these groups. The British Army's presence was not as strong as in earlier years, but they still patrolled, did checkpoints, and had large installations in Belfast, Derry, and Armagh. On any hills in these areas there were surveillance towers watching 24 x 7.

Belfast Mural

On my many trips to Belfast and Derry, I noticed that the Loyalist and Nationalist neighborhoods were very segregated and clearly marked off by flying the Union Jack or Irish Tricolor flags. Some of the Nationalist areas had "peace walls", i.e., high concrete walls with barbed wire on top to separate the neighborhood from the Loyalist neighborhood on the other side. These were put up long ago when there was fierce rioting in the Nationalist neighborhoods where homes were often burned out. The walls were also high because the Loyalists would throw bags of urine, feces, or Molotov cocktails onto the roofs of the Nationalist homes close to the wall. These walls remain to this day, Good Friday Agreement or not.

On one of my early trips, I took one of the Black Taxi tours of the neighborhoods, each with its own murals. The Nationalist murals would usually be about the IRA, the Hunger Strike, Bloody Sunday, Bobby Sands, or other important figures in Irish history. The Loyalist murals were inevitably about groups like the UVF or UFF paramilitaries, praising Loyalists who had murdered Catholics or chasing figures like Gerry Adams to kill them. They tended to be glorifications of violence and showed very little history of the North of Ireland or England for that matter. Nationalists conducted the Black Taxi tours, and they supposedly had agreements with the Loyalist areas to drive into their neighborhoods for their murals. The tour I took was late in the day, and when we drove into the Shankill area (notoriously violent Loyalist area), the taxi driver told me to jump out and take a quick picture that we wouldn't be staying long. I didn't see what the problem was until I stepped out and saw multiple people coming out of their houses, checking out what I was doing there. Later, I would find out that any Catholic/Nationalist or anyone wandering into their neighborhood that they didn't know would be beaten up, shot at, or chased out. They would even look to see what road you came in on or left from their neighborhood to determine whether you belonged there or not. I quickly took my photo in the previously deserted area and, got back in the taxi, and we drove away. One of the creepiest places I had ever been.

For most trips, I would stay at the Belfast Hilton because I had points to stay there for free. Given it was downtown and one of the newest and nicest hotels in Belfast, the only cabs that would come, were usually Protestants or Loyalists. I was usually exhausted by the time I reached Belfast because I was unable to sleep on the 7-hour flight to London. I was then waiting an hour or so for my flight from London to Belfast, and then arriving in Belfast at 11 AM Belfast time (4 AM my time). I needed to stay awake at least until 9 PM to get my body used to the right time.

Once, on a flight over, I read about a play called "Ballymurphy" – a famous Nationalist neighborhood in Belfast – that was going to be put on by residents acting out many of the events that had happened to their neighborhood over the years. I decided I just had to be there. Unfortunately, it was at 6 PM that night, which meant I would be watching it exhausted and getting to bed late. Deciding it was worth it, the hotel called a cab for me, and I remember telling the driver I wanted to go to the Ballymurphy Community Center. It was starting to get dark, and when the driver looked at me like I was crazy, that was when I figured out that he was Protestant and likely never drove anyone there, especially not from a nice hotel. When we arrived, he said, "Are you sure this is the place?!" Probably because the building was dark, deserted, and surrounded by barbed wire. Being younger than I am now, I assured him that this was the right place, gave him a big tip, and sat outside on the steps, waiting for people to show up. Within about ten minutes, people started coming in and the door was opened. The play was one of the most amazing dramas I have ever seen. The whole play was vignettes of violent or tragic scenes that had happened to people in the neighborhood, played by people from the neighborhood and watched by many people from the area. I was the only one who was not from there. When everyone was getting in their cars and leaving, I realized I had no way of getting back to the hotel. There was no way a regular cab company would come at 9 PM and pick me up. Luckily, someone noticed my concern and called one of the Nationalist cabs in the area for me.

Most of my activism in Ireland took place in the years leading up to the Good Friday Agreement and in a few years afterwards. During one ten-year period, I traveled to Ireland every year on what I would call my "political vacation." I was usually attending a festival,

Free Derry Wall in Bogside Neighborhood

Bloody Sunday Commemoration, working with Coiste, and doing work for Sinn Fein. I attended two Sinn Fein Ard Fheis which was their big convention each year. During those conventions, I noticed how socialist they sounded, which was very different than when they presented at Friends of Sinn Fein events in the U.S. Given the bad connotation being socialist has always had in the U.S., this code switching by Sinn Fein wasn't surprising. The Ard Fheis just before the Good Friday Agreement was a very intense one. There was a great deal of conflict around joining the Unionists and the potential decommissioning of IRA arms. The great majority of members supported this new direction, likely a result of the extensive discussions Sinn Fein leadership had with all their constituent groups, including activists in the U.S. At one point, both INA and Clan na Gael (the original Irish Republican organization in Chicago) members were told there would be a meeting with a well-known Irish Republican in the basement of one of our favorite Irish Republican pubs.

Joe Cahill

He turned out to be Joe Cahill, a very famous lifelong member of the IRA who was on their "Executive Board". (A good book to read on his life is *Joe Cahill: A Life in the IRA* by Brendan Anderson.) He was in his 80s and was greatly respected. Sinn Fein had sent him to the U.S. to explain to activists what was being negotiated and their reasons for doing so. His trip demonstrates how Sinn Fein worked hard to keep the Irish Republican movement together. At the meeting, I was happy to give him a copy of the book *The Committee: Political Assassination in Northern Ireland* by Sean McPhilemy which had just been released in the U.S. but was banned in the North of Ireland. It was one of the first books that described in detail the system of collusion between the British government and the Loyalist paramilitaries.

Free Derry Wall Supporting Palestine

One organization I worked with extensively was the Pat Finucane Centre (PFC), named after a lawyer whom Loyalists murdered for representing Irish Republicans in court. The PFC is a non-sectarian support organization for victims of state sponsored killings. They were not lawyers but would work with family members and victim support groups to get justice for their loved ones. During all of the 1970s, 1980s, and 1990s, there were many cases of collusion between the British security services and Loyalists, where information was handed over to Loyalists to help them target Irish Republicans. The PFC would work to get independent inquiries into these cases that were often stonewalled or swept under the rug. Usually, the RUC (Royal Ulster Constabulary) or the PSNI (Police Service of Northern Ireland, renamed after the Good Friday Agreement) were either involved in the collusion or simply did only a cursory investigation of these murders. My involvement with the PFC was to help publicize the major cases they were working on by publishing information in the U.S. or having the INA support speaking tours of PFC spokespeople here in the U.S.

This was the time when I developed a very healthy suspicion of the news media. I would personally be at some event in Belfast or Derry, and then I would read the writeup in one or more American newspapers where the event would be described very differently. In the U.S. press, any activities of the Irish Republicans were viewed as supporting terrorism and any stories of collusion were completely ignored. One of the main reasons for this was that all the U.S. news came from reporters based in London or directly from the British themselves. AP or Reuters, which are used by multiple newspapers without their own reporting staff, would also use the London-based stories ensuring that all the newspapers were promoting the same British propaganda. This is the same approach used today in many of the major news outlets and cable services that cover Israel-Palestine news. The reporting comes primarily from journalists based in Tele Aviv. It's very rare they even have Palestinian spokespeople to provide alternative views. *The New York Times* and CNN are well-known for their Israel bias. With the Gaza War happening now, the Israelis have literally not allowed any journalists into Gaza and have just closed *Al-Jazeera* down even in the West Bank.

Visitor Badge for Sinn Fein Ard Fheis

One of my trips to the North of Ireland occurred during the very first election after the Good Friday Agreement (GFA). Much of that time, I spent in Fermanagh observing and helping with the local Sinn Fein MP campaign. I reviewed lists of past voters to create call sheets for other campaign workers to call on potential voters in the area. As is typical in these elections after the GFA, local city councilors, MLA (members of the Northern Ireland Assembly), and MPs (members of the Parliament in Westminster) are all elected using a "Single Transfer Vote" or "Proportional" voting system. Voters can spread their vote across multiple parties if they wish, meaning they select their first choice, second choice, and so on. They can vote for as few or as many as they want. Each area has a certain quota of election officials. The number of first and second votes a candidate gets counts more than others and, in each round, whatever second votes a losing candidate gets are transferred to the other candidates still in the race. This continues until the quota of candidates for that area has been met. So, even small parties may have an attractive candidate who can still win.

As an example, in the election I worked on, one of the Alliance Party members won a seat in Belfast. (The Alliance Party takes a middle position between Unionists and Nationalists.) I remember thinking this was a much more democratic voting system than we have in the U.S., where your choice is only between a Democrat or Republican, and third parties never have any chance. The argument against this system is that it leads to government by coalition, which, given the dysfunctional state of American democracy, would not be a bad thing. The Sinn Fein candidate I supported in Fermanagh did win and I was impressed by the organization of the campaign even though it was in a smaller, more rural area.

In the year leading up to the GFA and two years after, INA membership got smaller as most people were focused on the possibility of peace in Ireland and were not as interested in protesting or working with ex-prisoners. During that time, I also joined a new group called the Irish American Unity Conference (IAUC). This was the more "acceptable" Irish Republican group who were focused on lobbying the U.S. government for Irish Unity. They would participate in some INA events as speakers or in the Hunger Strike Commemoration but would mainly focus on lobbying. I saw that they were doing worthwhile work, so I stayed in both organizations.

After the GFA, the IAUC organized a sort of "reconciliation" conference in Belfast, holding meetings where Loyalists and Nationalists would speak with each other over common issues. The events I attended were always very tense, and once, there was a man whose father had been killed by the IRA sitting next to someone else whose family member had been killed by the RUC or Loyalists. These events were worthwhile attempts, but I didn't see how these few meetings would change the feelings of large communities.

At times, there was a push for a "Truth Commission" (reconciliation was considered impossible until the victims of state violence had been served) by the PFC and victim groups where an independent panel could investigate killings during the war and be able to offer immunity to those willing to testify. Both INA and the IAUC worked in the U.S. to try to get U.S. legislators to support such a panel. The British, who were key to any panel's success, were never interested in this because the collusion of the British government would have likely come out in any review.

We also found that the U.S. had no interest in pursuing this panel at all nor pressuring the British government to participate. It was as if, now that there was "peace in Ireland," everyone could move on. No comparisons to the South African experience with the Truth and Reconciliation Commission made any difference. Shortly after this frustrating time, I kept working with the PFC, but when INA folded, I left the IAUC. This brought an end to my Irish Republican activism.

Palestine Activist Years (2001-Present)

Ireland/Palestine Mural on the Falls Road in Belfast

Becoming a Palestine Activist

Earlier I talked about how Nationalist and Loyalist neighborhoods are usually marked with the British or Irish flag. One other common approach was for neighborhoods to paint their curbstones the color of the flag. When I first saw this on one of my trips to Belfast, I was very puzzled and did not understand the connection between Irish Republicanism and Palestine. Often, I would see Nationalist areas flying the Palestinian flag and the Loyalist areas flying the Israeli flag, which made even less sense to me given that Loyalists were typically very racist and antisemitic. Even the famous "Welcome to Free Derry" wall would be painted over with Free Palestine themes and it was common for Sinn Fein to invite Palestinian speakers to Belfast and Derry.

One time, Leila Khaled, the famous activist from the Popular Front for the Liberation of Palestine (PFLP), was on a speaking tour of Ireland, but the authorities refused to allow her to come to Belfast. We had to settle for listening to her speech from Dublin on live video. I knew that Sinn Fein as a party and the Nationalists in general were big supporters of the Palestinians. (Gerry Adams, head of Sinn Fein, was the first Irish politician to meet with Hamas leaders in 2006.) Still I was surprised to see so many Palestinian flags flying there at the event.

The more I talked to Nationalists, the more I understood the parallels between the North of Ireland and Palestine. Both Ireland and Palestine are settler colonial states: in the 17th Century, the English planted English and Scottish settlers on land belonging to the Indigenous Irish, who were pushed off their land violently and had few rights. In the case of Palestine, before the British colonial mandate in Palestine ended in May 1948, the UN passed resolutions allowing Palestine to be partitioned between newly arrived Jewish settlers and the indigenous Arab peoples from all religions who had lived together in peace for generations. The head of the Jewish Agency, David Ben-Gurion, proclaimed the establishment of the State of Israel, ignoring the UN partition plan. In that same year, the Israelis implemented their plan to control all of Palestine by force. During the Israeli-Arab War which followed, the Nakba, meaning "catastrophe" in Arabic, occurred when the Arabs were violently displaced from homes and cities they would never see again. The majority of the refugees ended up in settlement camps in Jordan, Lebanon, and other areas of Palestine. All of those settlement camps still exist, and these Palestinians have never been allowed to return. Both Ireland and Palestine are under military occupation and have had a history of groups resisting that occupation, including the IRA and PFLP, among others. Indigenous people are discriminated against, and both Nationalists and Palestinians are portrayed as terrorists.

Al-Awda Chicago

After one of my trips to Ireland, I decided to look for Palestine solidarity groups in Chicago. I was at a "Café Intifada" at a Youth Center in a near Southside Palestinian and Black neighborhood that highlighted singers, rappers, dancers, and especially spoken word poetry. All of these performances highlighted Palestinian and Black youth culture and solidarity. (I would later perform some of my own spoken word poetry at the Students for Justice in Palestine (SJP) DePaul and at the Arab American Action Network.) Someone passed around a sign-up sheet for something called "Al-Awda Chicago" – a Palestine Right of Return group. Al-Awda focuses on the right of return of all Palestinians to go back to their original homes in what is now the Apartheid State of Israel. At the time, I had no idea what the group was about but I signed up to check it out. The group in Chicago was small and leftist, but Al-Awda itself is a large nationwide organization, mainly in New York and LA.

Al-Awda Poster for the Tour with the Mexico Solidarity Network

Like what I experienced in Ireland, the Palestine activist groups were all about actions in solidarity with other oppressed groups. The more that I read about the history of the Palestinian resistance, the more I could see the parallels to the Irish

Republican resistance with the Unity of Ireland as the goal. The resistance in both places was made up of political arms like Sinn Fein, the Irish Republican Socialist Party (IRSP), the 32 County Solidarity Committee for Ireland, and Fatah, PFLP, and Hamas for Palestine. The military wings were the IRA, the Irish National Liberation Army (INLA), and the Real IRA for Ireland. For Palestine there was and al-Aqsa Martyrs' Brigade and A-Qassam Brigades for Palestine. Apartheid Israel has designated both the political parties and military wings as terrorists. The British and the U.S. designated the Irish military wings as terrorist groups, but that designation was removed after the Good Friday Agreement in 1998.

When I was with Al-Awda Chicago, I worked on a tour with the Mexico Solidarity Network at locations across Chicago, focusing on the parallels between the Palestinian freedom fighters and the Chiapas in Mexico. (Chiapas is the southernmost state in Mexico that at the time was controlled in autonomous zones by the Zapatista Army of National Liberation or EZLN.) We showed short films about each struggle and led a discussion afterward. One of the stops we did in the Pilsen area was well attended with a lot of supportive energy from the crowd.

Al-Awda Chicago also organized a rally promoting the right of return for Palestinian refugees that included about 500 people in Federal Plaza, Chicago. Out of this effort came a well-designed T-Shirt with stylized images of a Palestinian as well as a Chiapas fighter with "Intifada" and "Palestine Will Be Free From the River to the Sea" on the front. On the back, it said "Al-Awda Chicago, We Are All Palestinians," and the date of the rally was "September 2020." For a long time, it was very controversial to wear that T-Shirt, but it definitely got a lot of negative attention, mainly from counter demonstrators and Zionists. (Zionism is a Jewish political movement that believes all of Palestine was given to the Jews by God and that Apartheid Israel should be an exclusively Jewish state.) Even now, in 2025, Zionists and all pro-Israel people believe that the "River to the Sea" slogan is antisemitic because it means killing all the Jews and ending the Israeli State. In actuality, it has always meant freedom for Palestinians in ALL their homeland, and for an end to the Israeli Jewish state, i.e., there should be one democratic state for both peoples regardless of their religion or lack thereof. In this case, Zionists are terrified of a truly democratic state as they will be outnumbered by the Palestinians and not be the dominating group running the country and oppressing Palestinians.

Al-Awda Chicago Rally T-Shirt

During this time before 9-11 and during President George W. Bush's first term in office, I attended the largest pro-Palestinian protest ever held in Washington DC. There were thousands of people waving Palestinian flags from all over the country, filling the streets between the Lincoln Memorial to the White House and beyond. I have never seen any larger pro-Palestine protest since then. On the flight from Chicago, I was sitting with several Syrian doctors who were going to the protest. I remember being surprised that they had voted for George Bush and saw no conflict between their vote and supporting Palestinian rights. This would all change after 9-11.

Palestine Solidarity Group (PSG) - Chicago

The Al-Awda Chicago group collapsed when most of the members moved to New Jersey to go to Rutgers, and I was left as the sole member. After that time, I joined the Palestine Solidarity Group – Chicago (PSG) after being invited to join by one of the main Palestinian leaders in Chicago, Hatem Abudayyeh who was and still is Executive Director of the Arab American Action Network (AAAN). Palestinians ran PSG, and I remained in that group for many years until the leaders of the group were subpoenaed by a grand jury investigating "material support for terrorism". But that story will need to wait. The group dwindled in membership, and the US Palestinian Community Network (USPCN) was formed as a Palestinian only organization, which also greatly reduced some of the leaders and members of PSG-Chicago.

During the time I was with PSG, the group organized and participated in several Boycott Divestment Sanction (BDS) campaigns, protests against the Iraq War, and protests over the continual wars in Gaza. PSG was one of the many groups that mobilized in the lead up to the Iraq War in 2003. I always remember how well organized the planning was for the thousands who would show up to protest the War in Iraq. There were easily over a hundred different organizations represented in the planning meetings. The meetings were run according to the Roberts Rules of Order and had very effective leaders like Pat Hunt of Code Pink, who knew how to manage all the widely varied groups represented. One significant result of these meetings was being sure that Ending the Occupation of Palestine was added to the demands of the protest. During this time, there was the "Progressive Except for Palestine" phenomenon, where some activists would complain about Palestine being added to any protest because it wasn't "relevant". Hatem Abudayyeh, a PSG member at the time, led the effort to shut down these complaints, and no one was going to argue with a Palestinian leader of his stature.

Another innovation in tactics during these protests was to effectively take over major streets beyond the "approved" protest routes. The size of the crowd was so large the Chicago Police Department (CPD) had difficulty directing it, so the protestors would go around the police to access Lake Shore Drive from Michigan Avenue blocking at least one lane of one of the largest roads in the city. The police would try to block off that access road, and the protestors would just continue to the next one and get back on Lake Shore Drive. Finally, the police invented their own tactic that would come to be known as "kettling". They would close off all the roads where the march ended and trap hundreds of people with nowhere to go. In this case, I remember a friend Tom Burke, walking up to the police to negotiate, and was arrested immediately. They clearly intended to do a mass arrest, which they did for about 500 protestors. After a short while, they opened up a small path and let some people (I was one) leave. Since I'm counting, this was the third time I was close to being arrested and was not. I was part of the group that protested and offered jail support for those arrested. For all these protests and many more to come, people like Jerry Boyle and his partners from the National Lawyers Guild were instrumental in insuring many more protestors did not get arrested, negotiated with the police along the way, and were immediately on hand to give anyone who was arrested legal support and representation.

Many of the PSG campaigns were in support of the Boycott, Divestment, Sanctions (BDS) movement based upon the success of the BDS movement against apartheid South Africa. On July 9, 2005, "Palestinian Civil Society Calls for Boycott, Divestment and Sanctions against Israel Until it Complies with International Law and Universal Principles of Human Rights". This was based on an open letter published in ten different languages with all of the civic and human rights organizations in Palestine. This included all academic and professional organizations, tourism, sports, and the arts. The actionable part of the open letter is reproduced below. The full letter can be found at https://bdsmovement.net/call

> In light of Israel's persistent violations of international law and
>
> Given that, since 1948, hundreds of UN resolutions have condemned Israel's colonial and discriminatory policies as illegal and called for immediate, adequate, and effective remedies and
>
> Given that all forms of international intervention and peace-making have until now failed to convince or force Israel to comply with humanitarian law, to respect fundamental human rights, and to end its occupation and oppression of the people of Palestine, and
>
> In view of the fact that people of conscience in the international community have historically shouldered the moral responsibility to fight injustice, as exemplified in the struggle to abolish apartheid in South Africa through diverse forms of boycott, divestment and sanctions; and Inspired by the struggle of South Africans against apartheid and in the spirit of international solidarity,

moral consistency and resistance to injustice and oppression.

We, representatives of Palestinian civil society, call upon international civil society organizations and people of conscience all over the world to impose broad boycotts and implement divestment initiatives against Israel similar to those applied to South Africa in the apartheid era. We appeal to you to pressure your respective states to impose embargoes and sanctions against Israel. We also invite conscientious Israelis to support this Call for the sake of justice and genuine peace.

These non-violent punitive measures should be maintained until Israel meets its obligation to recognize the Palestinian people's inalienable right to self-determination and fully complies with the precepts of international law by:

1. Ending its occupation and colonization of all Arab lands and dismantling the Wall

2. Recognizing the fundamental rights of the Arab-Palestinian citizens of Israel to full equality and

3. Respecting, protecting, and promoting the rights of Palestinian refugees to return to their homes and properties as stipulated in UN resolution 194.

At this time in 2005, multiple human rights organizations such as Human Rights Watch and international figures like Desmond Tutu had declared Israel to be an apartheid state based on the treatment of Palestinians as second-class citizens even within the state and the laws that favored Jewish citizens in housing, representation, ownership of land, marriage, and many other aspects of life. BDS was a global movement especially effective in European countries like Ireland, Britain, and France. With the strength of the Zionist, pro-Israel forces in the U.S.,

BDS campaigns were particularly hard to gain any momentum in the U.S. But there were still successes.

One of the BDS campaigns PSG participated in included SodaStream, a product used to create your own carbonated drinks that had a plant in the occupied West Bank. There were multiple pickets in front of Target and Marshal Fields (now Macy's) to stop selling the product, letters written to management at headquarters, and stickers that were placed on SodaStream boxes in the stores warning the consumers of the boycott. We considered this campaign a success as the product was very popular for a short time and then sales nosedived. We also worked with the American Friends Service Committee (AFSC) on TIAA-CREF for their investments in Israel, which involved protests outside their Chicago headquarters. In July 2013, TIAA-CREF announced it was divesting $9 million from SodaStream.

Two of the longest running and most significant BDS campaigns were against Caterpillar (for selling mechanized bulldozers to Israel for the destruction of Palestinian homes, orchards, and farmlands) and the Petach Tikva Chicago Sister City campaign. Petach Tikva is a city built on stolen Palestinian land near the Palestinian village of Mulabes, and is the site of one of the most notorious Israeli detention centers for Palestinian prisoners. Apartheid Israel also has a long history of detaining and torturing Palestinians without charge, including women and children. (I will talk about this history later when I describe one of my trips to Palestine.) Even today, during the yearlong genocide in Gaza, the Israelis abducted hundreds of Gazans to use as "hostages" for any future ceasefire deal. As reported by Addameer Palestinian Prisoner Support and Human Rights Association, as of February 5, 2025, there are 10,000 Palestinian political prisoners; of those, 15 are women and 365 are children (https://www.addameer.org/statistics).

From this point onwards, in my memoir, I will be reproducing articles written by me or our allies describing how many of the protests and actions happened in real time. My hope is that these articles will give my readers a feel for how these protests were represented in alternative news sources. It was rare that any of these protests were covered in the mainstream media unless it was a very large protest with thousands of people. Even then, it was common for crowd size and the goals of the protests to be under-reported.

The first article is by Stephanie Weiner from *Fight Back! News* is describing the protest at the Chicago Sister City Office against Petach Tikva being included as a Sister City to Chicago. This action by the city was especially egregious as there were many protests going on at this time against the U.S. Guantanamo prison.

Here is a *Fight Back! News* report on a protest at the:

Chicago protest demands city government drop ties with Petach Tikva – Israel's Guantanamo

Fight Back! News
By Stephanie Weiner
July 12, 2010

International Israel Boycott, Divestment and Sanctions (BDS) Day of action in Chicago, July 9th. (Fight Back! News/ Chapin Gray)

Chicago, IL – Activists took part in the International Israel Boycott, Divestment, and Sanctions (BDS) Day of action by holding a demonstration at the offices of the Chicago Sister City Program July 9, to demand that the Chicago drop ties with the Israeli city of Petach Tikva.

Protesters were outraged when they saw the closed wooden door on the fourth floor of the Chicago Cultural Center and realized that Leroy Allala, the Executive Director, had closed the entire Sister City office early to avoid dealing with our protest. The group left a list of demands and continued the protest outside.

The crowd grew to 50 people, with many Palestinian flags tucked into the trees in front of the building. Students from the University of Chicago, DePaul, Wright College, and Northeastern held a very large center banner that read "No to Israel's Guantanamo." One activist who was dressed in an orange jumpsuit and had his hands handcuffed to educate the passersby about the torture that happens in the detention center in Petach Tikva said, "I know that this campaign is part of freeing political prisoners tortured there like Ameer Makoul and I am determined to keep up the pressure."

Last month, former police commander John Burge was convicted for the torture of hundreds of Chicagoans. Protesters made the connection that Israel's Guantanamo, Petach Tikva, where Palestinian BDS leaders like Ameer Makhoul are tortured, must be closed too. Maureen Murphy, in her closing speech, said, "This sister city relationship is a key link in helping Boeing, Caterpillar, and United Airlines do business in the Israeli occupation." She invited people to join in the call-in campaign on July 14 to the Sister City program office and for the next protest at the Sister City Festival at the end of August.

An important approach that this article illustrates well is that these protests and the BDS campaign itself were often linked with other common struggles at the time. In this case, Petach Tikva was tied to Guantanamo, where prisoners were also tortured without any due process, and to freeing Ameer Makhoul, a Palestinian leader who was imprisoned at Petach Tikva. In another common tactic was the inclusion of a protest with events happening in Chicago itself, such as Petach Tikva being a Sister City, but even more importantly, the campaign going on against Chicago police brutality that led CPD Detective and Commander John Burge to be convicted of torturing hundreds of innocent suspects.

The PSG led action was joined by multiple other organizations because of our ability to tie the protest to the calls to close Guantánamo and the campaign against Chicago Police brutality and torture. As the article says, the next major protest was at the Chicago Sister Cities Festival, where about 100 of us disrupted the festival where there was a Petach Tikva booth chanting slogans and handing out leaflets. There were some arrests at the end when the Chicago Police were called and when the police targeted Arab-looking protestors for arrest.

They were released shortly afterward. This was the last of the Chicago Sister City Festivals ever held. We also made sure that the Petach Tikva brochures on display at the Chicago Cultural Center were always missing when they were restocked.

The Caterpillar campaign involved persuading Caterpillar to stop selling militarized bulldozers to Apartheid Israel, who would then use them to demolish Palestinian homes and orchards. These sales made up only 1% of Caterpillar's worldwide sales. This destruction happened when Apartheid Israel was evicting Palestinians from the land where new settlements were planned. These bulldozers have been used to destroy an estimated 18,000 Palestinian homes. Multiple groups across the country launched the campaign and was active for several years. Both Human Rights Watch and Amnesty International had also condemned the sales. The Stop Cat Coalition that led the protests was made up of 50 different groups, including PSG, Jewish Voice for Peace, the U.S. Campaign to End the Israeli Occupation, International Solidarity Movement (ISM), DePaul Students for Justice in Palestine, Coalition for Justice in Palestine – Chicago, and many more. The main action was to disrupt the annual Caterpillar stockholders meeting held at Harris Bank in downtown Chicago. For a long period of time, different groups of shareholders would float resolutions to end the less than 1% of sales that went to Israel, but every year the resolutions would be voted down. Finally, the decision was made for more disruptive tactics. I participated along with ten others whose shareholders had made proxies so we could attend the meeting. The ten of us took seats spread out across the auditorium. Every few minutes, one of us would stand up in place, usually in the middle of the row, and shout facts about Caterpillar's supporting the destruction of Palestinian homes and orchards. We didn't stop talking until people came to throw us out. The series of speeches and people chanting while they were led out disrupted most of the meeting.

Here is a report from the International Solidarity Movement (ISM) about the action at the time. ISM has sent activists to Palestine for many years to protect farmers, stop houses from being bulldozed, and other supportive actions. Rachel Corrie was a famous 23-year-old ISM activist trying to prevent the destruction of a Palestinian home that was run over by a Caterpillar bulldozer and killed in 2003. To correct their report, ten protestors from multiple organizations were involved, including PSG, not just three from ISM in the disruption.

Caterpillar Annual Shareholders Meeting Picketed and Disrupted by Palestine Solidarity Activists

International Solidarity Movement Online
June 14, 2008

International Solidarity Movement: In Chicago on June 11th, more than 50 Palestinian solidarity activists from numerous organizations gathered to oppose Caterpillar Corporation's annual shareholders meeting. Caterpillar, an American company, is responsible for building and outfitting militarized bulldozers to sell to the Israeli army.

These bulldozers have been used to destroy an estimated 18,000 Palestinian homes, uproot hundreds of thousands of olive trees, and build Israel's infrastructure of apartheid, including the apartheid wall, settlements, and Israeli-only roads. Additionally, several Palestinians and American activist Rachel Corrie have been murdered by Israeli Occupation Forces using Caterpillar's equipment.

For the past five years, Palestinian solidarity organizations in the United States have waged a campaign against Caterpillar, demanding that the company stop all sales to the Israeli military. This year, activists picketed outside the meeting at Northern Trust Bank in downtown Chicago. Three activists with the International Solidarity Movement's Chicago chapter were able to get inside the meeting. Each of these activists separately disrupted the meeting, remembering Palestinians who have suffered because of Caterpillar's sales to Israel. The three following statements were given to the CEOS and shareholders alike:

"I am Samir Nasrallah from Rafah Palestine. My home was demolished by a Caterpillar D-9 bulldozer, leaving my family homeless and robbing us of our life savings."

"I am Ahmed Kasem, a farmer from Palestine. In 2001, the Israeli army used Caterpillar bulldozers to destroy my olive groves, the only source of income for my family. More than 200,000 olive trees have been uprooted using caterpillar bulldozers, impoverishing thousands of people."

"My name is Nabila al Shu'bi. In 2002, my family and I were murdered inside my home by a Caterpillar D9 militarized bulldozer. The attack killed 8 of my family members, including three of my children."

Each activist ended their statement by chanting, "Take responsibility and do the right thing!" as they were quickly surrounded and ejected from the meeting by security guards. Caterpillar Corporation will continue to be targeted for its support for the occupation and apartheid in Palestine until it agrees to end sales to the Israeli military.

···

As the article suggests, there was an attempt to make the protest more personal by quoting from Palestinians who had their homes, orchards, and families killed by the Israeli Defense Forces (IDF) using Caterpillar militarized bulldozers. The very next year, they held their stockholders meeting in Joliet at their headquarters, where large protests were much more difficult to organize. To this day, Caterpillar is still selling militarized bulldozers to Apartheid Israel.

Other targets of PSG protests were the Friends of the IDF (FIDF) and the Jewish United Fund (JUF). Both of these organizations raised millions of dollars in private money for Israel and its army.

Below is a flyer for one of the Friends of the IDF protests. What was typical for these events was the security was very high around the hotel, and no protestors were allowed inside the hotel. We were picketing in front of the hotel and at least were able to heckle attendees arriving in cabs and limousines. This picketing became a normal event at all of the FIDF and JUF events to the point that their number was reduced or held in less central locations.

The Friends of the IDF (FIDF) was also a very common target. They held fundraisers, often at large hotels like the Chicago Hilton or small night clubs, to raise money for the Israeli Defense Force (IDF) or the Israeli Occupation Force (IOF), as protestors called them. I could never understand how the IDF could be legally fundraising in the U.S. I always tried to imagine some another country, even one that is an ally, being allowed to fundraise for their country's army. There were multiple attempts to declare the FIDF and American Israel Public Affairs Committee (AIPAC) as "foreign agents" so they could not fundraise. Foreign agents cannot raise money that goes to a foreign government. All of these efforts were unsuccessful because of the very high level of support among politicians from both parties for Israel. Protests at these events were usually picketing outside or making attempts to disrupt the event inside, but these events had very heavy security, so getting inside was usually impossible.

ISRAELI WAR CRIMINALS FEAST AT THE CHICAGO HILTON WHILE PALESTINIANS HUNGER FOR JUSTICE WE ARE HERE TO PROTEST

FRIENDS OF THE ISRAELI DEFENSE FORCES (IDF) ANNUAL FUNDRAISER

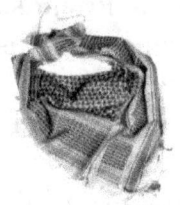

The guest speaker is an Israeli Vice Prime Minister and Minister of Strategic Affairs and was chief of the IDF in suppressing the Palestinian resistance to occupation from 2002 to 2005.

NO TO IDF KILLING OF CIVILIANS AND TORTURE OF PRISONERS, NO TO ISRAEL DRAGGING US INTO A WAR WITH IRAN, NO TO THE OCCUPATION - NO TO THE SIEGE OF GAZA YES TO JUSTICE FOR THE PALESTINIAN PEOPLE

Get Involved!Palestine Solidarity Group – Chicago www.psgchicago.org

Jewish Voice for Peace – Chicago www.jvpchicago.org

US Palestinian Community Network – Chicago www.uspcn.org

Endorsed by: Palestine Solidarity Group – Chicago, Jewish Voice for Peace – Chicago, US Palestinian Community Network – Chicago, Chicago Movement for Palestinian Rights, American

Muslims for Palestine, Gay Liberation Network, Episcopal Peace Fellowship – Chicago Chapter, American Friends Service Committee, Committee Against Political Repression

One thing you will notice about the flyer is the wide range of different groups that supported the protest. This strong level of solidarity was very typical for pro-Palestine events in the city.

The JUF often held fundraisers and sold Israeli Bonds to multiple organizations, including the State of Illinois. The money raised goes to support the Israeli government, the IDF, and illegal settlements in the West Bank. During one protest, I dressed up like a banker, i.e. dark suit, white shirt, and tie, and handed out fake Israeli Bonds while holding onto one of the PSG members dressed in an orange jumpsuit. This act reminded onlookers that the money also goes to detention centers where Palestinian prisoners are tortured. There were usually protests held at every event the JUF organized.

The following is a description of one of the protests against the JUF held when Trump was President that included the Jewish Voice for Peace (JVP) – Chicago. The protest involved a JVP report that documented money that the JUF had given to multiple anti-Muslim organizations. As my article points out, the JUF was funding anti-Muslim groups at the same time that anti-Muslim and antisemitic acts were on the rise. The article provides some information from the report. (It was common for me to cover protests for the *Chicago Monitor* when I worked there.)

Chicago Jewish Activists Tell Jewish United Fund "Stop Funding Anti-Muslim Hate Groups"

Report Details Jewish United Fund Ties to Anti-Muslim Groups

Chicago Monitor
By Bill Chambers
March 23, 2017

This morning, at a press conference held in front of the headquarters of the Jewish United Fund of Metropolitan

Chicago (JUF), Jewish Voice for Peace – Chicago (JVP-Chicago) called on the JUF to cut ties with anti-Muslim hate groups. The just released JVP-Chicago report reveals over $700K in donations from the JUF to Islamophobia network groups from 2011-2014.

The JUF is a not-for-profit social welfare and advocacy organization for the Jewish community and for Israel. They have already come under fire for their failure to denounce President Trump's appointment of Stephen Bannon, who ran the anti-Semitic website Breitbart News, to the role of White House Chief Strategist. This appointment was widely celebrated by white nationalists, who see it as an extension of the racism, Islamophobia, xenophobia, misogyny, anti-LGBT bigotry, and anti-Semitism that were all elements integral to Trump's campaign.

As detailed in the JVP report, a review of the JUF's 2011-2014 Form 990 filings reveals that the Jewish United Fund:

- Contributed $683,750 through its donor-advised funds to organizations identified by the Southern Poverty Law Center as "anti-Muslim fearmongers:" Daniel Pipes' Middle East Forum and Steven Emerson's Investigative Project on Terrorism.
- Contributed $100,000 to Donors Trust, a funder of both these organizations.
- Received $5.1 million from Donors Trust affiliate Donors Capital Fund. Donors Trust/Donors Capital Fund is identified as a key funder of the Islamophobia network by the Center for American Progress.
- These organizations are members of what the Southern Poverty Law Center describes as activists, which spreads the Islamophobic ideologies that

enable the promotion of anti-Muslim policies such as the current administration's desired Muslim Ban.

Representatives of this "Islamophobe Network" have also been involved with multiple figures in the Trump administration, including Stephen Bannon and Stephen Miller, who developed the Muslim Ban; Kellyanne Conway with Steve Gaffney's Center for Security Policy; CIA Chief Mike Pompeo with the anti-Muslim group ACT for America; and Attorney General Jeff Sessions who has won awards from both the Center for Security Policy and the anti-Muslim hate group David Horowitz Freedom Center. At a time when both anti-Muslim and antisemitic acts have risen since the election of President Trump, the JUF's support for these same anti-Muslim organizations is a complete contradiction to the prominently displayed slogan on their website: "Together for Good."

In its report, JVP-Chicago calls on the JUF to:

- Immediately cut off all funding to anti-Muslim hate groups through donor-advised funds or other funding streams
- Commit to rejecting future contributions from funders that are contributors to anti-Muslim hate groups
- Make a written and public statement addressing JUF's funding of anti-Muslim hate groups and affirming JUF's commitment to the above actions.

Leslie Williams – JVP-Chicago
(Photo by Eli Massey)

"In a time when working together to challenge hate and discriminatory policies is more important than ever, these financial ties show that the JUF's priorities lie elsewhere," said JVP-Chicago member Lesley Williams.

"As a Black Jewish woman, I am outraged, although not surprised, by the JUF's funding of such racist organizations, and I hope that all members of the Chicago-area Jewish community who believe in solidarity with marginalized communities will join us in calling on the JUF to end its financial ties with groups that target Arab, Muslim and Palestinian communities."

Daniel Pipes, whose Middle East Forum received over half a million dollars from JUF funds, has also described acceptance of transgender people as a sign of "a civilization in decline."

Stephanie Skora, JVP-Chicago: "The JUF's contributions to anti-Muslim, anti-queer, and anti-trans hatemongers speaks volumes about who they think belongs in the

Jewish community. Clearly, it is not people like me or other queer and trans Jews.

*Stephanie Skora – JVP - Chicago
(Photo by Eli Massey)*

"Their cowardly exporting of virulent homophobia and transphobia, so that their bigotry can be spouted through the likes of Daniel Pipes, is yet another nail in the coffin to the JUF's claim that they represent all Jews. They can't even pretend to care if Jews like me live or die."

The JVP-Chicago report closes by describing how the JUF, the Middle East Forum, and the Investigative Project on Terrorism share a common agenda of defending the State of Israel's repressive policies towards Palestinians. JUF's relationships with groups that dehumanize Arabs and Muslims must be understood in the context of its own agenda to justify Israel's brutality toward Palestinians. As outlined in the report, JUF President Steven Nasatir has asserted that Palestinians "revel in destruction" because of their "vile, extremist Islamic ideology."

*Hatem Abudayyeh – USPCN
(Photo by Eli Massey)*

"The JUF has never legitimately supported the rights of oppressed people, despite their claims," said Hatem Abudayyeh of the U.S. Palestinian Community Network (USPCN). "Instead, they have historically spewed Zionist propaganda; been apologists for Israeli crimes; and supported military attacks on Palestinians and Arabs in our homeland, as well as racist, political attacks on Palestine support organizing in the U.S."

JVP–Chicago is the local chapter of the national, grassroots organization that works for a just and lasting peace according to principles of human rights, equality, and international law for all the people of Israel and Palestine. JVP has over 200,000 online supporters, over 60 chapters, a youth wing, a Rabbinic Council, an Artist Council, an Academic Advisory Council, and an Advisory Board made up of leading U.S. intellectuals and artists.

JVP-Chicago plans to follow up on their report by reaching out to other organizations and individuals in Chicago's Jewish community, in particular funders, grantees and others officially affiliated with JUF in any way to urge them to pressure the JUF to stop supporting anti-Muslim and anti-Arab organizations.

****

Whenever any Israeli government official came to town, like Prime Minister Ehud Olmert (2006-2009) or Benjamin Netanyahu (who I like to call Netanyahoo), there was always a large and very vociferous protest. One of the protests of Olmert happened in downtown Chicago in front of a Middle East Studies conference. All attendees were met by loud chanting protestors and were given fake programs that listed the Palestinians killed in his two invasions of Gaza. The last appearance Olmert made was at the University of Chicago with a large protest of up to 1,000 people.

The first and last trip of Netanyahu to Chicago is described in this *Chicago Monitor* article when he came to visit President Trump. The cover photo for the article is one of my favorite photos of all time.

No Walls From Mexico to Palestine – Chicago Protests Netanyahu Visit

"Justice is Our Demand, No Peace on Stolen Land."

Chicago Monitor
By Bill Chambers
February 16, 2017

Three hundred Chicagoans rallied and marched to Trump Tower last night to protest the meeting of Israel's Prime Minister Benjamin Netanyahu with President Trump. The protesters represented human rights and immigrant rights groups as well as Muslim, Christian, and Jewish organizations. The message of the speakers and their supporters was to clearly draw the connection between the anti-immigrant, anti-Muslim, and pro-Israel policies of the Trump administration and the goal of Netanyahu to continue to deny Palestinians their human rights.

Tarek Muhammad Khalil

Tarek Muhammad Khalil from the American Muslims for Palestine noted the movement across the US protesting Netanyahu's visit. "This is not only happening in Chicago. Actions are being taken throughout the country – Boston, New York, Los Angeles, Sacramento."

He noted that at the press conference earlier that day, "Donald Trump reaffirmed the so-called unbreakable bond and the shared values as we know them to be, the shared values of racism and hate." Netanyahu clearly stated his conditions for a Palestinian state – Palestinians are to recognize Israel as a Jewish state and for Israel to maintain total security control of the entire area of the West Bank. Tarek pointed out that these conditions would mean "we must maintain the occupation, continue to build settlements, and the Palestinians must recognize our right to do so."

Dr. Mohammed Kaiseruddin

Dr. Kaiseruddin, representing the Council of Islamic Organizations of Greater Chicago (CIOGC) compared Netanyahu with Trump in describing Netanyahu as being one of the "most unjust persons in the world...Not just Muslims say that Christians and Jews are also saying that. Donald Trump throughout his campaign proved he is equally unjust and will be oppressive against minorities, whether they are Latinos, Muslims, African Americans, or any of the minorities. We don't care if Netanyahu and Trump are standing together. There are millions of Americans standing against them."

Lisette Castillo

Lisette Castillo, representing PASO (Proyecto de Acción de los Suburbios del Oeste) West Suburban Action Project, provided the connection between the Palestinian's experience and that of Latinx immigrants coming to the US. "Displacement when people arrive in this country in the form of deportations and raids and family separations. Our communities are targeted every step of the way. So we stand in solidarity with the Palestinian and Muslim community and fight for the respect of their communities, their homes, their families, here and in Palestine and in whatever other countries communities here may be from."

Eli Massey

Eli Massey from Jewish Voice for Peace (JVP) – Chicago emphasized the importance of intersectionality of all issues in social justice work. "To be committed to social justice means to stand up for those values consistently. One cannot attend a protest against Trump's Muslim ban on Monday and be conspicuously absent from the Palestine protest on Tuesday and claim to be an agent for social change."

As so many protests have focused only on Trump and his policies, Eli Massey reminded everyone that settlement building in Palestine had been going on long before Trump took office. "We must remember we are resisting far more than Trump or even the Republicans. When we fight for justice in Palestine, we are defending the sacred bond between indigenous people and their land as we do when supporting the Water Protectors in Standing Rock."

Suzanne Akhras

Suzanne Akhras from the Syrian Community Network brought home the fight for Palestinian rights and the connection with the police in Chicago. "When we fight for justice in Palestine, we are opposing militarism and state violence whether it's perpetrated by an IDF soldier in Al-Khalil or a cop in Chicago."

Don Wagner from the Friends of Sabeel, a Christian Palestinian group, described the "great peace deal" described by Trump in the press conference as just "another settler colonial Zionist plan to ghettoize and delegitimize the Palestinians."

The marchers stopped in front of the Trump Tower with Palestine flags waving and continued with statements from Claudia Lucero Soto from Alianza America, Suzanne

Akhras from the Syrian Community Network, Zaher Sahloul from the Syrian American Medical Society, Vivian Khalaf a Palestinian attorney from Khalaf & Abuzir, LLC, Rahef Awadallah Alkouk from the US Palestinian Community Network, and Abdallah Altamimi from the UIC Students for Justice in Palestine.

In a press conference earlier in the day, Trump had extolled "Israel as a symbol to the world in the face of oppression and an open democracy in the face of violence." He continued saying that Israel needs security "against people who don't value human life...America and Israel value all human life. The US will fight the isolation of Israel and is against all boycotts of Israel."

Netanyahu responded by saying we "appreciate you treating Israel fairly in the international forum and that we will resist all slander and boycotts." Both Trump and Netanyahu affirmed their opposition to the world-wide Boycott Divestment Sanction (BDS) movement and its goals to end the occupation of Palestine and support Palestinian human rights.

The Palestinians only referred to at the press conference by both Netanyahu and Trump as "teaching their children to hate Israel from a young age" and "who need to give up their hate" was far from the Palestinians described by the protestors. Those were the indigenous people of Palestine who have been oppressed for over 60 years and continue to fight for self-determination and their basic human rights.

This protest was another example of the tight solidarity between religious, community groups, and social justice organizations in the city. The quote from Eli Massey from Jewish Voice for Peace (JVP) – Chicago in the article demonstrates this principle, i.e., the importance of the intersectionality of all issues in social justice work. "To be committed to social justice means to stand up for those values consistently. One cannot attend a protest against Trump's Muslim ban on Monday and be conspicuously absent from the Palestine protest on Tuesday and claim to be an agent for social change." The protests against Olmert and Netanyahu were so disruptive no other Prime Minister ever came to visit Chicago afterward and their U.S. trips to Washington, DC were also limited.

There were also protests at this time against Boeing who had recently moved their headquarters to Chicago. As a supplier of weapons to Israel, Boeing was a target of PSG and other Palestine solidarity groups. The article also describes Boeing's involvement in providing weapons for two previous wars on Gaza. It was originally published in the *Chicago Monitor* where I was Editor-in-Chief, but a new publication called *Palestine in*

America had just started in Chicago by Palestinians. This year, 2025, *Palestine in America* published their 15th edition, and as their website www.palestineinamerica.com explains:

"Palestine in America Inc NFP is a nonprofit organization dedicated to creating print and digital magazines that highlight Palestinians in the United States. We also pride ourselves on being a platform for Palestinian journalists to jumpstart their careers."

The article on Boeing was my first article for them. I have added to the Appendix another piece I wrote for them on "Palestine Support and Solidarity in Chicago: 2000-2016."

Boeing Faces Increased Opposition On Weapons Sales To Israel

Bds, News, *Palestine In America*

The following article was originally published in Chicago Monitor: www.chicagomonitor.com

Reporter: Bill Chambers

For the fourth year in a row, anti-war activists protested outside the annual Boeing shareholders meeting in Chicago yesterday. For the first time this year, Boeing shareholders who oppose weapons sales to Israel have presented a resolution calling for the corporation to prepare a report detailing these arms sales. Boeing fought to have the resolution disallowed from the meeting. But they not only lost that fight, but with over 5% of the shareholders voting for the resolution, it will be brought up again next year to likely even greater support.

Why is there opposition to Chicago-based Boeing selling weapons to Israel? How is it different than any other country they sell weapons to?

Boeing has been a target of the global movement to Boycott, Divest, and Sanction (BDS) Israel for many years as its weapons were used in Israel's military attack against the Gaza Strip in 2008-09, during which 1,300 Palestinians were killed, and again in 2014 when over 2,200 were killed. In both cases, the majority killed were civilians. Boeing produces the Hellfire missile, AH-64 Apache attack helicopters, and laser guided one ton "smart" bombs used in these attacks. Israel's actions have been condemned by multiple international NGOs and humanitarian organizations, such as Amnesty International and Human Rights Watch.

During July of 2014, Boeing was a target in a nationwide call-in campaign demanding cessation of weapons sales to Israel, and 24 doctors and scientists published an open letter in a renowned medical journal stating, "In the aggression of Gaza by Israel...we witnessed targeted weaponry used indiscriminately and on children, and we constantly see that so called intelligent weapons fail to be precise unless they are deliberately used to destroy innocent lives." Protests were also held outside of the Boeing stockholders meeting in Chicago that year.

Seven major universities in the United States have passed divestment resolutions that included Boeing due to the company's ongoing arms sales to Israel.

This year several members of the Anti-War Committee (AWC) of Chicago purchased shares in Boeing to bring a resolution before the stockholders demanding transparency and a risk analysis of sales to Israel. According to Richard Berg, who submitted the resolution, "The Boeing board initially refused to submit our resolution to the stockholders, saying it interfered with the regular business of the company."

The core text of the "Shareholder Proposal on Arms Sales to Israel" states

> RESOLVED: Shareholders request that, within six months of the annual meeting, the Board of Directors provide a comprehensive report, at a reasonable cost and omitting proprietary and classified information, of Boeing's sales of weapons related products and services to Israel.
>
> We believe it is reasonable that the report includes:
>
> 1. Processes used to determine and promote sales to Israel.
>
> 2. Procedures used to negotiate arms sales to Israel, government-to-government, and direct commercial sales and the percentage of sales for each category.
>
> 3. Disclosure of sales and other arrangements with local security forces.
>
> 4. Categories of military equipment or components with as much statistical information as permissible, such as contracts for servicing/maintaining equipment.
>
> 5. Detailed risk analysis surrounding business relations with countries like Israel that have been accused of violating Geneva and Hague conventions and international human rights law.

In light of the flight of investment from Israel, the worrisome prospects of growth, including maintaining partnerships with higher education institutions, for a company that is at the center of Israel's controversial wars, contributing to the deaths of thousands of civilians and children; and the overall moral and ethical questions raised by selling weapons that contribute directly to illegal occupation, apartheid, and human rights violations, we urge you to vote for this proposal.

The focus of the shareholder proposal is not to prohibit Boeing from selling products to Israel but to bring the process out in the open. According to the AWC, most people have no idea that Boeing is a major weapons contractor. "If the public knew how many weapons were being provided to the Israeli military for its wars on Gaza, opposition to the weapons sales would grow," said Kait McIntyre of AWC.

The Boeing Board of Directors argued against acceptance of this proposal.

We recognize particular sales may be controversial to a small number of individual shareholders. However, singling out one particular customer for detailed disclosures would serve no purpose other than to allow those shareholders to second guess these important decisions to the detriment of long-term shareholder value.

The Board of Directors failed to respond to the reasons "one particular customer" would be singled out and how these sales can put the company at financial risk due to the impact of the BDS movement. Soon, when the vote would be taken, the Board would find out that it was more than "a small number of individual shareholders" who were concerned.

Israel recently completed their largest arms deal with the U.S. to purchase almost $2 billion in ordnance. Boeing manufactures the largest components of the bombs and missiles, including the guidance systems that turn regular bombs into "smart bombs." A report by Amnesty International showed that the bombings which caused the most casualties in Gaza came from Boeing's laser guided, one-ton bombs, the MK-84/GBU-31. Israel is purchasing 10,000 of these smart bomb kits.

With the current struggle between the US government and Israel over finalizing a ten-year military aid deal, there is much more attention directed at the large sums of money being paid to Israel when budgets for public education, housing, social services, infrastructure, and healthcare are being cut in states across the country. This is especially true in Illinois where education and social services funding has been cut due to the budget impasse. Democracy Now recently reported on the latest negotiations with Israel in this way.

> The Obama administration has proposed an unprecedented military funding package to Israel that could top $40 billion over 10 years. It is the largest military funding package the U.S. has ever offered to any nation. Israeli officials are reportedly demanding even more funding. The U.S. currently gives Israel $3 billion a year in military funding under a deal slated to expire in 2018.

> The increased pressure on Boeing to address its arms sales to Israel reflects the national movement questioning US spending on military aid to Israel, especially as these weapons are used by the Israeli Defense Forces to enforce a military occupation and to kill Palestinian civilians.

Sarah Simmons, an AWC member, also described the increased focus the actions of the government of Israel are getting in the media and among human rights activists.

"The actions of the Israeli government are coming under increased scrutiny. Several major universities and investment firms have divested from companies profiting from the occupation. The human rights of Palestinians have become a topic in the presidential campaign."

In the past several years, members of the AWC purchased shares in the Boeing Company to bring a resolution before the stockholders. They joined together with the Interfaith Council on Corporate Responsibility (ICCR). Sister Gwen Farry of ICCR and the 8th Day Center for Justice spoke in favor of the resolution during the company meeting.

At today's board meeting, AWC was also joined by a group of indigenous Lumad activists from the Philippines. In their traditional lands on the island of Mindanao, the Lumad people have also been victimized by the U.S. "war on terror." Boeing produces drones called Scan Eagles, which have been used in targeted assassinations there.

When the votes were counted, the Board of Directors reported that 5% of their stockholders voted in favor of the resolution. The directors had stated that 88% of the stockholders had cast votes.

The company has a threshold for shareholder activism. To continue to press an issue, a resolution must achieve 3% of the votes. Newland Smith said, "With 5%, we can continue to press this issue next year. By then, we hope to reach the next threshold, which is 6%."

The AWC and their supporters will once again be back at the Boeing shareholders meeting next year as a part of the national movement protesting US weapons to Israel.

This article talks about the ongoing campaign to stop arms sales to Israel and ties Boeing to this campaign by reminding the public that this new company for Chicago had sold many of the arms to Israel used to kill 2,200 Palestinians in Gaza in 2014. The protest also reflected one of the BDS strategies at the time to pressure companies like Caterpillar, discussed above, and Boeing to end their sales/investments in Israel. The focus was to bring shareholder proposals to the shareholder's meeting to highlight and publicize the issue and, failing that, to disrupt the shareholders meeting if possible. Unfortunately, this strategy did not work as far as affecting the companies' actions, but it did publicize the complicity between American companies and Apartheid Israel.

Chicago Coalition for Justice in Palestine

PSG was heavily involved with the Chicago Coalition for Justice in Palestine, organizing the protests against the multiple invasions of Gaza by the Israeli Occupation Forces. At this time in 2025, the current war on Gaza began on October 7, 2024, with the Palestinian incursion into Apartheid Israel; it has reached the level of genocide, with over 48,000 Palestinians killed, with more than half being women and children. Much of Gaza has been destroyed as the Israelis have targeted all parts of Gaza and destroyed hospitals, schools, and mosques. Finally, there has been a global response to these war crimes.

But there have been major invasions of Gaza in 2008-2009, 2012, 2014, and 2021, with the worst in terms of civilian casualties being over 2,000 in 2014. But in every Gaza war, there has been the destruction of Gaza's infrastructure, including schools, hospitals, clinics, homes, and power plants. It is also important to remember that during all of these invasions, Gaza was under siege and cut off from the outside world. The protests we organized against each Gaza war were multiple actions over the time of the war, usually starting at Federal Plaza and ending outside the Israeli Consulate, which was in an office building near the Chicago River and Michigan Avenue. At one point, tiring of the continual protests outside the office building (probably from other tenants), the Consulate moved to the Ogilvie Transportation Center on an upper floor where they could not be reached, given the heavy security at the train station. All that this move did was create chaos at the train station when protests would be called during rush hour. These protests were always well attended, with anywhere between 500 and 5,000 people.

In 2014, protests about the civilians killed in the Gaza war were combined with another protest of the JUF, which was helping fund the war. In this case, unlike the JUF protest described above in 2017, this protest was directly tied to a large number of protests against the war on Gaza, the worst invasion so far. The tactics used this time were more aggressive in that Jewish Voice for Peace and Jews for Justice in Palestine were able to infiltrate the venue and completely disrupt the speeches of Mayor Rahm Emmanuel and former Israeli ambassador to the U.S. Michael Oren.

Chicago Protesters Disrupt Israel Fundraiser

Protesters march in support of Palestinians killed in Gaza and the West Bank.

By Bill Chambers
Chicago Monitor
August 22, 2014

Attendees of the Jewish United Fund "Chicago Stands With Israel" fundraiser at the Chicago Hilton last night were met with over 250 protestors picketing outside as well as a die-in representing the continued Palestinian civilian deaths in Gaza. What they didn't expect was multiple protestors from Jewish Voice for Peace and Jews for Justice in Palestine inside the venue disrupting the speeches of Mayor Rahm Emmanuel and former Israeli ambassador to the U.S. Michael Oren.

The Jewish United Fund / Jewish Federation of Metropolitan Chicago held a fundraiser at the Chicago Hilton last night – part of the "Israel Emergency Campaign" needed because "the prolonged conflict with Hamas has created intense humanitarian needs in Israel".

Photo by Ali Abunimah

The Students for Justice in Palestine (SJP) – Chicago organized a die-in on the sidewalk in front of the main entrance to the hotel to highlight the over 2,100 (including over 500 children) killed and over 10,000 injured in Gaza since the assault began on July 8th. News media coverage has been scant since the ending of the last ceasefire on August 20th, so the activists were also emphasizing the 30 Palestinians including 10 children that Israeli forces have killed over the last two days. Throughout the event, protesters organized within the last three days by the Chicago Coalition for Justice in Palestine marched and chanted outside the Hilton in support of the Palestinians in Gaza and those killed and injured in the West Bank.

Late yesterday, it was announced that Mayor Rahm Emmanuel and Senator Mark Kirk were attending the function along with the keynote speaker, Michael Oren, former Israeli Ambassador to the U.S. Several activists from Jewish Voice for Peace (JVP) – Chicago, Jews for Justice in Palestine, and the Chicago Anti-War Committee interrupted all the speakers multiple times. The Electronic Intifada has published a video of the activists disrupting the event. Two JVP-Chicago activists interrupted Mayor Rahm Emmanual as he was announcing a $5,000 gift from him and his wife to the Israel Emergency Fund. The JVP activists stood up, shouting "We are Jews; Shame on You! Stop killing children now!" An attendee took away a sign they held, and they were threatened with arrest unless they left. Michael Oren's speech was also disrupted multiple times by activists holding a banner and chanting. All the activists were expelled from the fundraiser without arrests.

Outside, multiple speakers emphasized the injustice of the continued assault on Gaza. Nashisha Alam from SJP-Chicago said, "While they sip cocktails and raise funds for war criminals, we are here supporting the people of Palestine...They are inside listening to Michael Oren trying to justify the killing of civilians." Kait McIntyre from the Chicago Anti-War Committee and one of the activists arrested during a recent sit-in at Boeing headquarters described the outrage that "in Chicago with the largest Palestinian community in the country, Boeing is providing weapons to Israel to kill Palestinians in Gaza." Hatem Abudayyeh from the US Palestinian Community Network (USPCN) – Chicago reminded the crowd of major victories when all activists in the community stand together. He described activists in Oakland who prevented an Israeli ship from unloading its cargo. "The majority black dockworkers of the International Longshore and Warehouse Union refused to cross the community picket line." The fact that the mayor of Chicago made a prominent appearance at the event didn't go without comment. "How is it that Rahm Emmanuel, as our mayor, is taking sides in this political conflict?" Abudayyeh continued to emphasize one of the main messages of the protesters – "We are here to continue to tell the truth to the American people; this is the truth about Israel – they want to continue the siege of Gaza and continue the occupation."

As with many of the protests about Palestine in Chicago over the last month, this one was no different in having little local media attention. There was only one local outlet, CBS-News, who was there filming, and a scan of the local news media shows no reports at all, including CBS news. Even the fact that Mayor Rahm Emmanuel had decided not only to attend a high-profile fundraiser for Israel but also to give a speech about a sizable donation he was making to the Israel Emergency

Campaign does not even merit a few lines in local coverage.

Since the end of the last ceasefire, the main media outlets have moved on to cover important stories like Ferguson and Iraq, but the complete lack of reporting on the continued deaths and injuries of Palestinians in Gaza is deafening. It has been up alternative media like the [Electronic Intifada](), [Palestine in America](), and the [Chicago Monitor]() to provide coverage of issues that clearly matter to thousands of Chicagoans.

As is described at the end of the article, the main media outlets ignored all the protests during this time, and if they mentioned the ones with more than a thousand people, the number of marches was greatly reduced to "a few hundred." A common news tactic was to pick out one marcher who had a sign attacking Jews and focus on the antisemitism of the march. Usually these people were not members of the organizing groups and were surrounded by the march monitors and asked to remove their sign. In many cases, it is likely that the person was placed there as a provocateur to besmirch the goals of the march, i.e., end the war on Gaza. The marches were effective at keeping the public aware of the killing of Palestinian men, women, and children that was happening and exerted pressure on the Obama Administration at the time to push Israel to end the war. The Palestine activists now knew that even a "liberal" Democratic President would do little to stop Israel's murderous policies. It was events like this where Israel was allowed free rein to conduct their war on Palestinians to the eventual genocide in Gaza that happened in 2024-2025.

For a history of Palestine activism in Chicago, see the Appendix for my article in *Palestine in America*, "Palestine Support and Solidarity in Chicago: 2000-2016".

Huwarra Watercolors

In 2009, I published a book, *Huwarra Watercolors*, that documented, in poetry and photos, the experiences of my four trips to Palestine. In 2012, I published a Second Edition with this description:

> *Huwarra Watercolors* was originally published after my 2009 trip to Palestine when I stayed in Huwarra and worked with the Addameer Palestinian Prisoner Support and Human Rights Association. The poetry describes my experiences during that trip and many others. Over ten years later, conditions for the Palestinians have only worsened, and the world's longest military occupation continues. Palestinians remain steadfast and resist the destruction of their homeland. I can only hope that republishing my book will help inspire the next generation of Palestine activists.
>
> Free Free Palestine
>
> Bill Chambers - April 2022

I will be discussing these trips in detail later, but the following are some of the poems I wrote about the Gaza war. These are meant to be spoken word poems so to get the full effect read them out loud.

Bill Chambers

Taxi to Gaza

I am from Gaza
not Jordan, not Ramallah, not ZigZigLand
Gaza

Me
the white-haired suitman,
I knew where he was from.
Knew the children on the beach
blasted by an American shell.
Knew the fishing boats
rammed off the shore.
Knew the white apartment buildings
splintered into a maze of crosses.
Knew his family in a country of families,
without food and medicine.
And this was before the invasion.

A thirty-year exile,
each day returning home.
Where the visiting hours were twice a year
Where there was no work-study program.
No time in the exercise yard.
No barred window looking to the sea.
No escape from forced open doors.
No time off for good behavior.
No conjugal visits.
No pardons.

And this was before the invasion.

Did you watch the girl wandering
alone in the rubble of the factory?
Did you watch the white arc
of shells over the city?
Did you look through the pockmarked hospital window

and see the patient tents beyond?
Did you see the fingers of men through the chain link fence
grasping for food?
Did you listen to the scream of the medic
when he finally reached the four boys?
Was it your family's home with the flag flying high
over the pile of shattered concrete?

And now the invasion is over.

Have you returned and found them?
They are no longer there.
There are no more bombed schools,
dead medics, and blasted children.
Now only suitmen talking about tunnels,
not about aid for Gaza,
envoys for Gaza,
democracy for Gaza,
freedom for Gaza.

And now the invasion is over.

When you find them,
return to us.
They are here now
Holding the yellow tape across the door of the embassy,
Holding the bullhorn at the window of the occupied building,
Holding the mike singing songs of Palestine,
Holding the flag, the fifty-foot flag,
Down the streets of Pilsen.

We
are from Gaza.

Gaza Dead Sea

Convoy hospitals with
Palestinian flags flapping,
moon and red sickles flying,
round about, rounding
Egyptian dictators, pharaohs
and their new riot-geared
slaves, blocking
every way.

Red dead sea parts
or not, while
tunnel life crawls
on, delivering daily gas, soap, dignity,
defiance, resistance, radiators,
meantime meds in trucks, trucks,
trucks circle Aqba and
wait, circle Syria and wait
for their Moses.

Remember Operation Justified
Vengeance on
healthcare warehouses
short in over a hundred
basic medical items
even before forty-eight
percent white christmas clinics
phosphorus damaged.

No healthcare
No health
No care
No Obamacare
No Obama
doesn't care
No one

cares, but the Gaza dead
see and
remember.

Annual anniversary of
silence, annually
aversive to speaking
out. Remember red
dead sea of Gaza parted,
drowning four hundred dead
children, one thousand dead
parents

Remember red
dead sea of Gaza parted,
drowning memories of
mujadin in Khan Younis and
one hundred eleven dead, one
thousand nine hundred fifty
six date forgotten,
until now.

Moses message of deliverance
remembers, Mandela marchers
remember, Selma freedom
marchers remember, free
at last Egypt, free
at last Gaza, free
at last the West Bank, freedom
last for Palestine from
the river to the sea.

Bill Chambers

The next poem was written during the time of the Arab Spring when another attack on Gaza was going on. During this time, there was no problem getting immediate updates on the war from friends on social media. This poem is a good example of this happening in real-time.

No Fly Zones

Flipping, flickering, photos
flash, heads line
up, videos in bed,
dead with rebel corpses,
Gaddafi troops shell Benghazi,
Egypt military bans union protests,
Saudi troops shatter Pearl Square,
scroll,
scroll,
scrolling,
Yemen men, boys shot by snipers in Sana.
Still scrolling,
I "Like" nothing, zoning
zoning out.

Gaza - 3 minutes ago, comment on comment,
"Reports of 5 dead in the last attack on Gaza."

Another attack, another Operation Casket,
Operation Overlook, Operation Odyssey
Midnight in the Garden of Evil.
Even poetry no anesthetic for this.

Extension of the Libyan no fly
zone, beyond what we all, the Arab
in League with, expected. Naval base blasted,
in Tripoli pirates have airboats.

Gaza - again

My Chicago Activist Life

"20 minutes ago...4 kids, a woman
and 10 others injured!"

Like a jet pilot, visor down, looking
I see the blinking cross and click
the link. Noor.
Noor from Gaza.
I send a Friend Request.

Stop killing civilians.
No French flying zones,
no U.S. drones,
no Zionist zones.

Friend Request Accepted
2 minutes ago,
from Gaza.
She accepted a request
from me, from my doesn't-care-zone
America, my tax dollars bombing her,
now.

Noor - 1 minute ago.
"Last attack on Al-Helo family, kids,
8 years old Ahmed Hamed
11 years old Mohammad Jihad
15 years old Yassir Aed
20 years old Mohammad Saber Hararh
the father, 50 years old, Yassir Hamed."
Rest in Peace. Shaheeds.

Posts pile up like Afghan
wedding party guests, like Iraqis
in Wikileaks war logs, like white-phosphored
Gazan patients, all meant-to-be
mistakes, no fly, do kill zones.

Noor - 1 minute ago
"I just got news...2 of the martyrs
in the last attack are my cousins!"

47 comments, all strangers, all sorry.
I post - so sorry for your loss - we will remember them,
all Palestinians murdered with malice, here,
everywhere around the world.

No Tahir Square.
No Pearl Square.
Martyrs Square,
square prison miles
of sky death, soccer players, students
in recess, fishing boats floating, all
blasted by IDF manned
drone planes, flies with a thousand
blind eyes at the controls.
Posting I say,
No fly zone over Gaza,
over Al-Quds,
over Banks West and East.

Pounding keys I say,
enforce blanket BDS bombing.

We need no Tunisian fruit vendor
to burn himself alive. Leave
your screens. You,
all of you, are invited to an Event,
an out-in-the-streets Event -

Create Three, Four, Many Poetic Intifadas.

RSVP - Attending.

Palestine Delegations

One major activity of PSG was to organize delegations of students, activists, teachers, and professors to go on a two-week trip to Palestine in August and meet with a variety of Palestinian-led organizations. The idea of the delegation was to enable participants to come back and become well-informed activists for the independence of Palestine. Many of those who went joined organizations like Al-Awda NY/NJ, the American Friends Service Committee, Sumoud (Palestine prisoner support group), and Palestine Solidarity Groups in various cities, including Chicago.

When the delegation returned from the trip it was common that PSG would organize presentations at college campuses of the experience. Almost everyone who went and experienced the harsh occupation and treatment of Palestinians was forever changed. A common itinerary would be to visit Jerusalem (Al-Quds), Ramallah, Bethlehem, Haifa, Acre, Nablus, Nazareth, Beit Omar, and Hebron. We typically stayed and ate in Palestinian family homes, so the cost of the trip was the plane flight and to reimburse those families for room and board. The majority of time was spent with Palestinian civic organizations in the West Bank and the Apartheid State of Israel itself. During this time, Gaza was under siege, and it was not possible for us or for any activists to go there.

Before leaving on the trip, we gave everyone an orientation to Palestine including the political situation, the groups we were going to meet with, and cultural sensitivity lessons (like don't wear shorts and for women no tank tops). Some areas of Palestine are more conservative than others in dress and general behavior. We also went over security precautions as at that time (and still today) the Israelis would question any group coming over, any Palestinians, other Arabs, and African Americans for hours at Ben Gurion airport. They would be immediately suspicious of anyone who said they were visiting the West Bank.

Our recommendations would include not having anything relating to Palestine in your bags (searching bags was very common); and making a reservation for at least one night at a Palestinian-run hotel in East Jerusalem whether you were staying there or not (this was often asked for); don't travel together on the plane or approach the border guards together (they would be immediately suspicious if you were white and traveling with another person who wasn't your relative); if you happened to be Jewish play that up by wearing a Star of David necklace for example (you would be sure to get treated very well). Another important tip was to go to Israel first, avoiding stamps from other Arab countries, especially ones not on friendly terms with Israel. If you happened to be Muslim and they could tell because you were wearing a hijab, you would be interrogated. (That would be a problem for me on a later trip when I couldn't bring the paper I had showing I was a Muslim and had to convince important people that I was – which didn't go well.)

The danger of not taking these precautions would mean you would be questioned for hours; asked for your passwords to your email account (some people set up new harmless email accounts for this purpose); and if they suspected anything, you would be deported back to the U.S. on the next plane and detained at the airport until then. During this period, they were still allowing some activists into the country if they were on an academic or religious delegation or from the AFSC who had workers there. But some years later, they stopped all activists from coming, and if they caught you either at the border or anywhere else, you were deported and not allowed into the country for ten years.

All the people on the delegation were American citizens, but that makes no difference to the Israelis. On one of my trips, I tried to get the help of the American Embassy in Tel Aviv for two of our participants who were being detained at the airport to be deported (they mistakenly went up to the border guards together). In a story for later, I found out one of the two people was an undercover FBI agent monitoring our trip. Too bad her FBI job was frustrated by the strict Israeli border guards. The person I spoke to at the American Embassy said there was absolutely nothing they could do as the Israeli border guards could deny anyone coming into the country for any reason.

Two of my four trips to Palestine from 2007 to 2010 were part of a PSG delegation. On one of the trips, I traveled with the family of a Palestinian activist lawyer from NYC. I stayed with her family and worked with her and Addameer, the Palestinian Prisoner Support Organization, to gather evidence of Palestinians being tortured. On my fourth trip, I went to visit my son Devin, who was working with a Palestinian activist group in the West Bank. In the following section, I will describe my experiences on each one of these trips.

First Trip to Palestine

For my first trip to Palestine in 2007, I tried to be well-prepared by not having any Palestine material on me or in my suitcase. On a later trip, I hoped I wouldn't be strip searched as I had a tattoo of a Palestinian woman waving the flag on my upper right arm. My cover story was that I was an old Catholic guy coming to see the Holy Land for the first time and made sure I included a *Guide to the Holy Land* in my suitcase. I discovered the trick was not to give the border agents any reason to be suspicious or question you. This approach worked well each time except when I went into the West Bank from the Jordan border, which I will explain later.

Any delegates on my flight I ignored and pretended they were strangers. My flight went from O'Hare to Atlanta on Delta and then from Atlanta to Tel Aviv. My first surprise was going to O'Hare Airport, reaching my gate, and seeing an entirely separate area staffed by Israeli officials who searched everyone's bag. I had never seen something like that before, but I realized once I got on the plane, that at least 90% of the passengers were Israeli or Jewish. Other than some pleasantries, I didn't talk with any of my seatmates. Arriving in Atlanta, the Delta gate for the flight to Tel Aviv was extremely crowded and it was clear they had severely over-booked this popular flight. Luckily, I got one of the last seats on the flight as did some of my companions.

When I arrived at Ben Gurion Airport in Tel Aviv, I was exhausted because I had not slept on either plane flight. But I had enough adrenalin going to continue with my "old Catholic guy here for the Holy Land" routine to be waved through by the border agents without a problem. This was a time I realized my white privilege came in handy because if I was perceived as "non-white" in any way, I would have been stopped and questioned.

We were picked up at the airport and taken to a Palestinian home in a nearby village where we would be staying that first night. When we arrived, we were all led outside to a portico where we were seated at a huge table covered with plates mounded with meats of various kinds. I had remembered from our orientation that hospitality for visitors is a huge cultural principle for Palestinians, and refusing what was offered would be seen as rude behavior. I was exhausted and not hungry at all and the last thing I wanted to do is eat a heavy meal at 8:00 at night. Despite my discomfort I made sure I had at least a sample of everything that was offered. I would find out later that even the poorest of families would always offer whatever they had to any guest.

Our first trip was to the Alternative Information Center (AIC) which is a Palestinian-run NGO that provides alternative information and tours of Palestine for activists and journalists from around the world. They provided us a tour of Jerusalem, a Palestinian village that had been destroyed during the Nakba, and a short tour of the surrounding settlements.

Al-Aqsa Mosque in Jerusalem (Al-Quds)

Jerusalem (Al-Quds) is divided into West Jerusalem, which has an Israeli majority, and East Jerusalem, which has a Palestinian majority. During that time and continuing to today, the Israelis encroach upon East Jerusalem by pushing more settlers into Palestinian homes. All the infrastructure money and tours led by the Israelis are concentrated in West Jerusalem. Any of the tours of the Church of the Holy Sepulcher, for example, are taken through those areas and tourists are directed away from any of the Palestinian shops or restaurants in the area. It was obvious when we were taken through the Palestinian section of the Old City that the area was run down, dark, and devoid of tourists.

I would find out on a later stop in Jerusalem that many of the Palestinian shop owners were pressured by the Israelis to sell and leave the area. The pressure on the shop owners is effective and comes in the form of higher taxes and utility bills, along with attempts to direct the tourists away from their business. Along parts of East Jerusalem, I learned that there were many new or under construction condos on previously owned Palestinian property. Many of these very expensive condos are owned by people who only live in them for a portion of the year and have permanent homes outside the country.

Home in East Jerusalem taken over by Israeli settlers

There was usually an encampment of international activists in East Jerusalem working to protect the Palestinians from settlers who would come into their homes and take over if the owners left their houses. Even as late as 2024, Palestinian families were ordered to be evicted to make way for Jewish settlers. Below is a portion of an article from PBS News that explains the background of the ongoing dispute.

Israel orders eviction of Palestinian family from east Jerusalem property, reigniting a legal battle

PBS News
Apr 15, 2024, 2:44 PM EDT

JERUSALEM (AP) — An Israeli court on Monday ordered the eviction of a Palestinian family in a contested neighborhood of east Jerusalem, the latest in a legal saga that has come to symbolize the conflicting claims to the holy city.

The Sheikh Jarrah neighborhood has been the focus of a long-running battle between government-backed Israeli settlers and longtime Palestinian residents. It's part of a broader trend of settlers encroaching on Palestinian neighborhoods in contested east Jerusalem, and previous attempts at evictions in Sheikh Jarrah have led to violent clashes and helped spark an 11-day war between Israel and Hamas in 2021.

According to Monday's ruling, the Diab family was given until July to vacate the house in Sheikh Jarrah. The family said it would appeal.

The Israeli magistrate court described the case as a simple dispute over real estate, ruling that the extended Diab family was squatting in a property owned by Jews and had no legal rights to it. Palestinians say they have lived in the homes for decades.

The case against the family was launched by Nahalat Shimon Ltd, a Jewish settler organization that for years has been involved in legal efforts to evict Palestinian families from Sheikh Jarrah.

Israel captured east Jerusalem in the 1967 Mideast war and annexed the area in a move that was not internationally recognized. Israel considers the entire city its capital, while the Palestinians seek East Jerusalem, home to the city's most sensitive holy sites, as the capital of their future independent state.

Nahalat Shimon is trying to seize the property under an Israeli law allowing Jews to reclaim properties that were Jewish before Israel was established in 1948. Jordan controlled the area between 1948 and the 1967 war.

There is no equivalent right in Israel for hundreds of thousands of Palestinians who fled or were forced from their homes during the war surrounding Israel's establishment.

Saleh Diab, one of the men in the family, said his family of 20 has been living in the Sheikh Jarrah property since

1955. He told The Associated Press he was shocked by the decision and thought his family was protected under a 2022 Supreme Court decision that halted the planned evictions of four other Palestinian families in the same area.

Monday's decision comes at a time of heightened tensions in Jerusalem over Israel's ongoing war against Hamas in Gaza.

A high-profile eviction case in Sheikh Jarrah helped spark the 11-day war in May 2021. Israel's firebrand National Security Minister, Itamar Ben-Gvir, played a key role in rallying demonstrations in support of the settlers as an opposition lawmaker at the time.

During the genocidal war on Gaza in 2024, the Israeli government used the "distraction" of the Gaza War to push further into the West Bank and East Jerusalem. In another similar Palestinian neighborhood in East Jerusalem, Silwan, in September 2024, the Israelis began to bulldoze homes in the early morning hours. This was in a section of Silwan known as Al-Bustan, where the houses have long been targeted for demolition over municipal plans to replace the residential area with a biblical theme park.

As of this writing the Diab family and many others in the Sheikh Jarrah neighborhood had their cases to stop the evictions pending in the Israeli courts recently denied. It is likely, given President Trump's election and his recent executive order lifting the sanctions President Biden put on violent settlers, that these families will be evicted in the near future.

Mosque of a destroyed Palestinian village

We were also taken to a destroyed Palestinian village outside of Jerusalem, where all that was left was stones and rubble. The original village mosque was still there, surrounded by a barbed wire fence. One of the original villagers gave us the tour and said that when the villager group used to come back to the old mosque to hold services, the Israelis fenced it off to keep them out. It was likely the area was going to be turned into a park for settlers which had happened in several places in the area. Once the area becomes a park, there is no record kept of the original Palestinian village whose inhabitants had been driven away during the Nakba of 1947.

Settlement outside of Jerusalem

We were also driven through one of the large settlements that could be seen on the hills surrounding Jerusalem. The contrast between the Old City tour and the settlements was stark. The settlements were multi-floor, modern condo complexes surrounded by palm trees, fountains, and swimming pools. We were told much of the water in that general area was routed away from Palestinian areas for the exclusive use of the settlers. One reason for the numerous settlements is that the Israeli government will sponsor any Jewish person, no matter where they are from, and provide a condo or house for them to live in with very little ongoing cost.

Bethlehem

After the Jerusalem area, we traveled a short distance to Bethlehem. The first time I saw the city it came as a shock. All of Bethlehem is surrounded by a very high concrete wall with lookout towers every hundred feet or so. It looked to me like I was entering a concentration camp, except the outside of the walls were covered with Palestinian artwork. Going through a large checkpoint is required to enter the city and visitors are directed like cows through long rows of fenced in halls that end with an Israeli soldier who would check your identification and decide to let you enter or not. At that time, if you had an American passport, they usually waved you though.

Outside of Bethlehem

When we arrived at the checkpoint, we saw some soldiers harassing a very old Palestinian man on the side and wondered if this is how they treat all Palestinians, especially elders. We went on a tour through the very modern visitor center and the Church of the Nativity that was nearby. Outside of both these buildings, there was a large plaza that strangely was quite empty. I was puzzled by this until I was told that tourists were bused into Bethlehem, stopped at the two buildings, and then all left so they would not visit the Palestinian shops and restaurants surrounding the plaza.

Head of the Palestine Bar Association

Next when we were in Ramallah, we met with the head of the Palestine Bar Association that is an NGO that works to protect the legal rights of Palestinians. The most interesting story he told us was what happened during the parliamentary elections in the West Bank and Gaza in 2006. He described the USAID office providing them with pamphlets and various materials on how to run a democratic election. They received training on how to conduct the elections in the most transparent way possible.

When the results of the election had Mahmoud Abbas and his Fatah Party winning the elections in the West Bank and the much more popular Hamas winning the majority in Gaza, the U.S. and Israel immediately declared Hamas a terrorist organization, refusing to recognize their democratic win. Hamas easily won in Gaza as the Fatah Party was known to be corrupt, and Hamas was effective in providing daily services to the people in Gaza. The head of the Bar Association said that they threw out all the USAID materials after that.

Old City in Nablus

During this trip, we visited Nablus, a large city in the West Bank that had come under attack by Israeli forces multiple times in the past. It was easy to spot bullet holes in buildings in the Old City. We met with a former mayor of Nablus, who was in a wheelchair when we talked with him. He, along with the mayors of other Palestinian towns, had gotten together to protest the continued encroachment of illegal Israeli settlements on their lands. The Israelis reacted violently to this non-violent protest (which was a constant theme we heard on our trip) to the point that they planted a bomb underneath the Nablus mayor's car and blew his legs off.

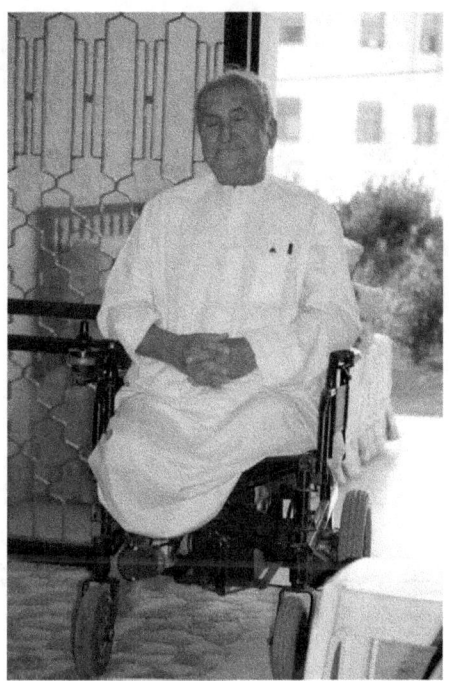

The people we met in Nablus were particularly welcoming, especially the members of the Palestinian Women's Committee, who organized job training for women, computer skills classes, and ran kindergarten and pre-schools for Palestinian children. When we met with the kindergarten teachers, they talked about the level of stress and trauma the children experienced because they never knew if a parent would pick them up or had been arrested by Israeli soldiers. Even though Nablus is designated as a Palestinian-governed area according to the Oslo Accords, the Israeli army would often raid the town to arrest people without warning. The majority of Palestinians in that area (and in the West Bank) had at least one or more family members who had been arrested and detained by the Israelis.

Mosque in the Old City of Nablus

In some cases, the children would be at home when the soldiers burst in and would be traumatized for a long time afterwards by seeing their father, mother, or brother taken away, not knowing when they would see them again.

Next, we visited Hebron (al-Khalil), a large city of 215,000 Palestinians and 500 Israeli settlers. The group of settlers there were known to be very violent and anti-Palestinian. The city includes the al-Ibrahimi Mosque or the "Cave of the Patriarchs." In Jewish, Islamic, and Christian traditions, it is the burial site of Abraham, Isaac, Jacob, and their wives. Because it is considered one of the four holy sites in Judaism, the small settlement of Israelis was located in the very center of the Old City. The street leading up to the Israeli settlements has a line of Palestinian shops that had been forcibly closed by the settlers. Above the shops are Palestinian houses that settlers have taken over. Providing a "roof" over the street is a chicken wire barrier that tries to provide "protection" for any Palestinian who might walk down the street. The settlers up above were known for throwing bags of urine, feces, and concrete blocks down on anyone walking down the street.

When I was there, I was used to taking many pictures of places like these. As I walked down the street with my group, it seemed eerily quiet even though it was the middle of the day. The street ended in a modern building in light stone with an iron gate and a watch tower guarding it. I kept taking pictures until our delegation leader said the soldier was yelling at me to stop taking photos or I would be arrested. He was saying all this with his rifle with live ammunition pointed at me the whole time. I was afraid he would confiscate my camera, so I walked away with the rest of the group.

Hebron (Al-Khalil) Street

When we were in that same area, I noticed two people dressed in what looked like UN soldiers' uniforms. Talking with them, we heard they were part of an unarmed team of observers from Norway that was set up after the Oslo Accords following a massacre of Palestinians in 1994 at the al-Ibrahimi Mosque. (A Zionist extremist killed 29 and injured 150 Muslims as they prayed in the mosque on the 15th day of Ramadan. He is still celebrated as a hero by the settlers.) We had heard many stories of Palestinians being beaten if they came anywhere near the Israeli settlement, so we wondered what the Norwegians were doing there. They told us if they saw any incident like that, they were not to intervene but just report it to the Israeli government and the Palestinian Authority. When asked what would happen then, they just shrugged. In other words, nothing. (In 2019, the Netanyahu led government at the time shut down the mission because they "were too biased".)

In approaching the al-Ibrahimi Mosque, the front entrance is guarded by Israeli soldiers who ask you whether you want to go in the mosque or the synagogue (the building is divided in two). I found out on a later trip that if you identify yourself as Jewish, which one of our group was, they force you to go to the synagogue side. After visiting the mosque, we were all to meet back in front. Sarah, the Jewish delegate, was terrified as she wasn't sure how she would get back to the front. Her fear was justified when she learned that the synagogue exits to the Israeli settlement had threatening looking men armed with rifles walking around. She was very relieved to make her way back to us finally.

Outside of Nablus, we visited some Palestinian agricultural worker collectives. These were organized collectives of farmers of a specific product for export overseas. For example, farmers with olive tree orchards would create pure olive oil to bottle and sell to other countries. Many of the main farmers were older men, with women doing the farmwork, such as gathering the olives. When we asked why that was so, they told us so many of the young men had been detained by the Israelis it was easier to have women as the main workforce.

The farmers had great difficulty exporting their products through the Israeli restrictions and checkpoints. All product shipments had to be searched in detail to see if they even made it through the checkpoints that were often closed unexpectedly. Even if products, especially perishable ones, made it through the checkpoints, they could be stalled for days, waiting for approved trucks to take them away. Much of their produce was spoiled in that way. This process didn't include the frequent raids by settlers who would come at night to burn down trees or crops.

Our way back to Ben Gurion Airport by train was uneventful until we entered the airport as a group with some of us having different flights returning to the US which made us automatically suspicious to the border security. All luggage was searched. (We were warned during orientation that anything we bought or picked up while in Palestine had to be sent back by Israel Post otherwise it would all be confiscated. The box that I sent back to Chicago had obviously been searched, but nothing was missing.) After some of us were interrogated and our luggage searched, we were allowed to get to our flights. The Israeli security is a lot less strict on the way out.

When the Chicago group returned, we gathered our photos and information to do trip "report back" presentations to multiple local colleges. What I learned on that first trip made me much more knowledgeable in debates with Israelis and Zionists on the topic of Palestine.

Second Trip to Palestine

On my second trip to Palestine in 2008, I went with a Palestinian lawyer friend and her family to Huwarra (near Nablus), where her family was from. Even though I spent time with her family, including her grandparents, who were still in Huwarra, our trip also had another purpose. I had been working with Addameer, the Palestinian prisoner support organization in Ramallah, since my last trip. This time, my lawyer friend and I went there to interview ex-prisoners about their experience in detention, including torture. We ended up interviewing several people, all of whom described some element of torture and beatings.

One interview was with a 16-year-old Palestinian girl who had been arrested when she was 15 for making a call to a friend in the West Bank (she lived within the Apartheid State of Israel's border). Phone calls like that were considered suspicious and could result in months long detention, which is what happened in this case. All Palestinians, no matter where they live, are subject to administrative detention for three to six months.

At the end of that period, the detention could be extended indefinitely and there are prisoners detained under that system for years. Palestinians are all subject to military law and military courts where the Israeli officials supplied no evidence. The Palestinian girl was detained for six months and often beaten or refused food or had her parents threatened because of her actions. I remember being proud of her when she said she helped organize other prisoners on a hunger strike for better conditions.

This was the only trip that I went into the West Bank from Jordan, and soon found out how long and difficult a trip that was. I had planned to spend some time in Amman and possibly visit the Petra site nearby. But when I got to the airport in Chicago for my non-stop flight on Royal Jordanian, the woman at the check-in counter before security said, "You know your passport is expired. They will probably let you through security and onto the plane, but you probably won't be let into the country." After I got over my shock, I found out that the same flight left the next day at the same time if I could get my passport renewed in a day. Amazingly, since the main U.S. passport office is in Chicago, you can pay an extra fee, make an appointment and get your passport renewed in a day.

With my time in Amman cut back to one day, I had no time to look around the city. The next morning, I met with my lawyer friend at the transport station to enter the West Bank. All Palestinians must go through on a certain bus, and everyone else pays extra to go on the VIP bus (just a regular bus without Palestinians). There are three sets of border guards you must go through. First is the Jordanians who take your luggage and put you on the first bus (and yes, there is more than one bus). You wait in a very crowded station early in the morning and try to listen to your garbled name on the faint loudspeaker to be called for the bus. This bus takes you to the Palestinian border guards, who put you on a separate bus for the rest of the journey while you hope your luggage is following you. During all this time, it is August and very hot with busses that don't have air conditioning.

The last stop is for the Israeli border guards, and you must search through a big pile of luggage in a large room and try to recognize your bag. This was the only trip to Palestine where I was detained for questioning. After answering a few basic questions, I had to go to the waiting area, presumably while they checked me out. While I was waiting, I saw my lawyer friend, who had arrived on her separate bus, being escorted to some back room for questioning. They took both her passport and Hawiya (Palestinian ID card) before they began questioning her. She did not let anyone push her around and was loudly complaining on her way out of the interrogation area that she refused to leave until they gave her Hawiya back, which they finally did. In other confrontations we had with Israeli soldiers at a checkpoint in Huwarra, she was always in the face of the soldiers, yelling at them. I found out later that the soldiers usually treat Palestinian women differently to avoid creating an incident with their male family members.

At this point, I am going to reproduce the poems I wrote before, during, and after this trip which gives a good idea of what I experienced on all my trips to Palestine. These poems are from *Huwarra Watercolors,* published by Community Road Publishing in 2012. Note that the person I am often addressing in these poems is my wife Elaine Fleming who I was, and still am, in love with.

Crossing Over

The Golden Tulip Hotel shines
in the dawn like a waxed
apple. A Mercedes murmurs,
mumbles, waits for me at the curb.

"Yellah, yellah, your VIP bus leaves early. "
Black cotton balls blow out the back and
mute concrete houses fall over each other,
while scavenger dogs scatter in our wake.

Suddenly, the station is there, a derelict mansion
busily cloning itself. A shriveled dog nudges rocks
with his nose across the lot; as I sit on my bag,
waiting for the tattered curtain to rise.

Bearded men arrive in VW vans, cigarettes hang
like fishhooks, women in pink, blue, and orange
headscarves, smoky-eyed children clutching
shirtsleeves
stare at my white hair and neon sign earrings.

Now, inside a dead grandmother's living room, golden
ceramic goats, drapes hang in mudslides from the
ceiling, a uniform yells, "Passport!" eyebrows
desperately trying to reunite with head hair; he grips
my tiny chart like an ER doctor.

Sadly clucking at my diagnosis, he sprints off,
passport deck fluttering in his hands. Behind
glass asylum office windows, a whirling fan
dervish spreads dust over five frowning men.

"Nabeel!" not my name, but here I am Nabeel, who
walks to the VIP bus,

smudged like broken finger paints on windows. My bus wheezes past
sallow school buses, where bearded men, headscarved women
wait in Jim Crow toilet lines.

We pant through back lot towns, Death Valley mountains, and over chalky rivers.
At another rasping stop, like yellow beads on dreadlocks, more buses
follow and spill passengers. Men in green box hats take my bag, all bags
hurling them into a river of black logs floating nowhere in slow motion.

Inside the terminal is a flea market auction, "Nabeel!" a stranger grabs my hand,
a warm hand shaking the good to see you again. In a sea of bobbing black bags,
mine surfaces, and together we are evicted out the door. My bus, my VIP bus
waits alone beyond barbed wire.

This stop, a camouflaged man in an outhouse window stamps Nabeel's passport. Seventy shuddering feet later, a 1950's airport without planes. Smiling green-suited woman asks
why are you here, where are you going, and who do you know. Waving my passport,
she vanishes behind blue partitions.

Suspended in the holding room, I adjust my mardi gras mask, painted with tourist eye shadow, but inside a minaret, a prayer song, a golden dome. Soon, a carnival barker

glads my hand, welcomes, you are sorry for delays,
welcome to our country, our land,
our white rivers, our crushed mountains.

I walk out, no buses, no barbed wire, only men chanting town names. My cab pulls
away, passing nomad camps with limp tents, sewer pipe rivers, empty guard tower storks, and endless roads crossing mountains twisted like badly rolled cigarettes.

Dreaming of river rain, hearing humming, calling from loudspeakers, my eyes cleansed with the call to prayer, my body answers the beating call. I have come back to this land. I am the prayer that rises and is heard.

Breathe your song loud in my heart. Lift me up, pierce these silences with your call.

Lunch in the Old City

An ancient dam of people bursts, from all streets surge
legless water sellers, tour barkers, tall women in green
jilbabs clutching boys in baseball shirts, grizzled men
holding brown babies and black rifles, all streaming by
almond trees gripping the ground, palm fronds fanning
this flood, jostling beneath the gate. Guns propped, green
soldiers smoke at the entry, leaning on smooth stones,
shaved slightly by all who pass by.

I walk through stone tunnels until the sun opens
to a traveling carnival of flags, pillows, dates, green
chipped stone necklaces, tree of life bowls, and golden domes
on plates. Men sitting in tattered lawn chairs creak to
life calling
"Mister, Mister" as I pass, smelling thyme, thieves, and
dust.
A white bearded man, resting on a pomegranate crate,
tobacco
pouches under his eyes, gestures down another bent
stone tube,
"alatool, alatool", straight, straight ahead.

Turning a corner, stillness rolls across an
empty square, the houses like misfit jigsaw pieces
jumbled, their pock marked doors open to staircases
suddenly disappearing like shy children. The carnival
has packed early, fleeing at dawn leaving a leaflet
fluttering across the square like a torn white butterfly.
A dark-haired girl runs by, staring at me, into an alley
where a door opens and shuts.

Retracing my steps like a boy in a snarled hedgerow maze,
I follow a smudged sign down an uneven street, shifting
underfoot like stepping on startled hard-shell beetles.
The road dead-ends at a scuffed and dented metal detector
jammed into a narrow-arched passageway. Two soldiers in camouflage
attached to a jagged sooty wall watch me approach, eyes like
walnuts under a raku bowl. "Right place, for you, opens at one."

Seven steps back, an archway yawns into a cathedral cave,
mesas of maroon-top tables, empty. I imagine the murmuring
of a hundred thawbed men, dust swirling at their feet smoking,
holding small white cups, these pilgrims preparing in this last sanctuary.
Looking up, there are stones, roughhewn, cemented in a quilted arch over
all below. Calloused, thick hands gently placed each rock, knowing its purpose, its
place in this heaven, where each holds open its palm, ready to receive the other.

I sip coffee, alone, underneath this dappled dome, waiting for
the gate to open, waiting for the rose-stained glass light
I know is there beyond the barrier, weaving
the ever-changing carpet below.

Traveling Out of Town

    The tawny mosaic of houses takes refuge
beneath barberry and almond trees
as the rumbling red van lurches down the road,
spitting gravel from all four wheels. Musa calls
from the house, pointing to our ride arriving.
Passing the outskirts of town, the sun
rises overhead like a mushroom cloud
of heatlamps. Dust from the road swirls
around the seats like swarms of burning gnats.
"This is our farmland, can't protect, we will show you."

    Brown, green-patched hills seep by, listless
waiting to be finally flattened. Curving
a corner, we see a small stone dome, assembled,
it must be, by broad sweating hands, lifting, setting stone
on stone, studying the image of a golden dome in the palm
of their hands. A path of overlapping footprints merges
into a rippling river that washes up to a blue door, painted
like a cloudless sky. The soundless door opens to a round room,
light-crossed from a solitary window. A handful of rugs, woven
by a hundred hands, all point to the east, the dust and
blue empty skies.

    We climb into the van and pass roads rising
and falling like swollen waves in the ocean. We come
to a valley, a carved notch in scorched land,
and see a deserted building, encircled by partly finished,
partly dismantled fencing. Looking in, we see a campsite

with walls, a fire suddenly snuffed out. "Settlers come
with guns, down those hills, see them? Too hot now."

On top of a nearby hill, houses like deflated brown
boxes with windows squint into the sunlight.
Beyond the empty building, a cave is roughly
scooped from the hill with shovels carving ash.
Pieces of grain like smoke-stained teeth scattered
inside. Jutting from the wall, a rock shelf barely holds
onto tattered, wool blankets.

We return to town, tired, unsettled. We eat mussakhan
for lunch at Musa's. Another van arrives. We climb
in silently for our trip away, beyond the now empty
checkpoint tower at the town's entrance. Still watching,
still a sentinel, the green iron gates are open, and the red
branded concrete blocks scattered, ready to join
like magnets when the time comes.

Kindergarten

Another taxi ride jerks down narrow
overheated streets, the sun dividing the car
into hell and cooler hell. We stop at a white
lego-built home with shuttered windows.

"This is our kindergarten. We only get money
from parents who have little money. There's no
government program for children, for adults, for us.
You've come too late, almost all children are gone."

A dark-haired boy is left sliding in and out
of holes in the indoor jungle gym, like a furless otter,
not smiling, not stopping, silently, endlessly
looping, as we watch from the center of the room.

"His mother is late, is gone, is dead. Stopped
again at her front door, leaving her street,
at the checkpoint, parking her car, by the police,
by the settlers, by her husband's interrogators."

I remember waiting for my mom, the purple shrieks
and scarlet bellowing of lilac bushes across our backyard,
walling off the short green patch of grass, hiding the alley
with its rivers of ruts that take everything away.

I dig, dig, dig into the sand beneath the hard green grass,
alone, paying no attention to the neighbor's growling
lawn mower. Through the curving windows, I see wallpaper
splattered with daisies on our breakfast nook walls.

Bill Chambers

Dad waves his arms, shouting at mom's back. I dig,
grass roots torn up,
dangling like green worms. Wind spreads the lilacs and
opens windows to the alley.
I see hairy garbage man arms hurling a can, its bent
top flying into
a churning mass of dead food, clanging.

The metal door claps open, the kindergarten boy's
loops
stop, suddenly, his mother runs in, her green headscarf
fluttering
behind her. All air is sucked from the empty room.
We watch them leave and not look back.

Balata Wedding

The call undulates in swirling waves,
like sand drifting from the distant
Haifa shore, car horns recoil across the ring
of hills, security cameras, and camp lights blink
like flickering stars above the wedding party.
Kaffiyehed ghosts, their bodies blown from
rooftop perches, watch as nomads leave
camels bellowing, pickup trucks spin
dust circles, refugees sit on scattered rocks
waiting to return. All watchers of the dance,
the spinning men, whirling
round the veiled bride, listening
to the shouts of the Balata camp.

The Poet's Gravesite

Green tear-shaped leaves erupt
between brown sage and rocks,
purple lilacs stitched in tree branches wave
to the Wall that climbs,
winds across the distant hills.

Across the hills, a giant has smashed
stone houses, scattering thresholds over each field
the smell of jasmine and almonds fills
the shimmering stillness in waves
over his homeland.

No longer an exile.
No country can expel him.
No siege can entrap him.
His soul has dissolved the Wall
and every boundary for his people.

My Chicago Activist Life

A family walks in the grass,
young girls pose behind his picture
and the boys run through the flowers.
We walk away from this hill
to the sound of children laughing.

Rooftop Debka

> The young men run in front of me. Ali, the one shot
> in the stomach during class, laughs the loudest calling me
> "Nabeel!" Dust parts like red sea waves over the path,
> almond leave shadows splatter like blossoms scattered
> before us.
>
> We run to their murdered uncle's tile shop, unfinished,
> white blocks, empty windows, doors without doors.
> Ali dances up the stairs in the dark, his flashlight a swinging
> incense burner blessing the concrete walls.
>
> On the rooftop, we look over the cypress trees to
> the deserted parking lot below. Radio Shack boom box
> music rises, lingers, falls with the air, the trees,
> the road, and the dancing teenagers.
>
> Bounding upstairs, dinette chair balanced on one hand,
> Ahmed places the chair in the middle, for me, the visiting king.
> Ten arms entwine in a swirling dance around me, until
> a blinding moon
> from the road freezes us like prisoners clambering over
> a wall.
>
> I smell the jasmine wilt as it floats like dust on the beam of light,
> seeping over the rooftop debka. The checkpoint jeep
> yells "Come Down!"
> to the shop, to the boys, to the boom box, to the chair,
> to the visiting king.

"Huwarra" by Elaine Fleming

Grandfather's Walk Home

    Down spiral stone stairs, grasping
    a rough-cut cane, Jamal grey-suited in the heat,
    leads his granddaughters, sons, and me,
    a stranger in procession behind him.

    The road, donkey-rutted and dark,
    winds by tumbled stonewalls,
    the smell of jasmine spread like
    sand across the powdery path.

    Owl eyes turn the corner,
    a jeep stares at us without blinking.
    His back still shining grey, he walks on,
    for him they don't exist and never existed.

    A few feet in front of us, where
    the dying light stiffens the road,
    a trail passes through a thicket of olive
    trees. Silent black hunchbacked spirits

Bill Chambers

walk down from terraced hills and past,
seeping into the orchard beyond.
We continue to walk, watching the fluttering
stillness of olive leaves.

Almond trees enfold an embroidered green
gate that swings open to embrace
Jamal and his followers as
his cane points upward to home.

On the porch steps, his wife Sileen
spreads her hands in prayer over this land,
deaf, but loud upon these stonewalls
that whisper softly of joy.

I am no stranger.
No jeep passing through.
No ghost walking the night.
Still, only a fleeting visitor.

The winding road arcs up and away
ignoring soldiers who pass by in the night.
The rock-strewn hills wait for them to leave,
but the land embraces those rooted in this place.

Going Home

    Anan hands me a rumpled paper bag with plums
    and dates, five of the family wave as I grasp
    the vibrating dusty door handle of the taxi.

    Windows cranked down, waves of whistling
    heat from a hundred blow dryers spin me
    round and round on the torn leather backseat.

    I am a package, delivered to the no-VIP bus,
    the anyone traveling in this heat bus, going home,
    leaving home, escaping home, and sweltering still.

    In a daze, I look through grease-smeared windows,
    a sepia sheen over low hills and houses, on the way
    to the bridge, to guards, to gates, and to the last hotel.

    The lounging waiter, glances up, squints, "you alone?"
    and smiles in a vast gilded room, full of disheveled
    tables deserted by the last supper guests.

    An earthen mound, a cairn of pita triangles, centered,
    exactly, on the white linen tablecloth, look stiff
    like tiny tan shovels for the bleached hummus.

    Golden Tulip musak seeps into the dining room
    conducting a cloud of white haired, khaki-clad travelers
    tumbling in like tourists into a refugee camp.

Yesterday white-robed camp elders gestured to me beneath
a leafless tree. Seeing me, one with the English of a 30-year teacher said,
"I look up and see your American planes.
What have we done to you?"

Even leaving, I walk with the laughing cousin who pulls up
his shirt showing the bullet hole, sit on a concrete block on
a stone roof watching debka, help an uncle carrying a crate
of breakfast fruit.

I'm lost in transition, crossing a smudged line, both feet in
heat-packed sand beneath almond trees, one hand reaching
for the handle of another taxi to take me to the cramped plane home.

Like sorting photographs in damp basement boxes saved
from flood, this home, these photos flash bright and move
steadily into my heart. I see you, my love, not home, but here.

My Chicago Activist Life

In the empty dining room chair, you smile over
the white linen tablecloth. I hear your laugh, a blue
thrush gliding over the jasmine bush potted in the
corner.

I am leaving this place with the smell of almonds
on my arms. Village lights on the hills still luminous
like day lilies stitched onto your black skirt.

I found you wandering in a stone house along a winding
rock-strewn road. The darkness curved in an arched
passageway over the open threshold to our home.

I am not leaving this place. I haven't left the poet
on the hill or his children laughing, but cradle my vision
of you here, in this middle space, in these dusty rooms
of my heart.

Ranya Returns Home

Returning to her abducted home, crossing barbed
barricades like thorns carving rivers in the dirt, she ends
at the terminal, a misshapen beige box stranded in a sea
of chalky stones. Tan boys with grey guns are laughing, while
women dressed as promoted prison guards, apologize
when they strip-search.

"Nabeel" is already passing through, freed
from Google searches, cursory questions, catalogued
a lone Midwest tourist, oddly cooperative,
a parolee sweating good behavior, yes siring
the traffic court judge. Escape clause sprung,
he sees Ranya led into a warren of offices.

Still, even now, returning to your stolen home, you resist
the grilling with the voice of those denied medicine, sitting
sleepless in white interrogation rooms, enduring hands
hung from clammy walls, feeding bawling babies
in sunless cells. They finish with you like sleepy
interrogators on break, sending you

back to start. But all those waiting in circular lines,
in cotton-pocked blue chairs, with folded hands in front
of shabby magistrate desks, recognize you --
and when you scream in fury, seven million voices
rush the chalked borders of a hundred lands, pouring over
the threshold of home.

Third Trip to Palestine

My third trip to Palestine was on my own to visit my son Devin who had quit his job in DC and was in Palestine all summer to work with a Palestinian-led group Beit Ommar, who worked on resistance to expansion of the wall and protected farmers from settlers. This trip was much more difficult for me as I was traveling alone and not with anyone who spoke Arabic. Navigating around to a hotel in East Jerusalem and even walking around Jerusalem itself was more difficult. When I was in Jerusalem, I spoke to a Palestinian shop owner who explained how difficult it was for him to keep his store open.

When I went into his shop, I was the only one in there, and it just confirmed what he told me about the Israelis sending tourists away from the Palestinian quarter of the Old City. The Israelis had continually increased his taxes on the cost of his water and electricity and were offering to buy his place so they could take it over. I bought several beautiful items especially jewelry he had in his store and of course, he was effusively grateful.

As I walked through that section of the city, it looked very deserted, as if no one lived in these very old houses. It also was likely they were avoiding the heat as I found out later that it was over 100 degrees. On this trip, I spent a lot of time just meditating by the Dome of the Rock and near Al-Aqsa Mosque. Before this trip, I had been studying the Quran and reading a lot about Islam as part of my long process of considering whether I should convert. As part of that process, Devin and I stayed with a Muslim family in Nablus. The father was a teacher at the local university. Along with giving us a tour of the city, we spent hours talking with him about Islam and I more and more realized how rational and sensible his answers were. (Later in this memoir, I will provide a more detailed account of my journey to Islam.)

For most of this trip, Devin stayed in the small village in the West Bank, where the activist group was located. It wasn't until years later he told me about some of the actions he was involved in. I never quite understood why he didn't tell me, but when I think about it now, he was likely afraid it would have gotten back to his mother and made her worry. In one case, he was a "witness" in a home that they had heard was going to be demolished by the Israelis the next day. But the Israelis never showed up. Even that action could be very dangerous as an American activist named Rachel Corrie had done the same thing a few years before and had been killed by one of the Israelis' militarized Caterpillar bulldozers when the operator just ran over her.

The other incident was when Devin was helping to protect a farmer from the settlers, who would often come down from their settlement on the hill and beat up the farmer or destroy his crops. The border police came and said nothing to the settlers and told Devin "You shouldn't be here", put a black bag over his head, tied his hands together with zip ties, and threw him in the back of their jeep. He was taken to some detention center, told to sign some documents in Hebrew, and was finally released the next morning. Likely, the document said he would not return to Israel for some period (later, they made it ten years for activists), and if he did return, he would be immediately deported.

Fourth Trip to Palestine

On my last trip to Palestine, I was part of one of the PSG delegations. This trip would be our very last delegation and would lead to the disbanding of PSG – Chicago. This time we were finally able to convince two Palestinians sisters from DePaul University to go with us once they got over their fear of making the trip. Most of the delegates were from the Chicago and Minneapolis areas including people from the Minneapolis Anti-War Committee.

We flew into Ben Gurion airport and as usual did not acknowledge each other on the plane. I was one of the first through border control once again playing the old Catholic guy there to see the Holy Land. My role was to wait in the airport until the other delegation members made it through. Once you make it through the border agents, they don't bother you further. The two Palestinian sisters were stopped immediately and interrogated for eight hours. One of them was smart enough to hide her phone so I could keep in touch with them while they were being questioned. I also gave their mother back in Chicago updates on how they were doing. The Israeli officials demanded their passwords to their email accounts, a common tactic at that time. Given we were prepared for this, both sisters had set up "clean" email accounts that didn't show any of their Palestine activism emails. They were finally released, and the initial group of us was picked up by our hosts in Palestine.

Once we arrived at our first stop at a village outside of Jerusalem, I started to make some calls to find out what happened to our other delegates whom I never saw at the airport.

I found out that two of the women from the Minneapolis Anti-War Committee made the mistake of approaching the border agents together which immediately made them suspicious. They were taken for questioning and detained at the airport to be deported on the first plane back to the U.S. The Israelis would put people they deported on any plane leaving Apartheid Israel and usually not to the city you arrived from.

I had a sympathetic lawyer contact in Jerusalem whom I called. She said there wasn't much she could do but would head to the airport to see if they were still there. In the meantime, being my naïve self, I called the American Embassy in Tel Aviv, sure that the Israelis couldn't just deport at someone with an U.S. passport. The official I got on the line said, "It's their country, and there really is nothing we can do about it" which I thought was true in many ways. By the time the lawyer got to the airport, they had already been deported. I would find out later that one of the two women was an undercover FBI agent.

Section of the Apartheid Wall

On this trip, we revisited many of the organizations from my earlier trips. We held meetings with the Addameer Prisoner Support Organization and were updated on the conditions of Palestinian prisoners still being held and tortured under Administrative Detention. As I mentioned earlier, I was working with Addameer regularly since my first trip to Palestine, and the Israelis often targeted them for the work they did. In one case, the Israelis raided their offices in the middle of the night, removing the hard drives from their computers, stealing paper files, and damaging their equipment. After that happened, I worked with them to get funding for new computers and other equipment.

On this trip, we learned the Israelis were becoming more restrictive in access to prisoners. This included any family as visitors and the International Red Cross who were supposed to be monitoring prisoner conditions. Shifting prisoners from one prison to another, a common occurrence made it difficult for their families to visit or even keep track of their condition.

When we returned to the U.S., the meeting with Addameer led to more than one tour with Executive Director Sahar Francis and former prisoner Ala Jaradat to the large cities in the U.S. With a follow-on meeting with Defense of Children International – Palestine; these tours focused on the detention and torture of children in Israeli detention centers. Israel does not recognize the categorization of children, even those under the age of 16. So, a 12-year-old boy who throws a rock at an Israeli soldier's jeep is arrested, detained, interrogated, and tortured with adults. When we would tell these stories to various church congregations during the Addameer tour, the shock on listeners' faces was palpable.

The American Friends Service Committee (AFSC) joined with DCI-Palestine to start a No Way to Treat a Child Campaign. Below is a short description from the AFSC of what this campaign led to.

> AFSC co-leads the "Israeli Military Detention: No Way to Treat a Child" campaign with Defense for Children International-Palestine, which seeks to challenge and end Israel's prolonged military occupation of Palestinians by exposing widespread and systematic ill-treatment of Palestinian children in the Israeli military detention system.
>
> Palestinian children have the right to a safe and just future. We believe the United States government must use all available means to pressure relevant Israeli authorities to end the detention and abuse of Palestinian children.
>
> The first bill on Palestinian children's human rights in U.S. history was introduced on November 14, 2017, by Rep. Betty McCollum (D-MN). H.R. 4391, "The Promoting Human Rights by Ending Israeli Military Detention of Palestinian Children Act," gained the support of 30 members of the U.S. House of Representatives. On April 30, 2019, Rep. McCollum introduced H.R. 2407, the "Promoting Human Rights for

Palestinian Children Living Under Israeli Military Occupation Act," a bill prohibiting U.S. taxpayer funding for the military detention of children by any country, including Israel. H.R. 2407 received 24 co-sponsors in the 116th Congress.

The bill met considerable opposition and was never passed. Upon our return to Chicago, we began what we hoped would be a series of "report back" presentations about our experiences in Palestine. Our first presentation was very well-attended at DePaul University, especially given two of the presenters were Palestinian DePaul students. After that event, I called one of the two women from Minneapolis who had been deported to see if they wanted some help in putting together a presentation for Minneapolis. At the time, I thought it was odd that the woman I called was very surprised and, in a stuttering voice sounded confused, saying she would let me know. Later, I found out that she was an FBI agent, and when I tried to call her again, the number was disconnected. In a later section, "FBI Campaign Against Palestinian Activists and Rasmea Odeh," I will cover the results of this attempt by the FBI to infiltrate our delegation.

Addameer Trip to Ireland

One of the tours I helped organize was Executive Director Sahar Francis and former prisoner Ala Jaradat from Addameer to visit multiple cities in Ireland and to establish a close relationship with Coiste, the Republican prisoners support organization. Having worked with both groups, it seemed they had a lot in common, which the tour confirmed. They started out being welcomed in Dublin and then I joined them on their stops in Belfast and Derry.

When they came to Belfast, they were welcomed by the staff at Coiste and taken on a tour of the city. We all had a great time going to the Felons Club and attending a Ska band concert. (The Felons Club was founded and frequented by former Irish Republican prisoners.) Wherever Palestinians go in Ireland, they are always celebrated in an over-the-top way. They also had some good discussions about cooperation and mutual support between Coiste and Addameer. On one tour of Belfast, we were all in a car with a guide who was the last Republican bomber arrested in London before the Good Friday Agreement. He also happened to be head of the Palestine Solidarity Committee. He asked everybody if they wanted to see the "Shankill" – which is a notoriously violent Loyalist (pro-British paramilitaries) neighborhood. Someone said, "Sure, why not." It wasn't me who said that. So, our driver took us down the road in the middle of the day. As I was watching people come out of their houses and bars to look at this strange car that had entered their neighborhood, our driver explained that they can tell who you are, Republican or Loyalist, by what street you entered on and what direction you left by. Nervously, I suggested we leave as soon as possible, and obviously, we didn't stop to say hi.

Sahar and Ala got a much better reception when we went to Derry. Raymond McCartney, one of the Republican hunger strikers who survived the 1981 Hunger Strike when Bobby Sands died, showed us around the city. We were in luck that in the most recent mayoral election, a mayor from Sein Fein was elected who welcomed them into city hall and gave them the keys to the city. The rest of our trip was very successful with several meetings with Derry citizens and college students to describe the prisoners' conditions in Palestine.

FBI Campaign Against Palestinian Activists and Rasmea Odeh (2010-2017)

A short time after we finished the PSG Palestine delegation report back at DePaul University, my wife Elaine and I went on a trip to Strasbourg, France, to visit my step-daughter Claire, who was studying abroad. We used our time to visit Tours and Paris and traveled then to Germany and Switzerland. While we were in Germany at our hotel, which was our last stop before Paris and the return home, I got a call from one of my good activist friends, Joe Iosbaker, who told me his home and that of Hatem Abudayyah (Executive Director of the Arab American Action Network – an organization I had worked with for a long time) plus some other people in Minneapolis and Grand Rapids all had their homes searched and files removed. The most disturbing thing Joe told me was that in their search of the Minneapolis Anti-War Committee office, the FBI left behind a list of 29 names to target, and mine was the last on the list.

The Department of Justice had impaneled a grand jury to review "evidence" that we were guilty of supplying material support for terrorists. I would find out later that they believed we were supplying money to Palestinian terrorist groups during our delegations, which we clearly were not, and they had no evidence that we had. It explained why the FBI informant tried to go on our delegation, and I always thought it ironic that the Israelis deported her before she could even enter the country.

McCarthyism
was WRONG in the 1950s...

SENATOR JOE MCCARTHY, 1950s   U.S. ATTORNEY PATRICK FITZGERALD

Why is U.S. Attorney Patrick Fitzgerald bringing it back today?!

U.S. Attorney Patrick Fitzgerald is heading up the Grand Jury that is attacking anti-war & international solidarity activists in the Midwest. He's responsible for the raids on anti-war activists' homes & offices on September 24. His Grand Jury witch hunt is menacing activists with jail on outrageous allegations of supposedly providing "material aid to terrorism". Fitzgerald is using "terrorism" the way McCarthy used "communism" - to carry out a witch hunt against those who speak out against US government policies. It's real purpose is to discredit and punish people for their ideas.

FITZGERALD'S MCCARTHYIST WITCH HUNT AGAINST ANTI-WAR & SOLIDARITY ACTIVISTS MUST BE STOPPED!

Contact President Obama—202-456-1111 or www.whitehouse.gov/contact and Attorney General Eric Holder— 202-353-1555 or askdoj@usdoj.gov. Demand that they stop the grand jury witch hunt against anti-war activists now! **STOPFBI.NET**

Elaine and I were in quite a panic because I was probably going to be arrested as I got off the plane in Chicago. Much to our surprise nothing happened at all when we arrived nor for the week after we got home. After about a week, I got a call from one of the Palestinian sisters who was on the delegation telling me the FBI was at her door and asked what she should do. I told her to tell them nothing and that she would get them the number of her lawyer. That day, about nine other people got subpoenas for the grand jury, the majority Palestinians who were on the delegation. In the end, a total of 23 subpoenas had been issued to compel grand jury testimony. This initial group was also given subpoenas to appear in front of the grand jury.

The activists liken the action to McCarthy-era political witch hunts. Jim Fennerty was an excellent lawyer who helped everyone through this ordeal. As far as we could tell, they were targeting the Freedom Road Socialist Organization, Anti-War

Committee in Minneapolis, Students for a Democratic Society (SDS), and the Palestine Solidarity Group – Chicago. These actions by the FBI were widely reported. Below is coverage from *Al-Jazeera*.

FBI targets US Palestine activists

Searches, subpoenas, but no charges for anti-war activists 'providing support to terrorists' in Colombia and Palestine.

Al-Jazeera
By Chris Arsenault
3 Oct 2010

Tracy Molm sometimes has a hard time paying rent, so it came as a surprise when American security forces banged on her door at 7 am one morning and searched her apartment under suspicions she had provided material support to a terrorist organization.

Warrants indicate that investigators believe Molm and at least seven other activists from the Minnesota anti-war committee and other groups provided material support to the Popular Front for the Liberation of Palestine (PFLP) and rebels from the Revolutionary Armed Forces of Colombia (FARC), groups the US considers terrorist organizations.

"My assumption is that material support means money and guns, but they [police] wouldn't explain anything," Molm told Al Jazeera. "I think the real thing is that they are trying to intimidate those of us who are standing in solidarity with the people of Palestine and Colombia."

Activists from Minneapolis and Chicago have been subpoenaed to appear before a grand jury investigation in October after coordinated police raids on September 24.

No charges

Despite the searches and seizures of computers, cheque books, mobile phones, documents, and photographs, Molm and other activists have not been charged with committing a crime.

"The searches were conducted pursuant to a warrant issued by a federal judge," Royden Rice, a special agent with the US Federal Bureau of Investigation (FBI) in Chicago, told Al Jazeera.

"No arrests have been made or charges filed in connection with this investigation," he said, leading activists to call the searches a trolling expedition targeting Americans who object to their government's foreign policy ventures.

More than 200 people demonstrated in Minneapolis on Monday, denouncing the raid, according to the Minnesota Daily, while at least 100 rallied in Chicago on Tuesday to support the anti-war activists. More demonstrations are planned in other American cities, and activists expect the numbers to increase drastically, as they only had three days to plan the first round of protests.

"The FBI does not investigate any person or group because of their political views," said agent Rice. "We investigate allegations that federal criminal law has been violated."

'Suppressing political activity'

Bernardine Dohrn, a law professor at Northwestern University in Chicago, thinks the police are trying to do one of two things. "Either it is a fishing expedition, as there is not enough evidence to indict [formally charge] anyone, or it is an attempt to suppress political activity. Neither is good news," she said.

As a legal scholar, Dohrn worries about the vague nature of national security laws instituted after the September 11, 2001, attacks on US targets.

"If you write articles, is that material support [for terrorists]? If you contribute resources for computers or healthcare clinics in occupied territories or territories resisting government control, is that material support?"

She says grand jury investigations, the legal maneuver activists are facing, represent a way to "circumvent other constitutional protections."

People who appear before a grand jury "cannot bring in a lawyer. It is the prosecutor, you [the person being investigated], and a group of grand jurors ... in short, it is a coercive method to get information."

Jessica Sundin, a clerical worker at the University of Minnesota, also had her belongings taken by security forces in the coordinated searches and seizures. Like Molm, she denies providing material support to any group and says she has done nothing illegal or unethical.

She believes that the "biggest task of our anti-war movement [in the US] is to educate our own people."

Visit to an occupied country

In that spirit, Molm and other American activists traveled to Palestine in 2004 to see the conditions there for themselves. "Everyday people [in occupied lands] go through checkpoints with guns pointed at their heads, and they have this horrendous situation, but they continue to live and laugh," she said.

"The occupation of Palestine is as brutal as it is because US tax dollars, my tax dollars, support that. Sending people there to bring back [personal] accounts and pictures is important to building solidarity."

Israel, the power responsible for occupying Palestinian land, received $2.55bn in American military aid in 2009, according to the US State Department. That number is expected to increase to $3.15bn per year from 2013 to 2018.

"I don't know why it would be a crime to have a scarf with the Palestinian flag on it, but they [police] took that," she said.

As for Colombia, the country has received at least $5bn in US military aid since 1999.

Amnesty International USA, a human rights group, said it "has been calling for a complete cut off of US military aid to Colombia for over a decade due to the continued collaboration between the Colombian Armed Forces and their paramilitary allies."

Justifying terror cash

Rather than a vast attempt by security forces to intimidate critics of US foreign policy, the searches may have a simpler motive: an excuse for police to justify the massive infusions of federal cash they received under the pretext of 'fighting terrorism.'

"In Minnesota [the state containing Minneapolis where most searches took place] a lot of money was put into anti-terrorism efforts," says Sheila Regan, a reporter with the TC Daily Planet who has been covering the issue for a local audience.

"It has one of the biggest terrorism bureaucracies anywhere; they [security forces] need something to do to justify their salaries," she told Al Jazeera.

Like other subpoenaed activists, Molm works for a group called Students for a Democratic Society (SDS), which had been critical in organizing major demonstrations against the US war in Vietnam back in the 1960s and 70s.

Dohrn was a national leader of the group from 1966-70 and has direct experience with the grand jury subpoenas, which a new generation of activists is now facing.

"When I was called before a grand jury and refused to collaborate ... I went to jail and was released eight months later by the same judge, who said 'apparently there is no evidence against you.' It is a strange way to have to prove your innocence."

Back in the anti-war movement of the 1960s, a few US activists did travel to Vietnam to see the effects of B52 bombers, toxic Agent Orange, and support for the western-backed government in South Vietnam.

Jane Fonda, the former activist and work-out video queen, famously stood next to an anti-aircraft gun with North Vietnamese communists and decried the US for what she called its "illegal" bombing campaign against the country.

The article does an excellent job of describing a tactic the FBI had been using for years for the Anti-War movement Puerto Rican independence movement, among many others. It is easy to get a grand jury to approve anything presented to them by the prosecutor. With little to no evidence, the FBI and Department of Justice (DOJ) can subpoena movement leaders and force them to focus their energies on the legal case instead of a free Puerto Rico or a free Palestine.

I was always puzzled why I never got a subpoena until I found out years later that it was likely I had missed some meeting while out of the country that the FBI informant had attended. What happened over the next year was a strong campaign by all those who were subpoenaed and their allies to refuse to talk to the grand jury. And no one ever did. The campaign focused on how there was repression of Palestine activism and treating all Palestinians as terrorists. With a lot of hard work and support from many organizations over a long period of time, the Justice Department gave up on using us as a target and decided instead to target one of the strongest Palestinian leaders in Chicago, Rasmea Odeh.

USA vs. Rasmea Odeh

Significant coverage in this memoir is given to the case of Rasmea Odeh initially being accused of "immigration fraud" and, when that was unsuccessful, indicted for being part of a U.S. designated terrorist organization. The case began under the Obama Administration and concluded under the first Trump Administration. The case was a significant event for Chicago activists as it brought together a number of campaigns for Palestinian freedom, immigrant rights, Black Lives Matter, and community control of the police. Supporters of all of these struggles joined in their support for Rasmea Odeh. There would be in the national Rasmea Defense Committee, over 50 organizations.

Rasmea Odeh was well-recognized as a major Palestinian community leader in Chicago especially in Arab women's rights. In 1994, she traveled to Detroit, obtaining her U.S. citizenship in 2005. From Detroit, she came to Chicago and joined the Arab American Action Network (AAAN), a social services organization, as their Associate Director and Community Adult Women Organizer. The AAAN utilized her broad experience with women's and workers' unions, family and domestic violence groups, human rights centers, and the Red Cross. She is the founder of the organization's Arab Women's Committee, which now includes over 600 members and in 2014, Rasmea received the "Outstanding Community Leader Award" from the Chicago Cultural Alliance. Odeh has devoted her time to working with Arab immigrant women, establishing projects related to civil and human rights, social justice, and community economic development. She promoted literacy and political education and organized workshops on domestic violence and anti-Arab expression.

Rasmea Odeh was arrested on October 22, 2013, by agents of the Department of Homeland Security and charged with immigration fraud. Allegedly, in her application for citizenship made 20 years ago, she didn't mention that she was arrested in Palestine 45 years ago by an Israeli military court that had tortured her into confessing to bombings in Jerusalem. When her trial started in the Federal District Court in Detroit, there would be a contingent from her women's group, plus many Palestine and human rights activists that traveled to every court appearance she had.

During this time, I was a journalist covering this topic for the *Electronic Intifada* and, especially, the *Chicago Monitor*, an online news publication sponsored by CAIR-Chicago. For about four years, I wrote articles and was Editor-in-Chief of the *Chicago Monitor*. To give you, the reader, the best feel for what was happening during this critical time for Palestine activism in Chicago, I am going to reproduce some of the articles I wrote during that time.

This first article I wrote for *The Electronic Intifada* describes the history of these attacks on Palestine activists. One of the effects of my experience with supporting ex-Irish Republican and Palestinian prisoners is seeing the big difference in how the U.S. government treated them. The following is an article that discusses this issue.

Why does US treat ex-prisoners from Ireland and Palestine differently?

Bill Chambers
The Electronic Intifada Chicago
12 November 2013

The Obama administration has excluded all Palestinian groups from the political process except for Mahmoud Abbas' Fatah party. (Issam Rimawi APA images)

With the Department of Homeland Security's recent arrest of former Palestinian prisoner and current community leader Rasmea Yousef Odeh for alleged immigration fraud, it is helpful to review the history of the targeting of former political detainees by US authorities when there is a US-sponsored peace process underway.

During Bill Clinton's presidency, groups such as Irish Northern Aid and the Irish-American Unity Conference conducted support campaigns for Irish political prisoners who were undocumented immigrants or didn't declare their jail time on immigration forms and were targeted for deportation after living quietly in the US for twenty years or more. Some actively supported equal rights for nationalists in the north of Ireland, and the US-sponsored peace process then underway, while others were not politically active at all.

Before 11 September 2001, very little attention was paid to the large numbers of undocumented Irish immigrants. If one was Irish and targeted for deportation, it was because one had been a political prisoner or was active in Irish Republican politics (generally, this meant supporting the use of armed struggle against the British state).

Influential politicians

During the time of the Irish peace process sponsored by the Clinton administration in the 1990s to early 2000s, Irish Northern Aid and the Irish-American Unity Conference among others, argued that these former Irish political prisoners who typically supported the peace process should not be re-criminalized and should be allowed to stay.

During the peace process, all the main paramilitary groups these prisoners belonged to agreed to a ceasefire and the decommissioning of weapons, whether they supported the peace process, like the Irish Republican Army (IRA), or did not support it, like the Irish National Liberation Army (INLA).

The Irish-American community was mostly supportive and had influential politicians in both main parties, including Edward Kennedy, the Democratic senator, and Peter King, the Republican representative, who promoted this message. Then Senator George Mitchell, who later became Clinton's peace envoy to Ireland, urged the president to grant Sinn Féin leader Gerry Adams a U.S. visa, even before the IRA had agreed to a ceasefire.

When Clinton granted the visa in 1994, against British objections, it demonstrated an understanding that the peace process could not advance without the recognition and inclusion of all groups, as George Mitchell wrote in his memoirs *Making Peace*.

In the case of Noel Cassidy, a former Irish political prisoner active in Irish Republican politics in the 1990s, a campaign to support him did not prevent his from returning to Ireland voluntarily to avoid deportation.

But such campaigning eventually did have an impact in 2000, when Clinton announced deportation proceedings against former IRA prisoners would be halted and given "deferred action" status.

The State Department, immigration authorities, and political opposition prevented the cases from being dropped entirely.

Why was the campaign even this successful? The Clinton administration was actively engaged in a peace process in Ireland that invited all groups to be involved, including those — like the IRA — previously on the State Department's list of "foreign terrorist organizations." Another key factor was the political influence of the very large Irish-American community.

While Clinton's announcement about former IRA prisoners was praised as a benefit of the Irish peace process at the time, but keeping their legal status in limbo became a huge problem after 11 September 2001. Following the atrocities of that day, deportation cases of former Irish political prisoners were once again activated. They once again were seen as terrorists.

Malachy McAllister, a former member of the INLA who had served three years in prison in Ireland in the mid-1990s, fled to the US after loyalist paramilitaries shot up his home in Belfast. After living an apolitical life for many years, he became a target for deportation by the

Bush administration that was going after anyone, anywhere, considered a "terrorist."

Ciaran Ferry, a former IRA prisoner released as part of the 1998 Good Friday Agreement, came to the US when his name was found on a loyalist paramilitary hit list.

In 2003, he was arrested when he went to a review meeting about his residency status and was accused of overstaying his visa even though he had been admitted to the US under a work authorization. Eventually, he was charged with lying on his immigration form about spending time in jail in Ireland as an IRA member. He spent almost two years in prison before finally agreeing to be deported for the sake of his American wife and two-year-old daughter. [I visited Ciaran in a Federal Maximum-Security Prison in Colorado where he was only allowed to see visitors including his wife and daughter, using a phone and behind bullet-proof glass. He was deported to Belfast over Christmas time. I visited him in Belfast, and he was having trouble finding work. Most workplaces are pro-British owned, and they don't hire former prisoners.]

Near the end of George W. Bush's second term, a group of former IRA prisoners formed their own lobbying group and, with the help of Irish American groups, started a new campaign to dismiss the cases against them. There was some support from Republicans and Democrats courting the Irish-American vote.

But the biggest factor was that the Bush administration was more focused on targeting the Arab and Muslim community, so the Irish ex-prisoners had their files "put at the bottom of the stack," as one official put it, where they remain today. With influential congressional representatives and mainstream Irish-American organizations like the Ancient Order of Hibernians taking up his case, Malachy McAllister has had his stay in the US extended year after year with the latest extension in March of this year. [Malachy was eventually deported back to Ireland.]

Excluding Palestinians

Another US-sponsored Israeli-Palestinian "peace process" is currently underway to pick up the pieces of the failed Oslo accords. But unlike Clinton's more even-handed and inclusive policy towards the Irish peace process, the Obama administration has favored Israel by continuing to supply military aid and by excluding all Palestinian political parties and groups except one — Fatah — from the political process.

Clinton made peace in Ireland a high priority of US foreign policy while also guaranteeing political support from the influential bloc of Irish-Americans. But under Clinton, another US foreign policy focus was support for Israel. The priority of supporting Israel during the Oslo negotiations overrode any desire to be equally even-handed during this peace process.

It was the Clinton State Department that originally placed all the major Palestinian political parties, except Fatah, on the designated list of "foreign terrorist organizations" because of their opposition to Oslo.

President Obama made a half-hearted attempt to emulate Clinton's handling of the Irish peace process by sending George Mitchell, the negotiator of the Good Friday agreement, to Palestine on Obama's second day in office. Yet Mitchell's mission was doomed to fail just like every other US-sponsored Israeli-Palestinian peace process because of the U.S. support for Israel and the blacklisting of all Palestinian political and resistance groups except one, Fatah, the leading party of the Palestine Authority.]

The Obama administration has also continued the Bush administration's endless war on terror by targeting members of the Palestinian, Arab, and Muslim communities.

What conclusions can we draw in comparing the domestic context during the Clinton administration's peace process in Ireland and the attempt of the Obama administration to broker peace in Palestine? For Clinton, all Irish political parties and the paramilitary groups they represented were eventually included in the peace negotiations with very few exceptions.

Irish activists in the U.S. were typically under surveillance but not targeted for arrest and deportation unless they were former political prisoners. The targeting of former political prisoners occurred either before the peace process was underway or after 11 September 2001 when they were swept up in the "war on terror."

During the Israeli-Palestinian peace process under Clinton and the current efforts under Obama, there has never been a genuine attempt to include all Palestinian groups. Nor has there been an attempt to distinguish between a political party and the resistance group that party may be associated with.

Unlike Irish activists in the 1980s and '90s, Palestine activists critical of U.S. policy toward Israel have not only been under surveillance but have been actively targeted for repression. From the cases of the Holy Land Five to Sami al-Arian, to the harassment of Students for Justice in Palestine groups, to the ongoing grand jury investigation of 23 anti-war and Palestine solidarity activists, the repression has continued during the Obama administration.

Palestinians and their supporters can't look to the Obama administration to be sympathetic to their activists or former political prisoners. We can't expect Arab-Americans to have the political clout enjoyed by Irish-Americans, especially as Arab and Muslim communities are both oppressed more generally.

Rasmea Odeh's arrest is just the latest attack on the entire Palestinian and Arab community and part of the ongoing repression of Palestine activists. Odeh has been a community leader fighting for Arab women's and immigrant rights in the US for more than twenty years. Any attempt to demonize her for "immigration fraud," threatening her with ten years in prison, and revoking her citizenship is nothing other than a vindictive attempt to destroy not only a successful Arab community leader but also a strong advocate for Palestinian rights.

Bill Chambers was a member of both Irish Northern Aid and the Irish-American Unity Conference. He is currently active with the Palestine Solidarity Group - Chicago and the Committee Against Political Repression.

The above article explains in detail how Irish Republican prisoners like Ciaran Ferry were not targeted for deportation until after 9-11 and the war on terror, when the terrorist label was broadly applied to many different groups. Palestine activists have been targeted for many years, and the repression just intensified after 9-11. In the current time, 2024-5, Palestine activism itself is being targeted, especially after Apartheid Israel's genocidal war on Gaza. Several students, faculty members, and student groups like Students for Justice in Palestine and Jewish Voice for Peace have been expelled, fired, or barred from campus. Given Trump's election as president, this repression is expected to continue and broaden to Palestinians in general.

Angela Davis and Rasmea Odeh

The following articles from the *Chicago Monitor* and *The Electronic Intifada* provide background on the case against Rasmea Odeh and the progress of her trial in Detroit. At every hearing, many activists from Chicago and her colleagues from the AAAN, where she was Associate Director, attended both inside and outside the courtroom. These first two articles are from early in the case against Rasmea Odeh and provide some good background on the case against her.

Rasmea Odeh Targeted for Palestine Activism

Chicago Monitor
By Bill Chambers - August 29, 2014

The defense team for Chicago Palestinian community leader, Rasmea Odeh has uncovered new evidence that confirms her alleged immigration fraud case is based on her being targeted for Palestine activism. Yesterday, they filed a motion to dismiss the indictment against her.

My Chicago Activist Life

Odeh supporters outside the Detroit Federal Court

Rasmea Odeh was arrested on October 22, 2013, by agents of the Department of Homeland Security and charged with immigration fraud. Allegedly, in her application for citizenship made 20 years ago, she didn't mention that she was arrested in Palestine 45 years ago by an Israeli military court that had tortured her into confessing to bombings in Jerusalem.

In the Chicago courtroom on the day of her arrest, Assistant U.S. Attorney Barry Jonas was seen conferring with the prosecutors. At the time, that was the first clue Odeh's indictment was related to the case of the well-known Palestinian and anti-war Midwest activists whose homes were raided by the FBI when the U.S. attorney alleged that they had provided material support to foreign terrorist organizations in Palestine. Eventually, a total of 23 activists were subpoenaed, but all refused to testify and were never charged, assuming because of a lack of evidence. Members of multiple organizations were also targeted, including the Anti-War Committee in Minneapolis, Freedom Road Socialist Organization, Arab American Action Network (AAAN), Palestine Solidarity Group – Chicago, and others. Assistant U.S.

Attorney Barry Jonas continues to lead this ongoing investigation. Odeh's supporters could easily presume that Odeh and the case of the 23 were related. Hatem Abudayyeh, Executive Director of the AAAN and one of the activists whose home was raided by the FBI, is also a colleague of Odeh, Assistant Director of the AAAN.

It's important to note that this ongoing investigation involves activists from multiple struggles, including the anti-war movement, Colombia, Cuba, and immigration rights, but it's primary focus is support for Palestine. Echoing what's happening to Odeh now, Carlos Montez, a veteran Chicano, anti-war, and immigrant rights activist, whose name appeared on a search warrant of the Anti-War Committee office in Minneapolis, was indicted in May of 2011 on unrelated charges related to a protest 45 years ago. The charges were eventually thrown out of court. This multi-year investigation that involves targeting social justice movements, in this case, Palestine activism, by criminalizing their activity and suppressing any coalition building among different groups has been a trend throughout U.S. Justice Department and FBI history. More on this trend later.

On Wednesday, the Rasmea Odeh defense team confirmed a direct relationship between the investigation targeting Palestine activists in 2010 and the records that led to the indictment of Odeh in 2013. The press release states, "Attorneys representing Chicago's long-time Palestinian community leader, Rasmea Odeh, have filed a motion and brief in Detroit's U.S. District Court to dismiss the indictment against her. They are doing so on the grounds that the charges are the product of an illegal investigation targeting both Palestine solidarity efforts and organizing in the Palestinian community."

In the motion to dismiss, Odeh's attorneys describe the indictment as "the product of an illegal investigation into the First Amendment activities of the Arab-American Action Network (AAAN) and intended to suppress the work of the defendant in support of the Arab community of Chicago." The motion goes on to describe how in January of 2010 the Assistant U.S. Attorney Brandon Fox "initiated a request through the Office of International Affairs Criminal Division of the U.S. Department of Justice from the State of Israel for records of the defendant."

In July 2011, the Israelis sent a set of documents to Assistant U.S. Attorney Fox, supporting the claim that Odeh "had been arrested, convicted and imprisoned by the military legal system imposed by Israel in the West Bank...Over two years later, with nothing to show for its raids in 2010, Ms. Odeh was indicted for falsely answering questions in 2004 in her naturalization application." The defense attorneys also speculate, not without reason, that "the United States Attorney in Illinois, which was the office that initiated the request for the Israeli documents and was carrying out the investigation, apparently passed the case to the office in Michigan, to divert attention from its failed efforts to criminalize the work of the AAAN in Chicago."

These are dots that are not difficult to connect. The initial investigation in 2010 broadly targeted activists throughout the Midwest but primarily focused on Palestinians and Palestine activists in Chicago. During the last four years, the Palestine solidarity movement has grown in numbers and impact particularly through the growth of the Boycott Divestment Sanctions (BDS) movement directed at Israel and the proliferation of Students for Justice in Palestine groups on college campuses. With the growth of the movement came the attention of the FBI.

As mentioned above, the FBI has a history of targeting growing social justice movements in the U.S., criminalizing those movements, and preventing coalitions they might form with other communities or organizations. Examples from Church Senate Committee Report on FBI Counterintelligence (COINTELPRO) Programs and other studies of FBI history include Dr. Martin Luther King, Jr. and the Southern Christian Leadership Conference (SCLC) accused of being communists and the undermining of attempted coalition building with unions and anti-Vietnam war groups; the Black Panther Party prevented from building coalitions with the Students for a Democratic Society (SDS) and politicized gangs like the Blackstone Rangers in Chicago; and the targeting of the Sanctuary Movement that supported Central American refugees in the 1980s accusing activists of supporting terrorists as a way of undermining the movement's broad support of faith-based, human rights, and socialist groups.

Several hundred statements of support from unions, human rights, civil rights, and faith-based groups and thousands of supporters from across the country for the 23 anti-war and Palestine activists seem to have prevented indictments in that case so far. It is not hard to imagine the prosecutors reviewing the evidence they had collected that had failed to convince a grand jury for an indictment, finding Odeh's file from the Israelis, and deciding to build a case for indicting another leader of Chicago's Palestinian community. There are few other reasonable explanations for why Odeh would be charged for an alleged offense that occurred 20 years ago based on a prison term resulting from a confession obtained through torture 45 years ago.

"Rasmea is facing up to ten years in jail and deportation. She is a Palestinian who has stood up for the Palestinian, Arab, and Muslim communities in Chicago and to end the occupation of Palestine as well. Rasmea suffered vicious torture and sexual abuse in Israeli prisons, and the U.S. government is trying to victimize her again," states Hatem Abudayyeh of the national Rasmea Defense Committee.

Odeh's defense team will be discussing this motion to dismiss at her next court hearing on September 2 in the United States District Court for the Eastern District of Michigan, at 231 W Lafayette Boulevard, in Detroit, Michigan. The Rasmea Defense Committee and the Committee to Stop FBI Repression (CSFR) – CAIR-Chicago is a member of both coalitions – are organizing a picket line outside the court building at 2:00 p.m. and filling the courtroom for the hearing beginning at 3:00 p.m.

This article exposes the prosecution of Rasmea Odeh in the case described above of the well-known Palestinian and anti-war Midwest activists whose homes were raided by the FBI when the U.S. attorney alleged that they had provided material support to foreign terrorist organizations in Palestine. The same Assistant U.S. Attorney Barry Jonas, who initiated the grand jury and subpoenaed the 23 who all refused to testify and were never charged, assuming because of a lack of evidence, was seen conferring with the prosecution team of Rasmea Odeh. It proved that out of frustration in having this case against Palestinian activists collapse, the Department of Justice would retaliate by going after Palestinian leader Rasmea Odeh. Not surprisingly the defense motion was denied.

The next article describes another hearing of Rasmea Odeh's case because the original judge recused himself as it was discovered he had business interests in Apartheid Israel. In the description of this hearing, it is clear the Department of

Homeland Security (DHS) was ratcheting up its targeting of Palestinians and their supporters who had once again traveled to Detroit to support Rasmea Odeh. The numbers of supporters (as well as DHS police) swelled to a larger turnout than usual given protestors were also there for the final phase of the City of Detroit bankruptcy case at the courthouse earlier that day.

USA vs. Rasmea Odeh: Detroit Hearing Update

Update on Rasmea Odeh case to set hearings and trial start.

Chicago Monitor
By Bill Chambers - September 3, 2014

Once again, the supporters of Rasmea Odeh came to Detroit for a hearing on her case. This time, they had to be content with chanting with confrontational DHS police outside the courthouse and filling up the hallway outside the judge's chambers during the closed hearing.

Yesterday, Rasmea Odeh, the Chicago Palestinian community leader charged with "immigration fraud" based on allegedly not mentioning on her citizenship application a conviction in an Israeli military court obtained through torture, had a hearing in front of U.S. District Judge Gershwin A. Drain. Judge Drain had been assigned to the case after her previous judge had recused himself because of undisclosed Israeli business interests.

Supporters from Chicago, Milwaukee, Louisville, Grand Rapids, Flint, Dearborn, and Detroit gathered in front of the courthouse, expecting to picket and chant as had happened multiple times before without incident. As soon as one of the group began to use a bullhorn, he was approached by Department of Homeland Security (DHS) police saying he had to move across the street because he was disrupting the court proceedings in the building.

Hatem Abudayyeh, one of the leaders of the Rasmea Defense Committee, challenged the lead officer of the DHS police detail to produce "the statute" that said bullhorns had to be used across the street and not on the public sidewalk as had been done every other time before. The statute was never produced, but the protesters agreed to have the chants led from across the street.

This interaction would be indicative of the attitude of the greater numbers of DHS police that day. The larger turnout of DHS police was also likely due to the over 100 protesters of the final phase of the City of Detroit bankruptcy case at the courthouse earlier that day. For those protestors who were fighting for public employee pensions and to stop the city from turning off water because of unpaid water bills, the DHS police had blocked off the street in front of the courthouse and seemed to have no problem with megaphones.

After chants of "DOJ, let's be clear, Rasmea is welcome here" and "When community leaders are under attack, what do we do? Stand up and fight back!" – Odeh's supporters passed through the security checks and filled up the first-floor hallway of the building only to find that Judge Gershwin was going to hold a private hearing in his chambers. The DHS police presence was also prominent within the building. While waiting in the hallway, one of Odeh's supporters overheard a DHS policeman's comment "these people are pathetic, bringing all these people here for this case."

Michael Deutsch and Rasmea Odeh

After the closed hearing, Michael Deutsch, one of Odeh's defense attorneys, reported that he had asked the judge to move the hearing into open court because of the many people who had traveled hours to be there. "He said that this was only setting dates, and this was how he did it. He wasn't hostile about it and just didn't want to treat this case any differently than any other." But as Deutsch pointed out, the judge knew this case was different than the others because of the effort of Odeh's supporters to be there even for a short hearing. Deutsch reiterated that the situation is still much better with the new judge on the case than the old one.

The result of the hearing was setting dates for the arguing of the defense motions and the beginning of the trial. On October 2 and continuing October 21, four defense motions will be argued.

Motion to dismiss the indictment as "the product of an illegal investigation into the First Amendment activities of the Arab-American Action Network (AAAN) and intended to suppress the work of the defendant in support of the Arab community of Chicago."

Motion to exclude any documents provided by the Israeli occupation military court.

Request for documents from the U.S. State Department that have interviews with U.S. citizens included in the 500 people arrested by the Israeli authorities at the same time as Odeh in 1969.

Motion to include expert testimony on Odeh's case of PTSD from being tortured while in prison.

The trial is set to begin on November 4 with jury selection.

After the report on the hearing, there were speeches from representatives of some organizations as part of the Rasmea Defense Committee. Jess Sundin, representing the Committee to Stop FBI Repression (CSFR), described how "people are mobilizing around the country to fight this indictment of Rasmea". CSFR sponsored a call-in day to the prosecutors coinciding with the hearing, and Sundin described the "thousands who had made the call, filling up the prosecutor's voice mailboxes".

Frank Chapman from NAARPR

Frank Chapman, from the Chicago Alliance Against Racist and Political Repression, expressed the solidarity of his organization with the Rasmea Defense Committee. "On August 27, we sent a request to the DOJ for an investigation into 65 victims of police brutality in

Chicago. Just like Rasmea, many of these were victims of torture."

Michael Deutsch had the last word, "The judge knows now this is a big case because all of you are here."

The Rasmea Defense Committee including over 50 organizations, CAIR-Chicago being just one, will be organizing Odeh's supporters to come out for both hearing dates on October 2 and 21 and for the start of the trial itself on November 4.

That hearing set the stage for the coming start of the trial and consideration of the motions of the defense for overturning the conviction.

The following article by Ali Abunimah from the *Electronic Intifada* describes Rasmea's first day in court on November 14, 2013. As expected, there was a large turnout of supporters due to the intense nationwide organizing the Rasmea Odeh Defense Committee had been doing. Ali Abunimah reminds everyone that the "Obama administration….has deported as many people as possible and split up more families than every previous U.S. administration combined."

Rasmea Odeh's Day in Court

Electronic Intifada
Ali Abunimah
14 November 2013

Rasmea Odeh (left) and attorney Jim Fennerty with supporters outside the US federal courthouse in Detroit on 13 November 2013. (Photo by Ali Abunimah)

United States magistrate judge Laurie Michaelson treated everyone who came before her with notable kindness and courtesy, whether for an arraignment, detention hearing, or to decide if an individual should be jailed for violating his bail terms.

She wished each of the men who stood before her bench at the U.S. courthouse in Detroit on Wednesday, including those wearing red vests bearing the words "Wayne County Jail Prisoner," a "good afternoon" before going through the motions of his case.

But her gentle manner could not conceal the violence manifest in that wood-paneled courtroom. Most of the defendants sat along the wall on one side of the room. Unable to afford lawyers, all but one required a federal defender.

On the other side of the room were the prosecutors – men and women in suits – secure in the knowledge that they had the unlimited resources of the United States at their disposal.

And there, too, was Rasmea Yousef Odeh, sitting in the front row with her nephew on one side and Chicago attorney Jim Fennerty on the other, waiting for her case to be called.

In the rows of seats behind, several dozen supporters packed the benches. I sat in the back row between a correspondent from Reuters and a local representative of Jewish Voice for Peace.

Many of us had come from Chicago, Rasmea's home, to be with her.

Outside the courthouse in the bitter cold, there were dozens more from Chicago, from Dearborn, Grand Rapids, and Detroit, Michigan, and from as far away as Milwaukee, Wisconsin. Supporters in several other cities, including Chicago, Minneapolis, Tampa, and Oakland held rallies as well.

A dozen students, including Farah Erzouki, traveled from the University of Michigan in Ann Arbor for the rally at the courthouse.

"We represent the [Students for Justice in Palestine] both in Michigan and nationally and came to show solidarity and support for Rasmea Odeh," Erzouki told Fightback News.

But inside, Rasmea had to wait her turn as other individuals were called up for arraignment – a procedure where the accused hears the charges they face, along with the penalties if convicted, and then has the choice of pleading guilty, not guilty or "standing mute."

All the accused but one were people of color, and Rasmea was the only woman. The first person called up, Mr. N., had been charged with "unlawful re-entry into the United States" – I presume from Mexico since he required a Spanish-English interpreter.

From the few details revealed in the hearing it appeared he has a wife in the United States. The penalty, if convicted, for wanting to stay with his family? Ten years and a fine of up to $250,000.

Another man, also requiring an interpreter, faced the same charge, and a third person, an African American man, was arraigned for "transporting an illegal alien within the United States." Again, up to ten years in prison and astronomical fines on conviction.

This is what the federal courts are busy with under the Obama administration, which has deported as many people as possible and split up more families than every previous U.S. administration combined.

This too, is the context for Rasmea Odeh's case, which was made vividly clear in that courtroom.

Men with guns

Then there was a young man, also African American, who faced a charge of "brandishing" a gun while committing a robbery (this is a federal offense because robberies interfere with "commerce"). Now, even though the man was not accused of firing the weapon or injuring anyone, this is still a serious charge that carries an additional seven years in prison on top of other penalties.

It struck me, though, how differently this country treats people brandishing – and firing – guns: in some cases, they are deemed "mentally disturbed," in other cases "terrorists" or reviled criminals against whom the full weight of the United States must be brought to bear.

Most of the time, of course, men with guns are considered patriots and heroes exercising a constitutional right or "serving their country." But it's not always easy to tell which is which.

Justice for Renisha McBride

I could not help thinking of Renisha McBride.

Just a few miles away from the Detroit federal courthouse, in the early hours of 2 November, McBride walked up to a house in the suburb of Dearborn Heights to seek help after a car accident.

But instead of helping her or calling 911, the homeowner shot McBride, 19, in the face and killed her.

Although he later claimed – implausibly – that the shooting was an "accident," the gunman has not explained why he waited several hours before calling the emergency services to report what he had done.

Police have refused to release the name of the shooter, although he was named on Democracy Now! on 13 November as 54-year-old Ted Wafer.

The Dearborn Heights police have not arrested him or charged him.

As outrage about McBride's killing grows, hundreds have rallied in Dearborn Heights to demand justice for her and her family.

Why has Wafer not been arrested? "His whiteness is the only explanation I can come up with; you know, her black body, justification, de facto," filmmaker and activist Dream Hampton told Democracy Now!

"We know that the ... Dearborn Heights Police Department is an all-white police force."

Commenting on her niece's shooting with – for now – total impunity, McBride's aunt Bernita Spinks asked, "Wow! Could I possibly do that? Somebody knocked on my door, and I pull my shotgun out, and I shoot them while they're leaving off my porch, instead of finding out what was the problem—would I be standing here? No, I'd be in jail without a bond."

But as we are reminded with tragic regularity, this is a country whose legislatures and courts are more interested in protecting sacred "commerce" and property than the sanctity of African American lives.

Rasmea's turn

Now it was Rasmea's turn, and she and Detroit attorney William Swor went up (a local lawyer is required in the court). The procedure was a formality for the ever-courteous Judge Michaelson, but I can only imagine what Rasmea must have felt when the court clerk called out "United States vs. Rasmea Odeh."

The charge was read: obtaining naturalization by fraud. Rasmea is accused of failing to disclose on her US citizenship application twenty years ago that she had a prior conviction.

The conviction in question was in an Israeli military court 45 years ago – in which nothing is resembling due process – for involvement in two bombings in Jerusalem, one of which killed two civilians.

She spent ten years in prison before receiving a pardon and being released by Israel as part of a prisoner exchange.

If convicted for this omission, the judge explained, Rasmea could face ten years in prison and an exorbitant fine, and the trial court would "revoke, cancel and declare null and void" her United States citizenship certificate.

From Lifta to Chicago

Rasmea Odeh is from Lifta, Palestine. She was born in 1948, the year Lifta was ethnically cleansed by Zionist militias.

During her time in Israeli detention, she faced torture, including sexual abuse.

Despite her ordeal, after her release and expulsion to Lebanon in 1979, Rasmea made her way to Jordan, where she earned a law degree.

She moved to the United States in 1995 and, as the dozens of organizations expressing support for her have reiterated, she has dedicated herself to working with women to promote literacy education and to fight domestic violence and racism.

On 22 October, Rasmea was arrested in Chicago on behalf of federal prosecutors in the Eastern District of Michigan and released on bond the same day.

Like the other defendants, Rasmea "stood mute," and Judge Michaelson entered a plea of "not guilty" on her behalf, just as she did for every other accused person.

After the hearing, those of us in the courtroom joined those still rallying outside. Hatem Abudayyeh, executive director of the Arab American Action Network, of which Rasmea is associate director, reminded us why we were there.

Rasmea's case is not just one of alleged "immigration fraud." It is in every sense a political case and part and parcel of the ongoing assault on Muslim, Arab, and Palestinian communities, Abudayyeh said.

One must wonder why the government would decide to dig out her 20-year-old immigration file now. As Abudayyeh suggested, this may be another case of selective prosecution, where Rasmea Odeh was singled out because of the community she comes from.

No mercy

We know, from the great piece Bill Chambers wrote for *The Electronic Intifada* this week, that in the case of Irish political prisoners, U.S. authorities had acted with discretion when they judged that it would help the cause of peace and reconciliation. As Chambers, who was also in court for Rasmea's hearing, pointed out, Palestinians have never been shown such mercy.

And while the government doggedly pursues Rasmea Odeh, the impunity enjoyed by the killer of Renisha McBride also extends overseas to other men with guns.

My Electronic Intifada colleague Maureen Murphy writes: "Meanwhile, the U.S. provides Israel diplomatic cover at the United Nations and other arenas, ensuring [Israel] total impunity — even when US citizens are its victims."

These victims include Furkan Doğan, the American teenager extrajudicially executed by Israeli commandos while he held a small camcorder documenting their assault on the Mavi Marmara humanitarian aid ship in international waters on 31 May 2010.

Long road

Yesterday, after the hearing, as Jim Fennerty and Rasmea stepped out of the courthouse into the cold, they were received with warmth by those outside. In brief statements, the two expressed how much the public support meant, and how much it will mean as the case goes forward.

Rasmea's next court appearance – the date was not set in the arraignment hearing – will be for discovery and preliminary matters before the trial court of US District Judge Paul D. Borman in Detroit.

The road from Chicago to Detroit is long, and it is one that Rasmea and many of her supporters are likely to travel many times in the months and perhaps years ahead.

And while "standing mute" before the power of the government is the wise course attorneys counsel their clients to take at this stage in a case, it is not an option for us. We will also need to speak out as we travel that road with her.

For a short period of time there was hope that Rasmea would be granted a new trial. In February 2016, the Sixth Circuit Court of Appeals sent the case back to the original District Court Judge Drain, saying he had wrongfully barred the testimony of a torture expert that was critical to Rasmea's defense. The issue was that Rasmea was not allowed to tell the full story of her conviction of bombings in Israel in 1969, which was the result of a coerced confession made after she was tortured and raped by Israeli military authorities. This article presents the arguments made by the defense demanding a new trial based on the Appeals court decision.

Palestinian Community Leader Rasmea Odeh Moves Closer to a New Trial

By Bill Chambers
June 16, 2016
Chicago Monitor

On Monday morning, over 100 of Rasmea Odeh's supporters gathered from five states at the Federal Courthouse in Detroit to hear the results of her hearing on whether she would be allowed to present her full story and potentially be granted a new trial. In February, the Sixth Circuit Court of Appeals sent the case back to the original District Court Judge Drain, saying he had wrongfully barred the testimony of a torture expert that was critical to Rasmea's defense.

At her trial, Odeh was not allowed to tell the full story of her conviction of bombings in Israel in 1969 that was the result of a coerced confession made after she was tortured and raped by Israeli military authorities. Odeh was originally arrested in 2012 for a twenty-year-old "naturalization fraud" charge that was "discovered" while Justice Department investigators were frustrated in their failure to charge or indict 23 Palestine activists in 2010 for "material support for terrorism."

The appeals court ruling stated that the judge had misinterpreted existing case law when he excluded expert testimony that Odeh had post-traumatic stress disorder (PTSD) when she applied for naturalization in 2004 and denied having been convicted of a serious crime or served time in jail. As a result of that torture, Odeh was diagnosed with chronic PTSD by world-renowned psychologist and torture expert Dr. Mary Fabri, which, in the words of the appeal, "blocked [Odeh] from understanding the time frame in the questions that were answered falsely." The defense team argued she was not given the opportunity for a fair trial when the expert witness testimony was denied.

Odeh's supporters held a rally outside the court before, during, and after the hearing. Representatives from a wide range of organizations spoke of the connection between Odeh's case and many social justice issues.

Hatem Abudayyeh, one of the spokespersons for the Rasmea Defense Committee and national coordinating committee member of the US Palestinian Community Network (USPCN), provided the perspective on the day's hearing.

> "Rasmea did not get a full and fair shake at her trial. Hundreds of us took off work and left our families to come out and support Rasmea's rights and to support the rights of Palestinians to fight for their liberation in this country and in Palestine…We lost that trial. We saw the inequity of it…But the appellate court said we were right and Rasmea was right – that her story needs to be told. The story of Israeli crimes, torture, and rape and the US support of those crimes will now be on trial in the US."

Frank Chapman, field organizer for the Chicago Alliance Against Racism and Political Repression, tied the fight for justice for Odeh to justice for victims of police crimes and for all political prisoners.

> "It's not our country that is in a world of trouble; it's the people who rule our country who are in trouble. Troubled times for them, momentous times for us. In Chicago, we are in the streets almost every day demanding justice, fighting for a Civilian Police Accountability Council, and continuing to demand justice for Rasmea Odeh. No matter what it takes…we are going to get justice for Rasmea Odeh and for all political prisoners."

Odeh's prosecution has led to support from many immigrant groups who see her case as another example of an oppressed minority being persecuted for organizing for their rights. Nerissa Allegretti from the National Alliance for Filipino Concerns (NAFCON) stressed this point.

> "Many Filipino and immigrant people and targets of the war on terror are fighting against the war machine. Like Rasmea, we try to fight and say the truth, and there is repression. We are all Rasmea."

Many Detroit organizations came out to show their support. Tawana Petty, from the James and Grace Lee Boggs Center, reiterated Nerissa Allegretti's concerns for oppressed minorities, connecting Odeh's case to her own community.

> "As a domestic violence survivor, I stand here on behalf of Rasmea and on behalf of my community to say that Rasmea is welcome here. As a Black community and as Detroiters, we need to stand up for other oppressed communities…We must stand up for equality, justice, and democracy for all communities. We can't let what happened in Florida to go from homophobia to Islamophobia."

Kristian Baily, from BYP 100 in Detroit, drew the connections between the experiences of the Black community and the Palestinians under occupation.

> "Today, we stand in solidarity with Rasmea and Palestine. Detroit is doubly occupied land; it was stolen from the Anishinabeg people and is currently being stolen from the majority Black population in the city…Black women and families are being evicted and kicked out of their homes every day. Palestinians are being kicked out of their homes by people who should have no authority over them. Water is under attack in Flint, Detroit, and in Palestine. They are trying to control our resources to police our lives. Both here and in Palestine, there are systems of incarceration to police and control our communities, to make us afraid to resist."

Nadine Darwish from Students for Justice in Palestine described the widespread support Odeh has gotten on campuses across the country and how that support has led to solidarity between different student groups as well as with professors.

"Rasmea has been able to bridge the gap between campuses and communities for years...On campuses across the country, there have been actions large and small in support of Rasmea, bringing students from all different backgrounds and organizations together...On the day of Rasmea's guilty verdict came at the same time as Darren Wilson's non-indictment [killer of Michael Brown in Ferguson]...We saw that system that let the killer of an unarmed black teenager roam free while it jailed a community organizer...At Loyola, Black and Palestinian students joined together and organized a huge demonstration against the flaws in the justice system...This is not about unlawful procurement of naturalization. This is an attack on Arabs on Palestinians organizing in their communities. This is an attack on sexual assault survivors. We will keep organizing until Rasmea gets the justice she deserves."

David Finkel from Jewish Voice for Peace (JVP) – Detroit said there was no reason for the U.S. government and Israeli intelligence to bring the case against Odeh other than "to criminalize activism and most importantly to terrorize Rasmea's community." He echoed Hatem Abudayyeh's comments earlier when he described how Odeh's case in on the front line in the struggle for Palestinian rights. "The last thing that the US government or the Israeli government would want is an open and fair trial in which the long record of torture in the Israeli prison system would come to light."

Some of the other groups represented at the rally were the Cincinnati Palestine Solidarity Committee and the Anti-War Committees from Chicago and Minneapolis.

When Rasmea Odeh's defense team spoke to her supporters after the hearing, they said there was an entirely new prosecution team who appeared much more reasonable in their arguments. Jonathan Tukel, the prosecutor at the original trial, was conspicuously absent and appears to be no longer involved. Assistant U.S. Attorney Jonathan Tukel had often emphasized Odeh being a "terrorist" in his comments during the trial and in prosecution papers had referred to Odeh's supporters as a "protesting mob" in requesting additional security measures for the jury members. His removal from the case was likely a rebuke for his handling of the original trial leading to the appeals court sending the case back.

The Rasmea Defense Committee indicated that they would continue to organize support on her behalf and are prepared to mobilize her supporters once again for the November hearing. At a press conference after the hearing, Defense attorney Michael Deutsch announced, "There is a tentative date for a new trial on January 10 of next year…but first a hearing is scheduled for November 29, and we will argue for the PTSD experts to give testimony in a new trial. The government will argue against the PTSD expert testimony being allowed…My reading of the judge is that he seems to lean to the fact that he is going to have to let her expert testify." Deutsch indicated that the prosecution appears to be looking for a detailed evidentiary hearing, but he is hopeful that the next hearing will be more of a quick decision by the judge to approve the PTSD expert and move on to the new trial. A new trial will mean a new jury and the presentation of all the evidence from both the prosecution and, this time, the defense. Rasmea Odeh is still free to return to her community until her next hearing.

The article spoke of the tight connection that was made at the time of Rasmea's prosecution was not only an attack on the entire Palestinian community but also linked to the immigrant rights movement, Black Lives Matter, and the current campaign for community control of the police. Again, this is another example how the support campaign for Rasmea Odeh intersected with many other important social justice campaigns happening in Chicago.

Rasmea would lose her fight to have a new, more favorable trial. Her last hearing for her sentencing in August 2017 is described in the article below. This next article demonstrates the atmosphere of political repression that had gone on throughout the trial. It was clear that the case was unwinnable for the prosecution if it was only based on "immigration fraud". The political mood in the country had changed with the election of President Trump. It was no surprise when U.S. Attorney Barbara McQuade announced in December 2016 that a grand jury she impaneled returned a new, superseding indictment asserting that Odeh was involved in "terrorist activity" and was a member of a "designated terrorist organization," both grounds for revoking her citizenship. This new indictment came one month after the election of President Trump and shortly before Jeff Sessions was confirmed as Attorney General. This new indictment would prove to be much harder to fight.

Judge Tells Palestinian Leader Rasmea Odeh – the Occupation is "Not Important"

Judge Warns Odeh to Stop Making the Case Political.
Chicago Monitor
By Bill Chambers - August 19, 2017

On Thursday, August 17, over 250 of Rasmea Odeh's supporters from across the country packed the Federal courtroom in Detroit for her final appearance in the over three-year case against her. She was to be sentenced after agreeing to a plea deal to be deported without jail time forced by the antagonistic environment of a Sessions Justice Department determined to retry her as a terrorist.

Rasmea and her supporters, who had rallied outside the court in the pouring rain, expected that she would be sentenced to time served in jail (33 days), receive some form of fine ($1,000), lose her US citizenship, and be deported. What they didn't expect was a still proud

Palestinian community leader prevented from giving her full statement and threatened with contempt of court and jail by Judge Drain if she didn't stop making the case "political."

But examining the history of the case and the past statements of Judge Drain, his words were predictable.

At her trial, Odeh was not allowed to tell the full story of her conviction of bombings in Israel in 1969 that was the result of a coerced confession made after she was tortured and raped by Israeli military authorities. Odeh was originally arrested in 2012 for a twenty-year-old "naturalization fraud" charge that was "discovered" while Justice Department investigators were frustrated in their failure to charge or indict 23 Palestine activists in 2010 for "material support for terrorism."

The Federal Court of Appeals sent the case back to Judge Drain's court in February 2016 when they determined in the original trial, Judge Drain prevented Odeh's defense team from using a PTSD defense, and a new trial was needed. As a way to win a case that they now believed was unwinnable if based only on "naturalization fraud," U.S. Attorney Barbara McQuade announced in December that a grand jury she impaneled returned a new, superseding indictment asserting that Odeh was involved in "terrorist activity" and was a member of a "designated terrorist organization" both grounds for revoking her citizenship. This new indictment came one month after the elected of President Trump and shortly before Jeff Sessions was confirmed as Attorney General.

But this is not a political case.

Odeh's defense team believed with this new even more hostile prosecutorial environment, it would not be possible to get a fair trial. As Defense Attorney Michael

Deutsch stated at an event for Odeh in Chicago before 1,200 of her supporters, "There was no guarantee that the Immigration authorities wouldn't have jailed and then deported her even if we had won the case."

Michael Deutsch speaking to reporters.

On Thursday, Michael Deutsch was the first to speak in court and stressed that "anyone who was concerned with justice and was told this woman had been in the country for 20 years, beloved by members of her community, and given awards would have taken a step back...Someone who was concerned with justice would not have charged her with an immigration crime. This case should have never been brought."

Prosecutor Jonathan Tukel spoke next immediately before Rasmea Odeh's final statement and said, "I didn't intend to say anything, but need to say she did commit acts of terrorism...It is so clear in the historical record and in the court record."

But this is not a political case.

Rasmea Odeh began her statement, making clear who she was and whom she represented. (Her complete, uninterrupted, statement to the court can be found below and in multiple media reports.)

"On this court's platform, I'm standing today to raise my voice on behalf of myself as a Palestinian woman and on behalf of all Palestinian People, whether under occupation, in refugee camps, or scattered in exile across the world."

Odeh did not get very far before Judge Drain interrupted her the first time. "This case is about you making false statements in immigration applications."

Odeh interjected, saying, "This is my first and last chance to speak. Palestinians are not terrorists," and then continued with her prepared statement.

Odeh continued to tell the history of the UN conventions that say Palestinians have the right to resist occupation, questioning why, like the early Americans, Palestinians are not given the right to fight for their independence and that the US government has supported the Israeli occupation of Palestine by selling arms illegally to the Israeli government to use against the Palestinians. Judge Drain interrupted two more times, saying, "This is not important. This is not the place to talk about that."

After Odeh said, "This government must be held responsible for the Palestine occupation and the colonization of our country. Israel has no right to exist as an apartheid state," Judge Drain interrupted the last time with a threat. "If you continue, I fill find you in contempt, and you will find yourself locked up."

Undeterred by this direct threat by the judge, Odeh concluded, "It was unjust they locked me in jail, tortured me, raped me, and destroyed my house. I will raise my voice to say we have the right to struggle for our country."

Before his official sentencing, Judge Drain emphasized he didn't believe PTSD prevented her from answering the questions on the forms correctly and with a final jab at Odeh's community sitting in the courtroom – "I recognize you have quite a few degrees, have helped people in Chicago, especially the Palestinian women who presumably came here legally [italics mine]." Members of the Arab Women's Committee sitting in the courtroom could only sit quietly and listen to this insulting insinuation.

But this is not a political case.

Judge Drain has a history of making prejudicial or insulting comments to Odeh and the people in her community.

In October of 2014, Judge Drain refused to allow testimony from the defense team's expert witness that Odeh suffers from PTSD but allowed the prosecution to present the specifics of Israeli accusations against her including information about the 1969 Jerusalem bombings she confessed to under torture. This was the decision that the Federal Court of Appeals overturned in February 2016, admonishing Judge Drain and the prosecution in the process.

Upon her guilty verdict in November 2014, Judge Drain stated, "Odeh doesn't have ties to the Chicago community. She has apparently done good work at the Arab American Action Network, but that work is not a substantial tie to the community. She could do this in another country." With those words, he wiped away Rasmea Odeh's 20 years of work in Chicago, being an advocate for Arab and Muslim women's rights. The twenty Arab and Muslim women sitting in the front rows who had come to court as representatives of Odeh's 800-member women's group were erased as if they did not exist.

But this is not a political case.

Although there were times when Judge Drain resisted the prosecution's continual attempt to paint Odeh as a terrorist and to deny her bail, in the end, he returned to his earliest view that this was not a political case and that Odeh's years of service to a community he didn't seem to respect would not matter because she had filled out her naturalization forms incorrectly.

Rasmea Odeh was directed to report to the Immigration and Customs Enforcement (ICE) agent Stephen Webber present in the courtroom for some yet undetermined period before she is deported.

Rasmea Speaking to Supporters.

The day in court concluded with a press conference and with Rasmea Odeh's words to her many supporters "We will continue to struggle for Palestine."

Rasmea Odeh's Full Statement to the Court

"On this court's platform, I'm standing today to raise my voice on behalf of myself as a Palestinian woman and on behalf of all Palestinian people, whether under occupation, in refugee camps, or scattered in exile across the world.

Honorable Judge Drain: First, I would like to clarify that my following message is not directed at you personally.

I am a Palestinian woman who was born into a family that had simple dreams and desires to live in peace and tranquility, far away from bombs, explosions, murder, and displacement.

But those dreams turned into a nightmare at the hands of the Zionist Haganah gangs, whose crimes are hard to imagine. The Zionists committed massacres, killing children and the elderly without any consideration of human values. They displaced hundreds of thousands of my people and killed thousands more, in 1947 and 1948, upon the establishment of the state of Israel. They turned us into strangers in our own country and pushed us into the inhumane conditions of refugee camps inside Palestine and other Arab countries.

The Israeli goals were not satisfied in 1948, so they pursued the ambitions of Zionism and launched another war in 1967, illegally occupying the rest of Palestine and parts of surrounding Arab countries.

International law prohibits the following practices and considers them punishable offenses:

The Israeli occupation of Palestine is a crime; its use of biological and chemical weapons is a terrorist crime; demolishing schools, homes, hospitals, clinics, and places of worship is a crime; imprisoning hundreds of political organizers and resisters (including dozens of children) without charge is a crime; putting up the Apartheid Wall is a crime; killing people is a crime; and collective punishment is a crime!

Many countries in this world have struggled to win their independence. International law and all the United Nations conventions state that people have the right to fight for their independence and to expel the colonizer and the occupier.

People in the U.S. struggled against British colonialism for their independence, and that is the reason the 4th of July is celebrated. Why are the Palestinians prohibited from struggling for our independence?

When Palestinians have fought for our rights over the years, all U.S. administrations have responded by supporting Israeli crimes and brutal aggression, falsely describing Israel's acts as "self-defense." At the same time, the U.S. government calls us terrorists by placing all our legitimate resistance organizations on its terrorist list!

I wonder how the U.S. or any other country would respond if they were invaded by a foreign force. If people in the U.S. were to defend themselves, would they be considered terrorists, and would their resistance organizations be placed on a terrorist list?

I am sure that they would have the full right to protect their country, just as my people should have the right to protect our country.

The Arms Export Control Act of 1976 prohibits the U.S. from exporting arms in situations where such arms would "...aid in the development of weapons of mass destruction... [or] increase the possibility of outbreak or escalation of conflict...," and prohibits the use of such arms against civilians and innocents.

Thus, the U.S. government or any U.S. company violates the law if it exports weapons to a state or group that uses them in this way. The reality is that the U.S., as Israel's patron, violates its own laws by supporting Zionist aggression. That means the U.S. is also guilty of crimes against the Palestinians.

This country's military, political, economic, and diplomatic support allows Israel to continue its colonization and military occupation of Palestine and to commit crimes prohibited by international law and U.S. law. That is why we organize for Palestinian rights in the U.S. because it is this government that must also be held responsible for Israel's state terrorism against my people.

We, the Palestinians, have been struggling against oppression for one hundred years, ever since the British Balfour Declaration promised the world that it would support the colonization of our country. And for almost 70 years, the manufactured state of Israel has been doing the bidding of the powerful British and U.S. empires. This Israel has no right to exist as a racist state of white settler colonialists, just like South Africa had no right to exist as the racist, Apartheid state it was.

This Israel represents nothing but violence and ethnic cleansing against my people. Many years of negotiations for a political settlement have been a huge failure because Israel continuously demands recognition as a Jewish state, which goes against all notions of equality and democracy, and because it wants to liquidate all the rights of the Palestinians, including our rights to return, self-determination, equality, and political independence.

Each Israeli government moves more and more to the extreme right, and Netanyahu's is the worst of them, launching three horrible wars on Gaza. He destroyed homes, schools, health clinics, and our infrastructure as a whole, killing thousands and finally imposing a siege on the entire Gaza Strip.

Recently, Israel installed metal detectors and security cameras at the entrance to the Al Aqsa Mosque in Jerusalem, prompting weeks of massive protests. Three Palestinians were killed and a thousand injured before Israel was forced by our mass movement to remove the barriers.

At the same time, Israeli laws that discriminate against Palestinians in Jerusalem, as well as settler violence against Palestinians in Jerusalem and the West Bank, are official policies meant to force more and more Palestinians out of our country and to consolidate Israeli control over Greater Jerusalem. It is quite clear that many, if not most, Israelis do not want Palestinians around at all.

I personally experienced a harsh, unstable, and terror-filled life in Palestine, like all my people under occupation. I was pushed off my land two separate times, my family home was destroyed twice, and the trauma of war killed my young sister. I was a political prisoner who was brutally tortured and raped by Israeli soldiers and prison authorities and was almost killed more than once.

I continue to be terrified of the future for myself and my people. I can still almost feel the accelerated pounding of the people's hearts while they are running to find shelter, the horrific screaming of the children, the moans of the people under the rubble of their homes, and the sounds of them dying from bombs, missiles, and bullets.

My people have the right to struggle to rid ourselves of the Israeli occupation of our country. The U.S. government must stop disavowing our rights and stop working with the Israelis to prosecute activists and organizers here. Most of the people and governments in the rest of the world are with us. Millions of people are supporting the Boycott Divestment and Sanctions (BDS) movement.

Black-Palestinian unity and solidarity are at their absolute height in the U.S. because both peoples recognize that the racist nature of the U.S. government and the racist nature of Israel is the same. When I saw those white racists marching in Virginia, all I could think of was the white settlers in Israel burning Palestinian children to death or marching to attack my people in Jerusalem.

Many of the social justice forces—from the Women's March, the Movement for Black Lives, and anti-occupation and anti-Zionist American Jews to immigrant rights, anti-torture, and civil liberties organizations—that supported my defense campaign did it not only because they support me as a survivor of torture and injustice, but also because they support the much more important cause of the liberation of all of Palestine—a democratic, secular Palestine for all."

Rasmea Odeh would end up being sentenced to finishing months in jail before being deported to Jordan, where she remains today, still fighting for Arab women's rights. Even though Rasmea Odeh's hundreds of supporters and the 50 social justice organizations that stood by her side could not prevent her unjust deportation, her case demonstrated the strong ties between the Palestine liberation movement and all the social justice movements across the country. To quote once again from Rasmea Odeh's final statement:

"Many of the social justice forces—from the Women's March, the Movement for Black Lives, and anti-occupation and anti-Zionist American Jews, to immigrant rights, anti-torture, and civil liberties organizations—that supported my defense campaign did it not only because they support me as a survivor of torture and injustice, but also because they support the much more important cause of the liberation of all of Palestine—a democratic, secular Palestine for all."

This solidarity between the Palestinian, Black, Latinx, anti-Zionist Jews, and immigrant communities would never break in Chicago, no matter what campaign of repression was waged against them.

Becoming a Muslim Activist (2010-2025)

At this point in my story, it makes sense to transition to my time as a Muslim activist who continued to support my involvement in anti-racism, anti-war, Irish Republican, and Palestine solidarity work.

First, I will describe my journey to becoming a Muslim. When I was in my Catholic high school in Detroit, I did not learn who Muslims were or anything about them in world history, even though some of the largest and longest empires were Muslim. During the 1960s, Dearborn, a city of over 107,710 west of Detroit, had the largest population of Muslims and Arabs in the country. I knew nothing about the Nation of Islam and its founding in Detroit on July 4, 1930. This redaction of history and of an entire group of people continued until I came to admire Malcolm X when I was in college. Even then, I thought of him as a more appealing Black Nationalist than Dr. Martin Luther King Jr. My education was typical for a white middle-class young man from Detroit. Everything I learned about fighting racism was outside the classroom and "in the streets," as we used to say.

From my time in a Catholic high school in Detroit, I admired the Church's opposition to racism, its logical sense of morality, and being the champion of the poor and dispossessed. I took a religion course called "Social Responsibility" using a textbook that applied Catholic teachings to the major social issues of the day. Everything was fine until it came to the chapter on the Vietnam War. The entire chapter discussed the Church's rules about a "just war" and concluded the Vietnam War was such a war. Given that I was already an anti-war activist, that approach would not work for me. From that point, I realized the Church usually sided with the government in power and was often on the wrong side of many issues. Later, I confirmed that perception. As an Irish Republican activist, I would discover that the Church condemned the Republican struggle and usually sided with the pro-British authorities in the North of Ireland.

I remained a religious person, but without a religion. Universal values were more than just human rights. They were moral principles above all governments. As I described earlier, during my first trips to Derry and Belfast in the North of Ireland, the curbstones in Nationalist neighborhoods puzzled me. Nationalists painted them in the colors of the Palestinian flag with the Irish Flag in their front yards. In the Loyalist or pro-British neighborhoods, they would fly the British flag next to the Israeli flag. The Nationalists identified with the Palestinians as they too, were under military occupation and had their land taken away by settlers. I finally understood the connection between the struggle in Ireland and that in Palestine.

Al-Aqsa Mosque in Jerusalem

During my time as a Palestine activist, I met many Muslim Palestinians who fought for self-determination alongside their

Christian and Marxist compatriots to oppose the military occupation of their land. During my multiple trips to Palestine as I wrote about above, I spent hours walking through the Old City of Jerusalem (called al-Quds in Arabic). The city that is the second holiest city in Islam inspired me. On one trip, my son and I stayed with a Muslim family in Nablus that discussed their faith with us in this city that was a center of resistance to the Israeli occupying forces. I read the Qur'an and its commentaries, but especially books about the life of Prophet Muhammad. Here was Scripture that put social justice at its very center. Here was a Prophet who was not only a religious leader but also a political one who respected all other "People of the Book"—Christians and Jews.

This awareness came after 9-11 when Islam was in the news every day, but not for any positive reason. There was clearly a whole new group of minorities the American government was going to oppress. Zareena Grewal, in her book *Islam is a Foreign Country*, draws the important distinction that for Muslims and Arabs, there is a gap between legal citizenship and social citizenship. In the majority Arab Muslim city of Dearborn, MI, everyone understands that citizenship is more than legal status and that national belonging is fragile and can be withheld from those deemed foreign, even if they are technically legal citizens.

Grewal also said, "You may be invited to the table, but that doesn't mean you are welcome." Muslims would be only "social citizens" and considered Arab in a country where 25-30% of Muslims are Black. Unlike the Irish, Muslims were not "white" even though many were based on the color of their skin. Islam was not an acceptable religion or, for many Americans, not even a religion at all.

Almost 15 years ago, in a Sufi community, I said my Shahada, the statement of belief in one God and Muhammad as His Prophet, that makes someone a Muslim. The group attracted me because of the equality between men and women, all praying and working together. Unfortunately, for me, the group focused too much on the Sheik, a religious leader from Jerusalem, who was head of this Sufi order. In my mind, the person to focus on, learn from, and follow as a model was the Prophet Muhammad.

For several years, I tried out different mosque communities with varied ethnic backgrounds. Some were welcoming, and most were not. For each one I visited during Friday jummah, a service when all Muslims gather in community prayer, the women would go in the front door and then never be seen again. They ended up in a balcony or separate room praying on their own. This violated my inherent belief that men and women are equals and should at least be in the same room praying together. Later, I would realize, after being educated in Islam and the Quran, that there is no inherent justification for this separation of men and women. The Quran makes it very clear that men and women are equal, and at the most, they may have different roles. Much of the separation and inequality found in Muslim communities is based upon the culture that these Muslims came from and not from Islam itself. In fact, in Prophet Muhammad's time, men and women prayed together and were leaders in the community, such as Aisha, one of the Prophet's wives.

Masjid al-Taqwa and the *Muslim Journal*

I soon discovered the American Islamic College (AIC)—the first and only Islamic undergraduate and graduate school that is based on similar principles to American liberal arts colleges. Muslims from many communities, including first-generation immigrants, studied together with men and women in the same classroom. AIC also reflected this same diversity in the faculty. While I was there, some of my favorite professors and fellow students were in the Imam W. Deen Mohammed Community. (Imam W. Deen Mohammed is one of the sons of the Honorable Elijah Muhammed, who took over and transformed the NOI into the "A-Islam" Community when his father died in 1975. The community uses the term "Al-Islam to differentiate itself from the beliefs of the Nation of Islam. See my first book, *The Muslim American Fight for Social Justice: From Civil Rights to Black Lives Matter*, for a complete history of this community.) To me, this is the inclusivity that Islamic higher education needs to be based on. I received my Masters Degree in Islamic Studies from AIC and, for a time, was the Student Support Services Coordinator.

The following article is a history of AIC as an institution that I wrote for the *Muslim Journal*.

The college has just recently achieved full accreditation.

The Legacy of Imam W. Deen Mohammed in Higher Education

4/15/19
Muslim Journal
Al-Islam Community Founds America's First Muslim College

The American Islamic College (AIC) was originally founded in 1981 during a very important time in the history of Islam in America. After the death of the Honorable Elijah Muhammad in 1975, Imam W. Deen Mohammed enabled the transition of members of the original Nation of Islam to more orthodox Sunni Islam. Based in Chicago, Imam W. Deen Mohammad was an important leader in the African American community as well as in Muslim American history. He was a key figure in the founding of AIC as America's first Muslim College according to his strong belief in education as an important part of Al-Islam.

The second significant development in this period was the increase of immigrant Muslims coming into the country after the easing of immigration law and increased quotas for people educated in the sciences to support American Cold War efforts. This new wave of Muslim immigrants resulted in the growth of mosques, Islamic schools, and organizations in the U.S. Unfortunately, many of these new mosques, schools, and community centers became segregated with the immigrant community who built them, in most cases Arab and South Asian communities. This pattern was particularly noticeable in highly segregated cities like Chicago.

But early in the late 1970s and 1980s, there was more cooperation between these two major sectors of Muslim Americans, i.e., the majority African American Muslims and the first generation of immigrant Muslims. These communities came together in the dream of establishing America's first Muslim college. Imam Mohammad was also particularly interested in dialogue not only with other Muslim communities but also with other faith communities. His leadership in these areas, as well as his desire to have a college in the U.S. where teachers could take classes in Islamic Studies and learn Arabic without traveling to Syria, Egypt, or some other country in the Middle East. His vision for Al-Islam in America was one based on leaders who would be developed here within the country. In 1983, his vision became a reality when AIC purchased a Catholic girl's high school, Immaculata, which became America's first Muslim college.

When AIC opened in 1983, its founding President was the highly respected Professor Ismail Al-Faruqi. Ahmad Sakr served as Vice President and is well known for his decades of work in youth training. Thomas Irving who was the first to translate the Qur'an into American English, was the Dean. Imam Mohammad continued to be intimately involved in the educational programs of the College, and his two brothers, Akbar and Jabir Muhammad, were founding members of AIC's Board of Trustees. Both Akbar Mohammad and Jabir Muhammad brought different but equally important knowledge to the founding of AIC.

Imam W. Deen Mohammad and his brother Akbar were two of the sons of the Honorable Elijah Muhammad who read the Qur'an and learned Arabic from an early age and were taught at the University of Islam (Elijah Muhammad's school) by Palestinian Professor Jamil Diab. Given that background it makes sense that Akbar would eventually become an Associate Professor Emeritus of History and Africana studies at Binghamton University in New York, specializing in African History, West African social history, and the study of Islam in Africa and the Americas. His own writings were focused on slavery in Muslim Africa, Muslims in the United States, and integration in Nigeria using education. He was fluent in Arabic after spending so many years in Cairo. One anecdote is that the Honorable Elijah Muhammad listened to both Imam Mohammad and Akbar read from the Qur'an based on Professor Diab's classes. He decided Akbar, with his better pronunciation, should focus on learning Arabic, while Imam Mohammad should focus on understanding and teaching the beliefs of Al-Islam.

Jabir Herbert Muhammad served as a chief adviser to his father, the Honorable Elijah Muhammed. He also worked as the chief business manager for the Nation of Islam and, along with Malcolm X, founded *Muhammad Speaks* which is now the *Muslim Journal*. Along with Muhammad Ali and others, they built the Masjid Al-Fatir on the south side of Chicago. Jabir was the longtime manager of Muhammad Ali.

These prominent figures in the American Muslim community of the 1980s created a vision of an American Muslim College that would continue to the present day.

Imam Mohammed always emphasized the importance of education, especially the social sciences, based on the Quran. In one of his commentaries in the collection Education: A Sacred Matter, he said, "The most important tool in the Quran is the tool of education. The most important tool in the effort to advance the ummah, the community of Al-Islam, or the ummah (community) of Muhammed is education."

In discussing the "education" that is so important, Imam Mohammed emphasized the Quran, but also the world Allah had made. This is why establishing a college like AIC was so important because the college taught not only Islamic Studies, but also the study of both the Creation and the social sciences. Imam Mohammad always emphasized the inclusion of all people in all their diversity.

Muhammed, the prophet, said, "The Ink of the scholar is more precious than the blood of the martyr." He was saying that the most precious thing we must protect is life, and it is the ink of the scholar and its connection to education that will best protect life. From this link, we become educated....He created the world to educate us and where can we get this education except from the world that G-d made?

When AIC was founded, it was established as a four-year college that offered undergraduate degrees. It included multiple colleges, i.e., a College of Education to train teachers for the Al-Islam community and a College of Arts and Sciences to train Muslims in all the arts and social sciences.

Dr. Ismail Al-Faruqi was a unique Muslim academic in the 1970s and 1980s when the study of Islam in the academic community was not a priority and scholars identifying as Muslim were rare. He saw the importance of shifting the approach in academic studies as a professor who represented non-Eurocentric models of knowledge. His most significant contribution beyond challenging Eurocentric models of knowledge was to decolonize fields of study, particularly the academic study of Islam. Like Imam Mohammad, Al-Faruqi was heavily involved in interfaith dialogues and partnerships, and he initiated the first Islam section at the American Academy of Religion. It is no surprise that Imam Mohammad and Ismail Al-Faruqi's vision of an American Islamic College was so compatible. Faruqi was also a prominent Muslim thinker in Muslim responses to modernity and a proponent of Islamic thinking that was open to contemporary thought.

Imam Mohammad and Al-Faruqi's vision for AIC was reflected in interfaith work during a time before it was widely accepted among all faith traditions. AIC also reflected these founders by having a very diverse student community combining men and women as well as students of many races, ethnic backgrounds, African American Muslims, and immigrants. In 1985, AIC became the first accredited Muslim College in the United States. AIC also was utilized as a center for Muslim youth camps by organizations such as the Muslim Youth of North America (MYNA).

With the assassination of Ismail Al-Faruqi and his wife Lamya Faruqi in 1986, Imam W. Deen Mohammad's death in 2008, and other changes in administration and leadership, AIC went into a long period of dormancy before being revived again in 2010.

In 2010, American Islamic College entered its second phase as members of the American Muslim community came together to reopen its doors in the Fall of 2013.

Staying true to the composition and vision of AIC's early founders, the College prides itself in the diverse composition of its Board of Trustees, Staff, Faculty, and Students. AIC has a blend of students and faculty from different ethnic, racial, and age backgrounds. AIC has a balance between men and women in all segments of its composition, including administration and faculty positions. Sensitivity to diversity and inclusion are key principles that propel AIC's mission.

When you read the Mission of the revived American Islamic College, you can hear the echoes of Imam W. Deen Mohammad, Akbar Mohammad, Jabir Mohammad, and Ismail Al-Faruqi and their joint vision of a College that would represent and celebrate the diversity of Al-Islam in America.

> "American Islamic College is an institution of higher learning grounded in Islamic values, embracing students of all backgrounds. Our Chicago location uniquely positions AIC to represent and research the diversity of Islam in America. AIC promotes appreciation of the variety and richness of Islamic history and civilization both in the classroom and by means of public events highlighting Islam's intellectual, artistic, and cultural expressions. Through rigorous scholarship, civic engagement, and interfaith/intercultural activities, AIC prepares our students to become global citizens and visionary leaders."

AIC offers a B.A. in Islamic Studies and M.A. in Islamic Studies and a Master of Divinity (Chaplaincy). To find out more about the American Islamic College, go to www.aicusa.edu. One course I took for my Master's degree in Islamic Studies was called "African American Experience with Islam," taught by a leading scholar in the field, Dr. Aminah Al-Deen (McCloud). We studied the earliest Muslims that came to America, who comprised 25-30% of slaves from West Africa. They went on to establish The Moorish Science Temple, Ahmadiyya movement, the Nation of Islam, and the Imam W. Deen Mohammed Community.

On a "field trip" to an African American mosque with a Palestinian student friend, I had a major realization. When we both went to the mosque for Friday jummah, we saw all the men and women coming through the same front doors and into the main prayer area. Men were on the right, and women were on the left. No balcony, no separate room. They were separated but clearly equal. The jummah service was the same as any other Sunni service I had ever been to. The only point that I realized it was actually the Nation of Islam (NOI) Mosque Maryam was when Imam Ishmael Muhammad mentioned Minister Farrakhan in his khutbah (sermon). After this service, I did the interview with Imam Sultan Muhammad, the National Imam of the NOI, which you can read in my first book, *The Muslim American Fight for Social Justice: From Civil Rights to Black Lives Matter*.

Some members of Masjid Al-Taqwa with me

After that experience, I attended Masjid Al-Taqwa Chicago, part of the Imam W. Deen Mohammed Community (WDM), at the invitation of some fellow students at AIC. My very first experience there was very welcoming. Women were in the same prayer area as the men, and it became very clear women held equal positions of power in this community. I read many of the books of Imam W. Deen Mohammed, and his analysis (tafsir) of the Quran was some of the most psychologically intuitive and with real world application I had ever read. More and more over time, I became convinced that was the real American version of Islam. The community focused on social justice and the equality of every person, not just in belief but also in action and everyday life. Imam W. Deen Mohammed also has a very reasoned and approachable understanding of the Quran, emphasizing being a part of the public life of the country and promoting interfaith dialogue.

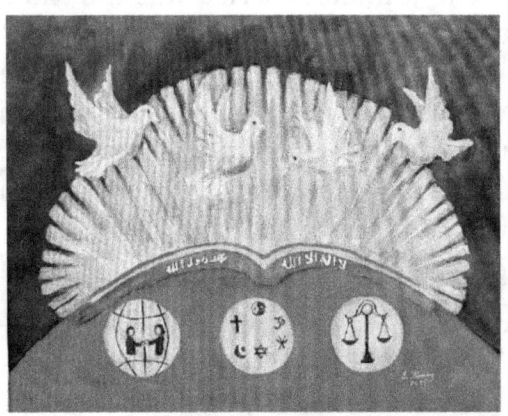

"The Four Birds of Al-Islam" by Elaine Fleming 2024

My own lived experience as part of the Imam W. Deen Mohammed Community and interacting with many members of the Nation of Islam for several years encouraged me to write my first book to educate both the white community and the non-Black Muslim community. My goal was to place the NOI and WDM Communities in their proper roles as pioneers in the Muslim American fight for social justice and to correct the popular misconceptions and false histories written about them.

All my experiences as an anti-racism, Irish Republican, and Palestine activist have led me to this community, and my first book *The Muslim American Fight for Social Justice: From Civil Rights to Black Lives Matter,* expresses the calling and the mission that I have had these many years.

Since becoming a member of Masjid Al-Taqwa I have written numerous articles for the *Muslim Journal. The Muslim Journal* originated as Muhammad Speaks in the 1960s as the publication of the NOI. It is one of the oldest independent publications in America and continues in both print and digital form.

In this next section of my memoir, I have included some of the major campaigns I was involved in as a Muslim, and not surprisingly, many of these social justice campaigns were some of the same ones that were happening in Chicago during this 2016-2024 period.

I have included the most relevant articles of my activist life as a Muslim including the genocide of Rohingya in Myanmar; Community Control of the Police; Mass Deportations under Trump; Palestine Nakba; BDS Movement; and the Chicago Black Muslim History Bus Tour that our masjid does twice a year. These articles will provide examples of some of the Muslim campaigns that were going on during this period. Increasingly over time, Chicago's Muslim community became a critical component supporting these social justice campaigns. The farther the community got from the repression that occurred after 9-11, the more the community came out to support those who had protested against the wave of anti-Muslim sentiment that occurred in the 2000s.

This first article is about the campaign among the Muslim community in Chicago to protect the Rohingya in Myanmar from being expelled from their country. Among the dominant majority of the country and the Myanmar military government, the Rohingya were not recognized as citizens and Islam was not among the "approved" religions.

Chicago Muslims Protest Genocide of Rohingya in Myanmar

By Bill Chambers
Muslim Journal
9/17/17

On Saturday, September 16th, over 500 Chicagoland Muslims turned out to hear a wide range of speakers condemn the ongoing ethnic cleansing of Myanmar's Rohingya Muslim minority.

The Council of Islamic Organizations of Greater Chicago (CIOGC) and the Burma Task Force organized this emergency rally to protest the brutal, barbaric killings of innocent Rohingya people, including children and women, in Myanmar. The number of Rohingya fleeing the violence in Bangladesh has increased to 300,000 in recent days.

Myanmar's leader, Aung San Suu Kyi, has launched a series of military assaults on the Rohingya civilian population in collective punishment for recent Rohingya militant attacks on police posts and an army base.

As recent as September 11, the New York Times reported that Zeid Ra'ad al-Hussein, the United Nations high commissioner for human rights, said the military's "brutal" security campaign was in clear violation of international law and cited what he called refugees' consistent accounts of widespread extrajudicial killings, rape, and other atrocities.

Mr. al-Hussein said the crackdown "resembles a cynical ploy to forcibly transfer large numbers of people without possibility of return," noting that Myanmar had progressively stripped its Rohingya minority of civil and political rights for decades.

(https://www.nytimes.com/2017/09/11/world/asia/myanmar-rohingya-ethnic-cleansing.html)

The rally in Chicago drew from multiple Muslim communities that were reflected in the diversity of the speakers.

Azeem Ibrahim, author of the definitive book on the crisis, *The Rohingyas: Inside Myanmar's Hidden Genocide*, spoke of the difficulty Bangladesh is having trying to receive thousands of Rohingya fleeing Myanmar. "I've seen the conditions of the camps there and they are not fit for human beings." He rejected the accusation by the Myanmar Buddhists that the Rohingya are not indigenous people but only "illegal immigrants from Bangladesh." As a teacher and researcher at the Harris Public Policy School, University of Chicago, his research has proven that the Rohingya have been native to Myanmar since at least 1799.

Imam Tariq El-Amin from Masjid Al-Taqwa in Chicago stressed, "Those who have not been oppressed, come to the aid of those who are oppressed. Those who have been left without have been aided by those who have. We see this with the hurricanes. Our people are opening their hearts and their homes to people they don't even know…As a descendent of a people taken from their homeland, and endured tremendous atrocities for centuries while the world was silent, I am moved by the suffering of other people. I am moved by the silence that exists that is an affront to humanity. Allah or God gives us an opportunity to come together so we can address those things that are wrong and against what it means to be a human being."

El-Amin continued, "We have been asked to do the very least to address genocide in Burma. Tweet Tillerson, UN representative Haley, your Senators…I know we can go a step further and share this information with someone not here."

Ahmed Rehab, Executive Director of CAIR-Chicago reminded the crowd, "Islamophobia is a world-wide phenomenon."

Elaine Doyo Siegel, as a representative of the Chicago Buddhist community, spoke of "mourning with all of you the deaths of the Rohingya…there is nothing in Buddhist teaching that allows these killings."

Among the other speakers were Suzanne Akhras of the Syrian Community Network and Abdul Jabbar Amanullah from the Rohingya Center of Chicago.

Abdullah Mitchell, Executive Director of the CIOGC Board and a Board member of the Masjid Al-Taqwa of Chicago, ended the rally by calling for all present to take action to stop the genocide of the Rohingya.

The CIOGC and Burma Task Force urged the protestors and all those who support the Rohingya to call the US State Department and Senators Dick Durbin and Tammy Duckworth to demand that they take immediate action to protect the Rohingya Muslims.

The Chicago Muslim community was very active in this campaign against the genocide of Rohingya in Myanmar, and this was only the first of many such protests.

The next piece is about the anniversary of the Nakba that the Palestinian community in Chicago celebrates every year. The Nakba, or catastrophe in Arabic, is what Palestinians call the ethnic cleansing of Palestinians from their homes and land by Israeli paramilitaries and the Israeli army in 1948. Palestinians see this as a continuing event that includes the destruction of their culture, identity, and political rights, and a refusal of the Palestinian Right of Return for all Palestinians and their descendants.

Chicago Marks 70th Anniversary of Palestinian Nakba and Protests Attacks on Gazans

By Bill Chambers
Muslim Journal
3/11/18

On March 11th, several hundred Chicago Palestinians and their supporters rallied and marched to mark the 70th year since the Nakba or Catastrophe in 1948 when Israeli troops forced almost 800,000 Palestinians from their homes and lands to establish the apartheid state of Israel. In cities across the country and around the world, thousands marched to protest this act of ethnic cleansing and the continued attacks on Gazans by Israeli troops who have killed more than 50 non-violent protesters with live ammunition. In Chicago, representatives of the Chicago Coalition for Justice in Palestine led by the Al-Nahda Center, American Muslims for Palestine (AMP), Palestinian American Community Center, Palestinian American Council, Students for Justice in Palestine (SJP)-Chicago, and the United States Palestinian Community Network

(USPCN) spoke at the rally before a march to the Israeli Consulate.

Hatem Abudayyeh of the Coalition for Justice in Palestine and the USPCN – "We are here to express our support for the Palestinian people who have been fighting against colonization and occupation for over one hundred years. May 15 marks 70 years of the Nakba, when the settler colonial state of Israel was formed and when almost 800,000 Palestinians were forced into exile. Those refugees and their descendants are now 5 million strong, and every single one of them is calling for the Right of Return to the homes and lands from which they were forced."

Jinan Chehade from Students for Justice in Palestine – DePaul reminded the crowd of the impact of these events on the Palestinians themselves. "Remember the mourning mothers of Palestine whose tears are still not dry from burying their children. Remember the thousands of peaceful protestors who have been shot and severely injured by the Israelis in the Right of Return March and all the other Palestinians who are now marching for justice and freedom." She followed her speech with a reading of the names of the Palestinians who had been killed in the March for Return.

The speakers represented the broad coalition supporting the Palestinian community, including those from the American Friends Service Committee (AFSC), Arab Jewish Partnership for Peace and Justice in the Middle East, Black Lives Matter (BLM)-Chicago, Chicago Alliance Against Racist and Political Repression, Committee for a Just Peace in Israel and Palestine (CJPIP), Jewish Voice for Peace (JVP)-Chicago, and the Pilsen Alliance.

Jazmine Salas of the Chicago Alliance Against Racist and Political Repression made the connection between the Israeli troops' occupation of Palestinian land with the Chicago Police playing a similar role in communities of color in Chicago – "We condemn the apartheid state of Israel for allowing its military to attack and murder peaceful protestors protesting their right to self-determination...We remember the atrocities that have occurred in Chicago. We know the CPD is the occupier of our communities...We demand community control of the police in our city."

Multiple members of the Jewish Voice for Peace (JVP-Chicago) made their presence felt with signs and chants.

Four days later May 15, an emergency protest was organized to protest the move of the U.S. embassy from Tel Aviv to Jerusalem, rejected by virtually every country in the world, and to publicize the ongoing attacks on Gazan unarmed civilians by Israeli troops that killed another 58 and injured more than 2,700. More than a thousand people turned out for the high-energy protest.

The Palestinians also claim Jerusalem for the capital of a future Palestinian state. As Michelle Goldberg described the embassy opening ceremony in an Opinion piece in the New York Times on May 14: "The event was grotesque. It was a consummation of the cynical alliance between hawkish Jews and Zionist evangelicals who believe that the return of Jews to Israel will usher in the apocalypse and the return of Christ, after which Jews who don't convert will burn forever... Religions like "Mormonism, Islam, Judaism, Hinduism" lead people "to an eternity of separation from God in Hell," Robert Jeffress, a Dallas megachurch pastor, once said. He was chosen to give the opening prayer at the embassy ceremony. John Hagee, one of America's most prominent end-times preachers, once said that God sent Hitler to drive the Jews to their ancestral homeland. He gave the closing benediction."

The Chicago Islamic Organizations of Greater Chicago (CIOGC) joined the hundreds in a rally in downtown Chicago. Many member organizations, including MAS Chicago and AMP-Chicago assisted with the organizing. G. Abdullah Mitchell, the CIOGC Executive Director, reiterated points from the CIOGC press release.

> "CIOGC condemns and denounces the use of deadly force by the Israeli military against unarmed Palestinians demonstrating against the opening of the U.S. embassy in Jerusalem.
>
> The demonstrations along the Gazan border, ongoing since late March 2018, have been met with an ever-increasing level of deadly force from Israeli military forces...Demanding the right to return to their land and practicing a legitimate right to protest, protesters should not be confronted with deadly force. It is inhumane for the people of Gaza to be subjected to such living conditions, and it is immoral for the response to their cries for relief to be met with military action.
>
> The killing and wounding of protesters must not be tolerated. We call upon religious leaders across the world to demand the end of military action against the people of Gaza, and we demand that the United States and the international community immediately supply needed humanitarian and economic relief for the residents of Gaza."

The large turnout from the Chicago Muslim community on Tuesday confirmed the outrage of the community by the move of the embassy to Jerusalem and the ongoing killing of non-violent Palestinian protestors by the Israeli military.

Once again, this protest demonstrates the wide support for the Palestinians among all of the social justice, and in this case, Muslim organizations in the city. The protest demonstrated well the continuation of the Nakba in Apartheid Israel's attacks on Gaza underway at the time.

During this period of the first Trump Administration, there were widespread protests against the mass deportations of immigrants. In cities like Chicago, there was a lot of fear in the Latinx communities of ICE raids on their homes and places of business. In my own view, I remember feeling this was a time of great political repression and fear that the city's most vulnerable communities were being driven to stay home from work and school to avoid these raids. It was very clear there was no compunction to separate families and to target any undocumented people whether they had committed any crime or not. It is important to remember now in 2025, during the second Trump Administration, that there is a history of resistance to these policies by the well-prepared immigrant rights groups organized to fight back. The next article describes a large protest in Chicago and across the country against the mass deportation of immigrants. The encouraging aspect of this march was the large turnout not just by immigrant rights organizations but also from the major Muslim groups in the city.

Thousands March to Stop Mass Deportations

Muslim Journal
By Bill Chambers
7/15/19

Last weekend, thousands in cities including Los Angeles, New York, and Miami marched to protest the mass deportations threatened by the Trump Administration. In Chicago, close to ten thousand people rallied in scorching heat and marched to the Immigration and Customs Enforcement (ICE) headquarters to demand an end to criminalization, detention, and deportations of migrants in Chicago and on the border with Mexico. Chicago is officially a sanctuary city. Mayor Lori Lightfoot said that the Chicago Police would be directed to not cooperate with ICE agents but resisted efforts to sign an executive order permanently barring the Department of Homeland Security from accessing the city's databases, especially the notoriously inaccurate gang database. She did not speak at the rally but did hold a press conference after the march at a church in Little Village.

More than 100 groups endorsed the march with immigrant rights, unions, social justice, civil rights, and faith-based organizations represented. Muslim organizations supporting the march included CAIR-Chicago, HEART Women and Girls, Illinois Muslim Civic Coalition, and the Muslim Community Center.

The rally had speakers including U.S. Representative Jesus "Chuy" Garcia and Illinois Lt. Governor Juliana Stratton. Rabbi Brant Rosen, Regional Director of the American Friends Service Committee, gave the invocation, saying:

> "Shalom to you angels of justice, angels of the moist high...show us how to fight for the liberation of anyone who has been forced from their homes, pursued, taken, and locked away...inspire us to take down oppressive systems that were built by the powerful to maintain the power of the powerful. Remind us there is a power yet greater that comes from a place that knows no borders, no deportations, no barrier walls, no prisons no guards, no soldiers, no police, a place where we no longer must struggle for justice because justice gushes forth like a mighty stream."

U.S. Rep. Jesus "Chuy" Garcia said that "It's about damn time we tell this racist president loud and clear: stop criminalizing desperation," reflecting most of the current migrants fleeing violence in Central American countries.

Those attending the march each had their own motivation for being there. Frank Chapman, a long-time civil rights activist and Field Organizer for the Chicago Alliance Against Racist and Political Repression, said,

> "We stand in total solidarity with the people at the border who are being inhumanely detained by the Trump Administration and violently denied their human rights. Separating children from their parents, concentration camp conditions...They must close these camps and stop these deportations. Glad to see Chicago is not cooperating with ICE, but we need to be here to protest and to make sure that happens."

Jackson Potter, Staff Coordinator of the Chicago Teachers Union, reminded us that.

> "We have a right wing, xenophobic white supremacist movement embodied in the White House that is a minority perspective within the country that is trying to divide the working class around race. What we have here today is the best we have in our country. A multi-national working-class resistance to that attack."

Branden McReynolds, representing the Church of God, an evangelical Christian group, said that, "We have come here today to promote a message of peace and believe that all of God's people should be together in peace no matter your gender, race, or economic status. We believe in the unity of all of God's people."

Laurie Hogetsu Belzer, a Zen Buddhist priest emphasized, "I am here in solidarity to counter the suffering created by the policies of our government against migrants and refugees. I'm here to support life and peace."

Stephanie Skora from Jewish Voice for Peace said

> "We believe deeply as Jews, it is our responsibility to stand up against any injustice. There are concentration camps in the United States being used on the border to house children. There are concentration camps being used to house indigenous people, including children, in Palestine. We believe all of these are atrocities and human rights violations and should never occur. We stand in solidarity with marginalized people around our city and around the world."

Muhammad Sankari, Lead Organizer from the Arab American Action Network (AAAN) described why his organization was there.

> "The AAAN is out here to stand shoulder to shoulder with all our communities, immigrant community, African American community, and other oppressed nationalities, and we are standing up with one voice saying no to Trump's escalated attacks against our communities. Saying no to any of our city's resources being used to tear up families and no to child detention centers and concentration camps."

Two Muslim students from Northwestern University, Sizzah Jaffer and Rwan Ibrahim, held signs saying

"ICE = Inhumanity" and "Abolish ICE."

Rwan said that "As human beings we need to stand up for anyone who is vulnerable and going through injustices...The fact that this is going on in Chicago, in our backyard, where ICE can separate these families from each other. It is important that as human beings, as Muslims, as anyone who believes in a greater good, can come together and support a cause like this."

Sizzah agreed, adding that "Islam is rooted in justice and human rights. This hits home because a lot of us are children of immigrants and have families dealing with the documentation process...Even though this is a problem happening all over the world, we must do what we can. It starts here, and it starts right now."

The march continued to the Chicago ICE Headquarters where people were encouraged to stay vigilant over the weekend, volunteer to patrol at-risk neighborhoods for ICE raids, and assist in handing out "Know Your Rights" pamphlets.

During both the Obama and Trump Administrations, the "war on terror" continued unabated. Much of this rhetoric fueled the deportation of immigrants discussed above.

At the time, the Obama Administration had deported the largest number of immigrants of any administration in a very long time. Many new programs were created to try to identify "home-grown terrorists" and to hand them over to law enforcement. The majority of these programs targeted Muslims even though a self-identified Muslim had not done a terror attack in years. There continued to be a rise in antisemitic and anti-Muslim attacks by white supremacist groups that were completely ignored. During this time, I was always aware of my special status as a white Muslim who could avoid any repression just by the nature of my skin color. I worried terribly for my friends and my community and worked to use my white privilege to speak about Islam and Muslims in settings that would listen to me and not someone who was an easily identifiable Muslim.

The next article describes one of these programs called Countering Violent Extremism (CVE). I was part of the STOP CVE Coalition led by the Arab American Action Center (AAAN). CVE was a COINTEL PRO like program that the Department of Homeland Security used to try to get Muslim communities to identify "home-grown terrorists" in their midst and to turn them in to law enforcement. (COINTEL PRO, Counterintelligence Program, was an FBI program initiated by J. Edgar Hoover in the 1960s to do surveillance, infiltrate, undermine, and destroy social justice groups primarily in the Black and Latinx communities.) It was particularly disturbing that this program was initiated by the Obama Administration, even with their supposed liberal orientation. Given the great resistance from Muslims across the country, the CVE Program ended up a miserable failure.

Countering Violent Extremism (CVE) Program: The New COINTELPRO for Muslims

By Bill Chambers
Muslim Journal
4/12/19

On March 20 at the Arab American Cultural Center at the University of Illinois at Chicago (UIC), the #StopCVE Coalition and community partners released the 2019 Report on Countering Violent Extremism (CVE) in Chicago. The 24-page report details how the Department of Homeland Security program is being implemented in Chicago and Illinois, disproportionately targeting and criminalizing Muslim and Arab youth. (You can download a copy of the Report at http://www.stopcve.com/chicago-report.html) UIC's Institute partially funded research for the Report for Research on Race and Public Policy.

The Stop CVE – Chicago Coalition includes many of the leading social justice organizations in the city, including the American Friends Service Committee-Chicago, Arab American Action Network, CAIR-Chicago, Organized

Communities Against Deportations, Asian Americans Advancing Justice-Chicago, Jewish Voice for Peace-Chicago, Chicago Teachers for Social Justice, Arab Jewish Partnership for Peace, Illinois Coalition for Immigrant and Refugee Rights, and many more community organizations.

The report provides an overview of what CVE is, how to identify CVE mechanisms and key players in Illinois, as well as policy recommendations and ways to take action. At the meeting, other StopCVE campaigns across the country were highlighted that have been organizing against CVE and resisting surveillance programs in their communities.

Before discussing the substance of the Report and the recommendations it offers, it is important to look back at the origins of programs like CVE.

The Long History of Surveillance of People of Color

In 1967, the FBI initiated COINTELPRO (Domestic Counterintelligence Program) targeting "Black Nationalist Hate Groups," including SCLC, Student Non-Violent Coordinating Committee (SNCC), Revolutionary Action Movement (RAM), Congress of Racial Equality (CORE), and the Nation of Islam. Ramsey Clark, LBJ's Attorney General, started a "community surveillance program" targeting black urban centers that coordinated the Department of Justice, military intelligence, and the FBI for preventive action against riots. There was an FBI "Rabble Rouser Index" that included anyone who was any threat to "domestic security".

Long before COINTELPRO was implemented, the FBI had been targeting, monitoring, and criminalizing the African American Muslim community from when the

Honorable Elijah Muhammad and the Nation of Islam was declared a Black Nationalist organization in the 1930s.

The CVE Program is square in the FBI tradition of monitoring, infiltrating, and targeting groups that have any connection to social justice or People of Color. The CVE Program is enhanced COINTELPRO for Muslims as now the entire program is focused on Muslims, and instead of the FBI needing to worry about infiltrators, they can have the Muslim community be their personal police force.

What is the Countering Violent Extremism (CVE) Program?

In 2014, the Obama Administration announced a new anti-terrorism initiative called Countering Violent Extremism (CVE) to deter U.S. residents from joining "violent extremist" groups by bringing community and religious leaders together with law enforcement, health professionals, teachers, and social service employees.

The CVE program is an inter-agency initiative led by the Department of Justice, DHS, the Federal Bureau of Investigation (FBI), and the National Counterterrorism Center (NCTC). When the CVE program was introduced, Attorney General Eric Holder announced a White House CVE summit and three CVE pilot programs to begin in Boston, Minneapolis, and Los Angeles. (None of the pilots have been successful.) The emphasis of the program is to work with local communities, local law enforcement, and community organizations to do Community Roundtables, Community Awareness Briefings, and multiple other community training exercises that can easily be transitioned into programs of surveillance, monitoring, interrogation, and "de-radicalization."

The Obama administration argued that this new model would offer a friendlier alternative to more aggressive counterterrorism initiatives. Unfortunately, CVE equates certain types of dissent or difference with violence and recruits community organizations to serve as terrorist watch-dogs, ultimately providing law enforcement access to spaces otherwise unavailable to them. Despite the promises made by the Obama administration, CVE, by design, has intensified, not mitigated, anti-Black, anti-Muslim, and anti-immigrant policing by expanding policy frameworks that historically have targeted these communities.

The Brennan Center for Justice that does research on the CVE program and remarks:

> "These programs are not new. CVE programs have existed for some time, often with dubious results. While purportedly aimed at rooting out all violent extremism, they have previously focused only on Muslims, stigmatizing them as a suspect community. These programs have further promoted flawed theories of terrorist radicalization, which leads to unnecessary fear, discrimination, and unjustified reporting to law enforcement."

In February 2016, The Brennan Center for Justice filed a complaint with DHS and the DOJ to obtain records related to the CVE strategy. As part of their complaint, the Center reiterated both the lack of empirical evidence supporting these strategies and their negative impact on the civil rights of Arabs and Muslims.

Using a Freedom of Information Request in 2016, The Brennan Center for Justice was able to determine how the CVE program is being implemented. In January of 2016, the DHS and FBI released its guidelines for "Countering Violent Extremism at School."

The definitions of suspicious behavior are very broad as are the "violent extremists" they refer to. "Animal Rights Extremists and Environmental Extremists," "white supremacy extremists," ISIS, and Al Qaeda are all listed as potential terrorist groups focusing on recruiting high school students even though there is no evidence of that happening. But it is very clear who is the real target of this document. All the photo examples of "extremists" in the document are Arab or Muslim except for one photo of a Nazi SS officer and one of Timothy McVee.

The DHS and FBI guidelines also provide a list of those who should be monitoring students that in education matches exactly those who have a "duty" to report suspicious behavior. These included teachers, grief counselors, principals, nurses, and guidance counselors.

One can only imagine what high school students would think if their "Guidance Counselor," "Nurse," or even "Grief Counselor" could report them to the FBI for something they said or did.

Radicalization "Research"

There are no indicators, risk factors, or warning signs that can predict who may commit an act of mass violence or identify who may be vulnerable to terrorist radicalization. Instead, these "signatures" or "red flags" criminalize constitutionally-protected speech, religious practices, and political activism expressed by Muslim communities." Males growing a beard, women deciding to wear a hijab, and increased attendance at the mosque are considered possible signs of "radicalization".

The Stop CVE Chicago Coalition Report concludes that there is no research that proves that "radicalization" occurs or can be identified in the locations that CVE targets, i.e., mosques, community centers, schools, mental health centers, or hospitals.

Even the targeting of the CVE programs to Arab, Muslim, and African American communities is not justified, given the statistics on terror attacks in the U.S. since 2014. The last terrorist attack by someone who identified himself as Muslim occurred in October 2017 in New York City. He was not a member of a local mosque and apparently was radicalized by social media.

Previous Muslim terrorist attacks occurred in Orlando in June 2016, in San Bernardino in December 2015, and in Chattanooga, Tennessee in June 2015. In every one of these cases, law enforcement stated that they appeared to be "self-radicalized" and were not an active member of any of the target locations where they might have been identified. This is four terrorist attacks since 2014 where the attackers were identified as Muslims. During this same period, there were eight terrorist attacks by those identified as white nationalists, white supremacists, or white right-wing political actors. There has been no attempt to apply the CVE program to white nationalists or concerted, sustained campaigns to target such groups.

How is it Being Implemented in Illinois?

The Report states – "The National Governors Association chose Illinois as one of four states to pilot its Roadmap on Preventing Targeted Violence...In Illinois, CVE is referred to as Targeted Violence Prevention (TVP) and is implemented through the state-wide Targeted Violence Prevention Program (TVPP) created by the Illinois Terrorism Task Force (ITTF). It is run by the Illinois Criminal Justice Information Authority (ICJIA), which is a state law enforcement agency.

"The Illinois Criminal Justice Information Authority (ICJIA) Targeted Violence Prevention Program (TVPP) is a new initiative funded by a $187,000 CVE grant from the Department of Homeland Security, in addition to $208,206 in state funding. ICJIA frames TVPP as a "non-punitive," "therapeutic," and "community-driven" approach to preventing violent extremism. More specifically, TVPP asks trusted community members like imams and mental health professionals to "off-ramp individuals who exhibit warning signs of radicalization to violence as well as those who exhibit behaviors signifying they may be in the early stages of planning an act of ideologically inspired targeted violence."

The Report states that "TVPP, in their 2016 CVE grant application, "Engaged Bystander-Gatekeeper Training for Ideologically Inspired Targeted Violence" named individuals as consultants from UIC, Chicago School of Professional Psychology, the DuPage County Board, Illinois Department of Public Health, and Illinois Department of Human Services/Department of Mental Health. In some cases, local interfaith or Muslim organizations are listed as assisting with the grant application when only a meeting was held, and the organization had no input at all.

Because TVPP is still in development, the Stop CVE – Chicago Coalition is still monitoring how it is being implemented. They did discover that ICJIA has conducted "community focus groups" to cultivate community relationships and develop its trainings aimed at "help[ing] community members intervene before crime or violence occurs."

ICJIA also has conducted at least one training for mental health professionals to learn how to prevent violent extremism in partnership with UIC. Participants could earn continuing education credits, which incentivized participation. Although ICJIA has sought to distinguish TVPP from CVE and downplay its relationship with law enforcement, training advertisements listed FBI Special Agents and a DHS representative as speakers.

The Chicago Police Department (CPD) is listed as a partner in the TVPP grant application and has helped facilitate the coordination of TVPP, despite the CPD's documented history of racial profiling against Muslim and Arab communities, condoning of anti-Muslim social media posts authored by its police officers, and systematic failure to respond to anti-Muslim hate crimes.

In one case, the Report concludes that the ICJIA "secured a nearly $200,000 federal grant earlier this year without approval from several 'partner' organizations listed in the agency's grant application." In addition, the ICJIA admitted in its own quarterly report that Albany Park's Makki Masjid "disengaged in the project, citing concerns over discrimination against the Muslim community."

Stop CVE – Chicago Report Recommendations

The Coalition's Report provided several recommendations that included:

1) When you are approached by someone involved in the CVDE-inspired Targeted Violence Prevention Program (TVPP), ask questions and refuse to participate.

- Who is hosting the event, and what is its purpose?
- Who are the listed speakers? Do they include key CVE/TVPP players? FBI agents? DHS representatives?
- Who provided the funding for these events?

2) ICJIA: Defund and End TVPP Immediately

3) UIC: Return CVE Grant Money and End CVE Research

But in my estimation, Muslim communities need to provide their own "solutions". Even though the research does not show that there is a problem of radicalization within Muslim American communities, there are still actions that we can take to support our marginalized youth and adult members, especially those who may be traumatized by the atmosphere of anti-Muslim bigotry that programs like CVE foster.

As Muslim communities, we need to invest in our own alternatives through funding from organizations like the Zakat Foundation or The Council of Islamic Organization of Greater Chicago (CIOGC).

- Create a database or list of psychotherapists, social workers, and counselors within the community who can be called upon to work with youth or adults who express more extreme or threatening behavior or may simply be responding to the increase in hate crimes.

- Provide Mental Health First Aid or First Responder Training for Imams, Youth, and Community Leaders offered by Khalil Center or American Muslim Health Professionals and The National Council for Behavioral Health that already exists and is available.

Following the Model of Other Successful Stop CVE Campaigns

In Los Angeles, Muslim community members and leadership, alongside organizations like MPower Change, VigilantLOVE, Advancing Justice LA, CAIR LA, ACLU Southern California, and the California Immigrant Policy Center, came together and organized against the program. The #StopCVE coalition in LA worked for over a year to defeat the program through Public Records Act requests, petitions, and lobbying visits. It's important to note that the Muslim community in Southern California, as represented by the Islamic Shura Council of Southern California, rejected CVE. Notably, Bayan Claremont rejected a grant totaling $900K. The #StopCVE coalition in LA is carrying forward its work after the victory by addressing Preventing Violent Extremism (PVE) programs targeting youth in local schools and organizing against surveillance programs across California."

By educating our communities about the CVE Program and supporting the efforts of the Stop CVE – Chicago Coalition, the Muslim community in Chicago can be as successful as LA in ending this criminalization of Muslim and Arab youth and the surveillance of our communities.

This article was my attempt to publicize this destructive CVE Program as widely as I could across all Muslim communities. One of the masjids that was considering this program was part of the Imam W. D. Mohammed community in DC. This masjid had a history of cooperating with DHS.

During Ramadan, many Muslim organizations like American Muslims for Palestine would remind Chicago Muslims to boycott Israeli produced dates. This is one article I wrote for the *Muslim Journal* describing the BDS Movement and that it involved more than just boycotting dates.

Support the Palestine Boycott Divestment Sanction Movement (BDS)

Muslim Journal
By Bill Chambers
4/19/24

"For every day on which the sun rises, there is a reward from God for those who establish justice among people."

- Prophet Muhammad (Sahih Al-Bukhari, Volume 3, Hadith 370)

Every Ramadan, you see articles about boycotting Israeli dates. This year, with the genocide and forced starvation happening in Gaza, it is even more important for us as Muslims to act against the oppressive Israeli state. But supporting the BDS movement is more than not eating Israeli dates. The bdsmovement.net website explains the movement in this way:

> "Boycott, Divestment, Sanctions (BDS) is a Palestinian-led movement for freedom, justice, and equality. BDS upholds the simple principle that Palestinians are entitled to the same rights as the rest of humanity. Israel is occupying and colonizing Palestinian land, discriminating against Palestinian citizens of Israel, and denying Palestinian refugees the right to return to their homes. Inspired by the South

African anti-apartheid movement, the BDS call urges action to pressure Israel to comply with international law."

The movement began in 2005, with all civic organizations in Palestine joining together and calling on the rest of the world for support. BDS is now a global movement made up of unions, academic associations, churches, and grassroots movements.

BDS falls into three primary areas: academic (cutting ties with Israeli universities and refusing to attend conferences); cultural (boycotting Israeli sports teams like the Olympics and soccer matches); and economic (boycott all Israeli-made products like dates and Sabra hummus). There is a long list of companies that support Israel in other ways, but the BDS movement has specific targets that make the boycotts more effective.

Specific U.S. consumer targets include:

Hewlett Packard Inc (HP Inc) - Computers and Printers

HP Inc (US) provides technology for Israel's Population and Immigration Authority, a pillar of its apartheid **regime.**

Chevron (including Caltex and Texaco brands) – Gas Stations

US fossil fuel multinational Chevron is the main corporation extracting gas claimed by apartheid Israel in the East Mediterranean.

SodaStream – Make your own soft drink product.

SodaStream is an Israeli company that is actively complicit in Israel's policy of displacing the indigenous Bedouin-Palestinian citizens of present-day Israel in the

Naqab (Negev) and has a long history of racial discrimination against Palestinian workers.

Ahava

Ahava Cosmetics is an Israeli company that has its production site, visitor center, and main store in an illegal Israeli settlement in the occupied Palestinian territory.

RE/MAX

RE/MAX (US) markets and sells property in illegal Israeli settlements built on stolen Palestinian land, thus enabling Israel's colonization of the occupied West Bank.

Another important area of the BDS movement that impacts our community directly is not to travel to Israel except for Palestinian led delegations. The Israeli led trips are propaganda exercises designed to gain support for the state of Israel and their apartheid policies. Many times these trips are advertised as inter-faith delegations to bring Muslims and Jews together. The Muslim Leadership Initiative (MLI) is one such organization that has organized such trips for imams from our community in the past. The MLI of Israel's Shalom Hartman Institute stated purpose is to shape the understanding of these participants with regards to Judaism and Zionism. MLI conflates Zionism with Judaism and violates our moral imperative as Muslims to act against an apartheid state.

Other Zionist organizations like the Anti-Defamation League (ADL) and the American Jewish Committee (AJC) also have inter-faith initiatives that try to include Muslims who are not educated about their political designs.

Another BDS area in the U.S. to be aware of is the national movement to make participating in BDS activities illegal. Boycotts are protected free speech from our Constitution and have been used for years in the Civil Rights and Black Lives Matter movement to bring about real change. As of 2021, 35 states have passed bills and executive orders to discourage boycotts of Israel. If you see your state attempt to pass these laws, know your rights and fight back!

So this Ramadan, take part in an effective BDS global movement to demonstrate that our community did not stand for apartheid in South Africa, and we will not stand for apartheid and genocide in Palestine!

This article reflected my strong belief that to be a good ally to oppressed people, it is important to follow the lead of their popular resistance groups and campaigns. The Palestinian BDS Movement is one of those groups that coordinates BDS campaigns around the world. With their designation of specific targets, they focus on the most winnable campaigns and have had great success, mostly from countries in Europe. Taking this being a good ally approach always helped keep me honest and reduce my ego from feeling like I was their "savior" of the Palestinians who couldn't help themselves. Just as in the case of the Irish, the Palestinians have a lot more experience than I will ever have in resisting their oppressors.

This next article describes another area of my activism, i.e., making sure the true history of social justice movements in America is told and recognized. In this case, the Masjid Al-Taqwa Chicago Black Muslim History Bus Tour provides an important set of Black Muslim history that has been redacted from U.S. history and that most Chicagoans do not know about. My first book, *The Muslim American Fight for Social Justice,* is all about recovering this history. This issue is particularly important in 2025 as the Trump Administration has issued executive orders that include "cleansing" of American history of events that might make white people uncomfortable including the genocide of the Native Americans and the brutal history of slavery.

Masjid Al-Taqwa Chicago Hosts First Black Muslim History Tour

By Bill Chambers
Muslim Journal
6/20/23

On Saturday March 18, Masjid Al-Taqwa (MAT) Chicago hosted the first Black Muslim History Tour in the city that was at the heart of the Honorable Elijah Muhammad's Nation of Islam and the Imam Warith Deen Mohammed Community of Al-Islam.

Chicago has a rich history of Muslim presence and influence that has contributed to the establishment of Islam in the United States. The tour traced the history of Chicago's African American Muslim community (in association with the leadership of Imam Warith Deen Mohammed), going from the historic Woodlawn and Hyde Park neighborhoods to Chicago's south suburbs. Some of Islam's most notable figures in the United States have called Chicago home, including Nation of Islam leader the Honorable Elijah Muhammad and wife Sister Clara Muhammad, former World Heavyweight Champion Muhammad Ali, and Imam Warith Deen Mohammed. During this Black History Month, Masjid

Al-Taqwa and The Taqwa Center for Community Excellence invited a wide variety of participants to experience and learn about this history that was unknown to so many.

The 56 seats on the bus were filled with many more on the waiting list asking for the next tour (which is planned for Juneteenth weekend this year). Our bus driver was Muslim and participated along with people from Interfaith America, Zakat Foundation, Lutheran Theological Seminary; McCormick Theological Seminary; chaplain, professor, and students from University of Chicago. President and staff from American Islamic College; President of the Illinois Muslim Civic Coalition; chaplain from Dominican University; members of the Wheaton Muslim Center; Greater Bethesda Missionary Baptist Church, and a member of the Focolare Movement. Even more impressive was the number of families and young people who came.

Feedback on the tour was universally positive, with people saying how impressed they were to learn about the history from elders on the tour who shared their personal involvement with each site. Some "had a new appreciation for the neighborhood where they lived" and said "The history was amazing. I learned so much I didn't know at all and know there is so much more to learn." Response from one of the families was "I'm excited that I had the chance to experience it with my family so we can get to know more about our black history."

One of the most important goals of the tour was not only to share the history of the African American Muslim community but also to communicate a strong sense of pride in what was accomplished and what continues to be provided by African American Muslims in Chicago. Another important goal was to share this history with other Muslim groups who have had a history of distancing themselves from all Black Muslims. This comment was only one example of how this goal was achieved. "My sister and I discussed how we wished we had known about this community when we were young in the 80s. The American Muslim role models we had were out of reach, like Hakeem Olajuwan and Kareem Abdul Jabbar. Growing up in the suburbs/rural town to immigrant parents, we just didn't know. Thank you for serving as a space to bridge the gap so another generation of immigrant Muslim children do not pass without this knowledge." At the end of the tour, there was going to be lunch provided by MAT and final summary presentations. Everyone who attended was so excited about the tour (and some of the traditional food) that they all stayed to discuss what they had seen.

This IS what it means to share African American Muslim history with people outside of the community, i.e., to inspire others with what has been done and continues to be accomplished. It also allows others to respect two great American religious leaders, Honorable Elijah Muhammad and Imam Warith Deen Mohammed.

Each bus rider was given a booklet with a picture of each stop, its address, and why it is significant. For each location, a member of the community described in personal detail each location and his/her own association with it. The first stop was Masjid Honorable Elijah Muhammad / Sister Clara Muhammad School at 7351 S. Stoney Island. Originally, it was a Greek Orthodox Church, and its purchase in 1971 was the largest of the Nation of Islam (NOI) under the leadership of the Honorable Elijah Muhammad. Brother Clyde El-Amin explained how this was the national center of all activity for every generation in the community. The school was called University of Islam and is known nationally as excellent and offering Black children a positive view of themselves. Imam W. D. Mohammed would rename all 47 of the schools to Sister Clara Muhammad Schools. In 1931 Sister Clara Muhammad began teaching children in her own home, then grew to be a nationwide system of schools.

The next stop was the Guaranty Bank at 6750 S. Stony Island Ave which was purchased in 1973 and kept by the NOI until 1980. This acquisition complemented the mission of African Americans controlling their community economics.

Honorable Elijah Muhammad House

The tour continued to the homes of the Honorable Elijah Muhammad and Muhammad Ali. Imam Rabbani Mubashshir emphasized the wide reach of Muhammad Ali expressing the teachings of the NOI, including impressing a teenage Rabbani to join in 1969. He also said that after the passing of Honourable Elijah Muhammad in 1975, many members were not oriented to see his death, and it was a shock for many. But they were fortunate that people like Muhammad Ali, the members of Elijah Muhammad's family, and the chosen successor Imam W.D. Mohammed, helped the community to get through his passing.

Next was Masjid Al-Faatir at 1200 E. 47th Street, the largest of Chicago's mosques and co-founded by Muhammad Ali. Brother Bashir Asad, often called the historian of the community, described this mosque being opened in 1987 in Kenwood neighborhood as the first free standing mosque in the city. It was opened under Imam W. Deen Mohammed, who was moving the NOI toward the Quran and the Sunnah of the Prophet. Now, it is part of nearly 70 mosques in the Chicagoland area.

Temple #2 at 843 East 43rd Street was next and served as the Chicago headquarters for the NOI from 1934. Temple #1 was at 11529 Linwood (Honorable Elijah Muhammad Blvd) in Detroit when it was purchased in the 1950s.

Next was the Lamb Processing Plant, 3900 S. Halsted St. which was a lamb processing and training facility providing food and educational opportunities for NOI members. This was an early effort to address the "food desert" issue in the community. Lamb was provided to local and national grocery stores. Brother Bashir Asad explained that lamb was a staple of many ethnic groups in Chicago and was part of the Honorable Elijah Muhammad's plan to improve the health of the African American community laid out in his book *Eat to Live*. This was an initiative to inform African American communities about a healthy lifestyle that would benefit and not harm their health.

The building at 2548 S. Federal St. was the production facility of Muhammad Speaks Press and the Muhammad Speaks Newspaper. During the 1960s, Muhammad Speaks was printing 600,000 copies a week. Latifah Wangara said Malcolm X El-Hajj Malik El-Shabazz started the paper in 1961 to get the message of freedom, justice, and equality and do for self out into the world. In 1977, Imam Mohammed changed the name of the paper to the Bilalian News and moved the production to the Pioneer Building 8300 S Cottage Grove which served as headquarters for the paper's last name change to the Muslim Journal. "The goal was always the same, i.e. to tell our own story. We watch other people try to tell our story or write our story out of history. The paper preserves our heritage and our history."

The Sister Clara Muhammad Memorial Foundation at 7900 S. Champlain was next. Their tagline is "Providing Quality Education to Humankind for Human Salvation Since 1931." The Foundation manages the nationwide system of Clara Muhammad Schools [grades k-8] and W.D. Mohammed High Schools [grades 9-12] that Clara Muhammad started in her house in 1931.

Salaam Community Wellness Center 613 E. 67th St. was established in 2020 and offers an integrative, holistic model of health and wellness. Dr. Constance Shabazz provided a tour of the Wellness Center while presenting how it fits into the vision of the Honorable Elijah Muhammad and Imam W. D. Mohammed to help build and support healthy communities by empowering them through the improvement of health, wellness, education, and economic development. The Center offers Primary Care, Addiction Treatment, Mental Health, Nutrition, and Case Management.

The next stop was the Ephraim Bahar Cultural Center 2525 W. 71st St. a community in association with Imam W. D. Mohammed led by Imam Omar Karim. In his talk on the Center, Imam Omar emphasized the work they do in the community throughout the year and their close partnership with Masjid Al-Taqwa on numerous events. The Center provides multiple classes, interfaith dialogue, feeding and clothing for the homeless, community meetings, the Annual Walk for Moral Excellence Parade, and many more services.

The Mosque Cares from Second Bus Tour

Originally, the last stop on the tour was going to be The Mosque Cares 929 171st St. Hazel Crest, IL, but due to time constraints of the bus, it had to be skipped. Brother Rod Bashir, a longtime resident of Hazel Crest, provided a commentary on The Mosque Cares, a non-profit Islamic da'wah project founded by Imam W.D. Mohammed in 2003 and currently led by his son, Wallace D. Mohammed II. Mosque Cares also has meetings with other Islamic groups, hosts the annual Saviors Day, and produces books on the teachings of Imam Mohammed. Brother Rod also explained how the city of Hazel Crest has also established a day in honor of Imam W.D. Mohammed.

Group from Second Bus Tour on Juneteenth

A hard-working team of Masjid Al-Taqwa members put together this tour that was such a resounding success. We thank Imam Tariq El-Amin for coming up with the idea. Inshallah, the next tour will be Juneteenth weekend this year with the expectation of many more participants and the retelling of the history of African American Muslims will have an even wider reach than before.

CAIR-Chicago and The *Chicago Monitor*

During the period of the Trump presidency, when Muslims were once again under attack, I was not part of any social justice group. The Palestine Solidarity Group – Chicago collapsed after the FBI campaign against Palestinian activists, as I described above. I had become a Muslim and was working toward my Masters in Islamic Studies at AIC, but I felt restless and needed to put myself out there in the resistance to Trump. The Council on American Islamic Relations (CAIR) was doing outstanding work at the time fighting Islamophobia and resisting the Trump Administration's attack on immigrants and especially when he banned immigrants from six Muslim majority countries in 2017. Trump issued an executive order to ban all Syrian refugees indefinitely and prevented anyone (including refugees) from Iran, Iraq, Libya, Somalia, Sudan, Syria, and Yemen from entering the U.S. for 90 days. This was also when the Syrian civil war was at its height. CAIR-Chicago mobilized its legal team to support immigrants denied entry as well as had lawyers at the airport assisting anyone coming in from those countries with their legal rights. Below is an article describing one of the CAIR-Chicago sponsored protests at O'Hare Airport in Chicago.

Given all the positive pushback that CAIR-Chicago did to the Trump Administration's attacks on the Muslim community, the organization seemed the perfect fit for my communication and writing skills. I volunteered at CAIR-Chicago in their Communications Department, I mainly worked on articles for the *Chicago Monitor*, an online news service run out of the CAIR-Chicago office, and eventually became Editor-in-Chief. The *Chicago Monitor* had been a lack-luster online publication for CAIR-Chicago interns to publish articles they wrote. The editing was typically poor, and the topics were usually not timely. I worked hard to change all that to make it truly an online news source providing in-depth analysis of mainstream news and uncovering under-reported and unreported stories on the local, national and international level.

Our topics covered everything from the burgeoning Black Lives Matter movement, community control of the police, oppression of the Palestinians, protests over Gaza, the war in Yemen, and the rising tide of Islamophobia. As Editor, I would mentor the interns on how to write journalism articles (when I was just learning to do so myself) and make sure that the topics they wrote about were those they were passionate about. During this time, I was often a reporter in the field, covering protests, press conferences, and other events happening around the city. Eventually, I applied to the CPD for a press pass and was able to use it to get into places I normally would be barred from. I loved being able to do that.

My favorite use of the press pass was when Trump was scheduled to speak in 2016 at the UIC Pavilion in Chicago at, one of the most diverse cities in the country and the most diverse university in the state. This was not a good idea on his part. The protesters were about 5,000, outnumbering the Trump supporters. The plan was to prevent him from speaking by having protesters inside the pavilion as well as thousands outside. I remember walking in with my press pass and showing it to one of the Trump handlers at the front desk. It was one of the many times I was glad that the *Chicago Monitor* sounded like a very official Chicago publication. I was handed my Trump Press Pass easily.

Inside the Pavilion, it seemed like there were more protesters than Trump supporters, mainly because of how diverse the crowd was. It was probably the most diverse Trump rally in history. My wife Elaine saw me on the TV coverage of the rally and was very concerned by the threat of violence, as many protesters were, but the violence was limited to a few skirmishes inside and outside the Pavilion. The main violence occurred after Trump refused to speak when the main body of protesters cheered, "We stopped him," and returned to campus. One group of BLM protesters decided to take over the nearby on ramp to the expressway and ended up getting attacked by the police. The following article describes my coverage of the event.

My Chicago Activist Life

Two protesters at Trump Rally

Thousands Of Non-Violent Chicago Protestors Shut Down Trump Rally

Chicago Monitor
Bill Chambers - March 12, 2016

There were about 3000 protestors outside the Trump rally in Chicago last night and about 1000 inside. While waiting for the never-to-appear Trump, small groups of protesters would chant or verbally spar with those Trump supporters wearing shirts like "All Lives Matter." Trump campaign officials called the Chicago Police Department (CPD) to escort individuals out while Trump supporters cheered. As the 7,000 seat Pavilion filled up, it became clear that if 15% of the crowd were protesters, Trump would not be able to make a show out of "get them outta here" as he has done at other rallies. But if you watched any of the local, national, or cable news immediately after the rally was called off, you would be sure that the "violence" of the protesters is what forced the rally to be canceled. And that is exactly what the media and the Trump campaign want you to believe.

The UIC Pavilion seats were filled as well, and about 300 people, including media standing on the floor in front of the stage when a Trump campaign spokesperson said:

> "Mr. Trump just arrived in Chicago and, after meeting with law enforcement, has determined that for the safety of all the tens of thousands of people that have gathered in and around the arena, tonight's rally will be postponed to another date. Thank you very much for your attendance, and please go in peace."

The CPD was quick to provide a statement that it was the Trump campaign that cancelled the event. According to the Associated Press, CPD spokesman Anthony Guglielmi said the agency never recommended that Trump cancel his campaign rally in the city and never told the Trump campaign there was a security threat at the UIC Pavilion. He said the department had sufficient manpower on the scene to handle any situation. Guglielmi said the university's police department also did not recommend that Trump call off the event. He says the decision was made "independently" by the campaign.

To all who were inside the packed venue waiting for Trump to appear, the announcement sounded as if Trump was "postponing" the event for people's safety, but neither the CPD nor UIC security believed it was a problem.

Trump continued to reinforce this message that protestors were creating a safety concern, and the decision was made with law enforcement.

In a telephone interview with CNN last night, he said the event was cancelled because he didn't "want to see people hurt or worse...We made the decision in conjunction with law enforcement...They said, "it would be better not to do it, and I think we did the right thing." In the combative interview with Don Lemon, Trump defended his previous statements about protesters being taken out on a stretcher and punched in the face by blaming all violence on protestors. "I don't take anything back…I've seen strong protesters hitting people, sometimes, it's the police."

Trump was not telling the truth about his "meeting with law enforcement" about there being safety concerns. When the cancellation announcement was made, the CPD has the thousands of protesters outside behind barricades across the street from the Pavilion. There was a lot of chanting and speeches from the very diverse group of protestors and very long lines of people peacefully waiting around the Pavilion itself to be admitted. Inside the venue, there were hundreds of protesters sitting in seats on the main floor, but most were waiting quietly for Trump to show up. The CPD took out some individuals, but only because they refused to stop chanting or wouldn't leave when instructed.

Protestors outside the UIC Pavilion

The most likely reason the Trump campaign canceled the rally was that as the Pavilion filled up, it was obvious that there were hundreds of protesters inside. More than they had ever seen at one of their rallies. Some whole sections of the stands were protesters so there was no way the CPD could cart them all out as security had done at other rallies. If Trump would have spoken, his whole speech would likely have been completely disrupted just by protesters chanting, which would have looked terrible on national TV. So, the Trump campaign "postponed" his rally and blamed it on the "violence" of the protesters.

So who were these protesters?

Many were UIC students from one of the most diverse universities in the area – Blacks, Asians, Latinos, Arabs, and Muslims. Student groups include the Young Democrats, Students for Justice in Palestine, the Black Student Union, the Muslim Student Association, and Mexican Students of Aztlan. Many analysts have commented that anyone Black or who looks Muslim (like a woman wearing a hijab) has been a targets for assaults by Trump supporters at previous rallies. In Chicago, there were hundreds of these "targets." Not only individual Trump supporters but also apparently the Trump campaign itself was intimidated. A protester's shirt said it best – "Your Fear of Black Men is Irrational."

Chicago groups, including Black Lives Matter – Chicago, Black Youth Project 100 (BYP100), We Charge Genocide, Chicago Alliance Against Racist and Political Repression (CAARPR), Immigrant Youth Justice League (IYJL), many Chicago Teachers Union (CTU) members, and others from the local Latino community were all part of a wave of solidarity protesting Trump. There was also a large contingent of Muslim students and community members both outside and inside the Pavilion standing up in large numbers to Trump's continued Muslim-baiting rhetoric. Just the day before, he had claimed "Islam hates us" in an interview with Anderson Cooper.

But this was a UIC student led protest – demanding that Trump and his message of hate and racism get off their campus and out of their community. In the Facebook event for the protest, the students were very careful to call for a peaceful protest.

"Trump has been known to provoke and encourage violence towards protesters in the past. Past protesters have been spat on, kicked, hit, shoved, and assaulted in various other ways. With, our strength will lie both in our numbers and our ability to show these Trump supporters a higher class of behavior. We do not condone and will condemn any physical contact with supporters attending the rally; please keep your hands and items to yourself. Our goal must be to show the attendees the empathy, acceptance, and love that we strive to see in the world. Keep any signs and chants aimed at Trump and his campaign instead of individual supporters."

And the students kept to their plan. But they were also very clear about what they were protesting for all who wanted to listen.

"**Reasons for protesting:**

- Trump has called for the complete and total shutdown of all Muslims entering the United States. He has claimed that Islam and Muslims are hateful and terrorists and must be barred entrance until he decides otherwise.
- Trump has generalized the entire Mexican immigrant community as criminals and rapists. He calls for the mass deportation of 11 million adults and children alike regardless of how long they have lived in the United States. He also calls for the building of a giant wall to separate us from our long-time allies in Mexico.
- Trump has advocated for war crimes such as but not limited to torture-interrogation, mass murder as a warning, the intentional murder of entire civilian families, and indiscriminately bombing of countries in the Middle East.
- Trump has consistently refused to disavow and condemn the white supremacist hate groups such as the KKK that support and work for his campaign.
- Trump has preyed on the fears of poor and middle-class whites while at the same time not offering any policies that would support them in overcoming the very serious and real challenges that they also face in America.
- Trump's nativist, nationalist, and fascist stances parallel the most evil leaders this world has seen such as Adolf Hitler and Benito Mussolini.
- Trump shows a childlike temperament that would jeopardize our national security and potentially start unnecessary conflicts."

Respecting the rights of free speech and the right of peaceful protest, security did not stop protesters who had tickets from coming to the rally. At one point, even on the main floor, there were UIC students with keffiyehs, Palestine scarves, Black Lives Matter T-shirts, and hijabs mixing peacefully with men in camouflage hats and Trump buttons.

Protesters inside celebrating Trump rally cancellation

When it was announced that the Trump campaign had "postponed" the rally because of security concerns, hundreds in the crowd started cheering, "We stopped Trump!" This was the point where many of the Trump supporters became angry at all the celebrating, and after several minutes, there were two or three fights between Trump supporters and Black protesters. The videos of these fights were the ones that the media showed repeatedly to mislead the public that there had been widespread violence by the protesters.

This is the first time that a Trump rally was canceled before it even started because of widespread protest. It will very likely not be the last. Now we know there are two things Donald Trump is afraid of – Megyn Kelly and the people of Chicago.

This was the last time Trump tried to come to Chicago and speak. Like Israeli Prime Ministers Olmert and Netanyahu, he would learn that showing up in Chicago would mean being met by thousands of protestors from every community in the city. He learned never to come back.

Being a reporter for the *Chicago Monitor* also helped me to be able to cover protests and press conferences and to be seen as an objective journalist (which I very clearly was not). This is another case that I used my white privilege to get into situations where I would normally have been barred. My age and grey/white hair were also useful to appear like an old reporter who might even potentially be on the side of the right-wing protestors. My "disguise", i.e., looking like an old white guy, enabled me to talk to the counter-protestors, who would always feel comfortable talking with a member of a press they had never heard of and getting their photo taken.

One good example of the strategy was Apartheid Week which was sponsored by the Students for Justice in Palestine at DePaul University. Apartheid Week was an annual week of events concerning Palestine where films were shown, and in many cases, mockups of the Apartheid Wall would be created with Palestinian students dressed as soldiers questioning students walking through the quad. This particular year, the pro-Israel group Stand With Us went to multiple colleges to do counter-protests and have their own tables praising Israel.

It was common for them to bring outside people from the organization to these campus events. I was covering this event as an "unbiased" journalist who wanted to interview those in the Stand With Us group to see if they were students or not. (Non-students are not allowed to set up tables or hold events on campus.)

In doing the interviews, it was clear that all the materials on the table had been provided by Stand By Us, and the pro-Israel "students" themselves were not all students. The non-students avoided me when I asked what student organization they were from. One did say they were part of a Students for Israel group but admitted it had only been set up recently. I doubted they were an approved student group, which they had to be to even have a table passing out literature. This event happened before it became increasingly common to attack Palestinian protests as being antisemitic.

Campaign Against Islamophobia

CAIR-Chicago is one of the leading Muslim organizations that fights and campaigns against Islamophobia. They provide lawyers for Muslims who have been involved in Islamophobic incidents. Given that history, the *Chicago Monitor* often covered anti-Muslim events locally and reviewed the media for slanted coverage against Muslims.

In one case I covered, two men on Facebook had made violent threats against the large mosque in Bridgeview located in a heavily populated Palestinian area. In my research, I found out that the FBI had been called in to question the two men, and the local police increased patrols around the mosque. But when I called the local sheriff and asked why the men hadn't been arrested, he said the FBI told him that nothing more could be done other than monitoring them because they had not taken any action. I realized someone could threaten to kill Muslims publicly, but they could not be arrested or even charged with a misdemeanor because of free speech laws. This seemed crazy to me especially at that time when threats and attacks on Muslims were commonplace. It inspired me to investigate "hate speech laws," which several countries did have, including Canada, where people could be charged with a hate crime for threatening to do bodily harm against any minority group.

The following article covers my research on the topic.

Bridgeview Mosque Threats Show Limits of Hate Crime Law

Chicago Monitor
By Bill Chambers - January 26, 2015

Two men who had made threats on Facebook alluding to shooting and killing Muslims at the Mosque Foundation in Bridgeview, a suburb of Chicago, were released on Friday by local police after turning themselves in. The local media only reported that the men were questioned by the Bridgeview Police Department and the FBI, but never explained why after such serious threats, they would be released without charge. Why were men who made threats, causing the local police to have regular patrols of the mosque, school, and surrounding community released?

The original threats, discovered last Sunday, involved two people messaging back and forth on Facebook, identifying the location of the Bridgeview mosque. The Mosque Foundation's vice president, Oussama Jammal, was quoted as saying the FBI and local Bridgeview Police immediately got involved after a screenshot of the conversation was provided.

"They were talking about killing people – you know, an eye for an eye, a tooth for a tooth – something of that sort. That's the specific words that have been said. So that is serious, that is not someone who is just saying, 'I don't like them, I hate them.'"

NBC News reported that the messages started as a status update on Facebook and threatened to put local Muslims "in check" for the actions of extremist followers of Islam on the other side of the globe.

"F****** Muslims burn down Christian churches in France! We got to start breaking some rules putting these n****** in check," one message said. While the post started as a generalized threat against Muslims, the discourse grew more specific in subsequent comments. "I'd like to start with that mosque down the street . . . Eye for an eye tooth for a tooth," another message said. Later someone else chimed in: "Haha . . . yep . . . maybe we should walk down the middle of the street without a worry in the world like they do shootin every one of them!!!!" Eventually, it was suggested that the two target a mosque near 87th and Harlem, according to the posting. The mosque near that intersection is the Mosque Foundation in Bridgeview.

On Friday, the men turned themselves into the Bridgeview Police Department and were interviewed by the local police and the FBI and released. ABC News reported that upon leaving the station, one of the men said to a reporter, "The threat was not real, I was never going to do that, it was all fake."

On Saturday, the *Chicago Monitor* interviewed Bridgeview Police Chief Walter Klimek on the puzzling question of the men not being charged and about the still ongoing investigation.

The men who turned themselves in are considered only "persons of interest" in the case. After the interview, the FBI determined that "no federal crime had been committed" and that for the men to be charged with a hate crime, "another criminal offense was needed to accompany it." Making threats against Muslims and a mosque on social media would need to be linked with some crime involving following through on those threats. The FBI is doing no further investigation and has left the case up to the local police. Chief Klimek explained that one of his detectives will be going to a grand jury on Monday to obtain a subpoena for six months of Facebook records of the "persons of interest," but it will take two to three weeks to get them back. Although the men were not charged and did not have a record of this type of behavior, Chief Klimek was taking the threats seriously and was keeping regular patrols out for the mosque, school, and surrounding community.

So this brings us back to the fact that in the U.S. unlike France, Canada, Germany, and several other nations, there is not a law against "hate speech." So someone can threaten to shoot Muslims at the Mosque Foundation or by Fox News host Jeanine Pirro, who called for the mass murder of "Islamists" by other Muslims whom we would "arm to the teeth," and if they don't shoot someone, they have not committed a crime. In the case of the Fox News anchor, they will not be questioned by the FBI, nor will they lose their job.

What is the difference between laws against "Hate Crimes" and those against "Hate Speech?"

Hate crime laws punish violent acts, e.g., assault, murder, bombing, and property damage, that target a person or group based on attributes such as gender, ethnic origin, religion, race, disability, or sexual orientation. The U.S. has a federal hate crime law that was updated in 2009 by the Obama Administration. As Benjamin B. Wagner, U.S. Attorney for the Eastern District of California, explains:

> "The Shepard Byrd Hate Crimes Prevention Act increased penalties for violent hate crimes, broadened and simplified federal jurisdiction, and for the first time recognized certain violent acts directed at individuals because of their actual or perceived sexual orientation as federal hate crimes. The Shepard Byrd Act provides investigators and prosecutors with

important new tools to deploy against hate crimes. Before the passage of the Shepard Byrd Hate Crimes Prevention Act in October 2009, there was no single federal hate crime statute, and prosecutions were based on a variety of civil rights statutes or other violent crime statutes."

But even with these enhancements to the U.S. federal hate crime law, it would not stop someone from just making online or any media threats against Muslims or any other targeted group. What would stop this?

Hate Speech laws prohibit name-calling, verbal abuse or expressions of hatred, and incitement to violence that targets a person or group based on attributes such as gender, ethnic origin, religion, race, disability, or sexual orientation. The U.S. has no laws against hate speech. But Canada, for example, does.

Canada — a country that has less of a violent history of hate speech against Native Americans, Catholics, Irish, Japanese, Germans, immigrants, African-Americans, Latinos, Arabs, and Muslims than the U.S. — has hate speech legislation. Under the current Canadian criminal laws, anyone found guilty of inciting hatred against an identifiable group — which the Criminal Code (Sections 318-320) defines as "any section of the public distinguished by color, race, religion, national or ethnic origin, age, sex or sexual orientation" — can be penalized by a fine or sentenced to up to two years in prison.

There are limits and exceptions on the application of the Hate Speech law that include:

- The accused establishes that the statements communicated were true.
- In good faith, the person expressed or attempts to establish by an argument an opinion on a

- religious subject or an opinion based on a belief in a religious text.
- The statements were relevant to any subject of public interest, the discussion of which was for the public benefit, and if on reasonable grounds, he believed them to be true; or
- "He intended to point out, for the purpose of removal, matters producing or tending to produce feelings of hatred toward an identifiable group in Canada."
- In Canada, as in the U.S., hate speech laws are controversial and have been accused of unfairly limiting freedom of expression. David Butt, writing last week for the Global Mail about the Charlie Hebdo tragedy, describes the utility of the Canadian Hate Speech law even though it is rarely invoked.

One glimmer of the law's utility might be seen in the decision by many Canadian media outlets not to re-publish the offending Charlie Hebdo cartoons despite being sincerely awash in "Je suis Charlie" sentiment. Our Supreme Court suggested the hate speech law has symbolic value such that even without being invoked, it silently validates a national ethic of multicultural accommodation and respect; and in the decision by Canadian media not to re-publish the cartoons, that very ethic can be seen in action. So it may be that our hate speech law was a silent point of resonance with the values, not the legal obligations, that motivated the media outlets who chose not to publish.

It's past time to have a debate in this country over passing a Hate Speech law that could not only protect the multiple groups targeted by hate speech, not only including Muslims and Arabs, but also Jews, African-Americans, Latinos, the LGBT community, and many more. A law that "silently validates a national ethic of multicultural accommodation and respect" and has Canadian safeguards protecting freedom of speech would be welcome at a time when men on Facebook or a host on Fox News can advocate killing Muslims without fear of repercussion.

The lack of hate speech law is an example of something that most Americans would not even consider a problem. Once more what seems so normal in America that clearly has a problem with hate speech against many different minority groups is considered a problem and classified as a crime by other "developed" countries who have less of a problem than we do. Again, the U.S. is an exceptional country only that it does recognize hate speech as even a problem.

Islamophobia had gone mainstream in 2015 when every newsperson and public figure seemed to find it acceptable to make anti-Muslim comments publicly. Popular cable TV figures like Bill Maher on HBO had no problem at all saying the most anti-Muslim stereotypes on his show without any adverse public reactions. As I pointed out in this article at the time, this Islamophobic atmosphere only encouraged attacks on Muslims and mosques.

2015 – Islamophobia Goes Mainstream In America

Chicago Monitor
Bill Chambers - December 28, 2015

With all the attention on Trump and the other Republican candidates for President making Islamophobic comments, one would think that the rise in attacks on American Muslims and Islam just began in the last few months. But 2015 will be remembered as the year that began with three young Muslims being killed in Chapel Hill and will end with attacks on Muslims and mosques at record highs.

The Year in Islamophobia

There have been any number of articles in the press pointing to the rise in attacks on Muslims since the Paris and San Bernardino shootings, but those incidents only encouraged an upward spike in a trend that had been simmering all year long.

This year has been the worst year on record for American Muslims since 9/11. Currently, the 38 suspected hate crime cases are 2.94 times the average monthly rate seen from 2010-2014.

There have been 63 recorded attacks on mosques (17 in November alone), with the previous high of 53 in 2010. Muslims were the target of 154 hate crimes in 2014. The total number for 2015 is expected to surpass last year's total.

"Islamophobia" has come to be used for any anti-Muslim or anti-Islam bigotry or prejudice with the assumption that it is always religion-based. The difficulty with the term is that it simplifies the multiple causes that can make up anti-Muslim speech or actions. Islamophobia can certainly have a pro-Christian, anti-Islam religious expression that dates to the hostility of Christian leaders in the 6th century to this new religion. Some of the Christian Right attacks on Muslims have this archaic tone to them and usually involve insulting the Prophet Muhammad. Pamela Geller's "Prophet Muhammad cartoon contest" in Texas reflects this thinking.

But there also is a political power-based component to Islamophobia that originated from the early Christian empires being challenged by the political growth of Islam. The equation in the media between "Islamist" (used to describe the mainstream Justice and Development Party governing Turkey as well as ISIS), "Radical Islam," "Jihadist," and "Islamic Terrorists" – all tend to make any Islamic group that seeks power in any way the same. In our modern world, many have suggested that "Political Islam" is the biggest threat to the West, replacing Communism. But it's important to remember that some "Islamists" are acceptable to the U.S. because they are allies and support American foreign policy goals. Saudi Arabia is the most obvious example. This year the U.S. had no difficulty supporting a Saudi-led coalition in Yemen that has been accused of huge numbers of civilian casualties in their fight against the Houthis, who are supported by another form of "Political Islam" – the Iranians.

Islamophobia also can express racism. As Evelyn Alsultany states in *Arabs and Muslims in the Media: Race and Representation after 9/11*, many Americans equate Arabs with Muslims (even though many are Christians, Jewish, or secular). There were numerous incidents, especially on Southwest Airlines in November and December, of Muslims and Arabs being removed from planes because fellow passengers said they felt "uncomfortable." There was no indication Southwest Airlines was ever reprimanded for supporting this racist profiling of their passengers.

There is also a cultural and "Other" component to Islamophobia where Muslims are perceived as having a different culture than the "typical" American. The fact that what is seen as "cultural difference" has often little to do with religion; the cultural difference is attributed to Islam. Twenty-five percent of American Muslims are African-American, and the majority of those have been in America longer than the Islamophobes.

The U.S. has a long history of anti-immigrant, xenophobic movements that have targeted each new generation of immigrants, and political parties have taken advantage of this fear and hatred of the stranger. But each group, whether it was the Italians, Germans, Irish, or Catholics, has slowly been "accepted" as they were perceived as having assimilated into American society embraced "American values," and especially because they were white. It can be argued that Black immigrants, just like African-Americans, have never been fully accepted. The multiple elements of Islamophobia, particularly the racist and cultural aspects, suggest that Muslims will also be in this same category. It will take specific laws to legally force Americans to provide them equal rights, especially in freedom of religion.

The last year saw an intense combination of all these facets of Islamophobia – the religious, political power, racist, and cultural – rise into a crescendo of hate crimes and attacks on mosques during November and December.

Charlie Hebdo and the Phantom Attack on America

The year began with the fallout from the Charlie Hebdo attack in Paris on January 7, 2015. This would be the first of two attacks in Europe by Muslim extremists that would result in increased attacks on American Muslims even though there was no threat to the U.S.

This is the first trend in 2015 that increased Islamophobia: When there have been no major attacks by a group of Muslims on the U.S., people act as if an attack in Europe was an attack on the U.S.

This approach turns the murders of twelve staff at Charlie Hebdo by two Muslim extremists into an attack on Western civilization and values by the Muslim world. When an event like this happens, there will always be statements made by some politicians that all Muslims should not be blamed for an attack by three people, but it will be their actions that will show the sincerity of their statements. After the Charlie Hebdo killings, there were understandably French soldiers dispatched to guard Jewish synagogues and centers, but none of those soldiers protected the mosques and Islamic centers that were coming under daily revenge attacks.

Chapel Hill and the Refusal to Recognize a Hate Crime

A little over one month later February 10, three young American Muslims, Deah Shaddy Barakat, Yusor Mohammad Abu-Salha, and Razan Mohammad Abu-Salha, were shot to death in Chapel Hill, North Carolina. Two were women who wore the hijab and were clearly identified as Muslims. The media initially focused on the local police department report of a "parking dispute" between the three young Muslims and the shooter. It took a concerted social media campaign #ChapelHillShooting, for the media to even begin covering the murders.

The shooter, Craig Hicks, was charged with "three counts of first-degree murder and a count of discharging a firearm into an occupied dwelling." Multiple civil rights and faith-based groups had to send a letter to Attorney General Eric Holder before the Justice Department's Civil Rights Division, along with the U.S. Attorney's Office for the Middle District of North Carolina and the FBI, opened "a parallel preliminary inquiry" to determine whether any federal laws, including hate crime laws, were violated. The FBI completed their report September 9, and the U.S. Attorney's Office in the Middle District of North Carolina is still apparently reviewing the report to determine what next action to take.

This is the second major trend in Islamophobia for the year: Attacks on Muslims are not taken seriously and are perceived as being done by loners.

Although there are specific leaders and groups who are advocating violence against Muslims and are clearly acting on this hatred, there is no public outcry and no systematic FBI investigation of these incidents. Later in the year, there would also be multiple arson and other damage to mosques throughout the country, but there would still be no Department of Justice inquiry. It is reminiscent of Martin

Luther King's questioning of J. Edgar Hoover after four young black girls died in the firebombing of a Birmingham church.

> "It would be encouraging for us if Mr. Hoover and the FBI would be as diligent in apprehending those responsible for bombing churches and killing little children as they are in seeking out alleged communist infiltration in the civil rights movement."

The FBI is more involved in surveillance of Muslim communities than in protecting them from attack.

Islamophobe Provocation

On May 4, Pamela Geller, characterized as "the anti-Muslim movement's most visible and flamboyant figurehead" by the Southern Poverty Law Center, sponsored a purposefully provocative "prophet Muhammad cartoon contest" in Texas. When two ISIS sympathizers took the bait and arrived with weapons, they were shot and killed. Most of the media focused on these men being a "sleeper cell" for ISIS, with little attention paid to Pamela Gellar purposefully trying to be offensive and spark a violent reaction so she could prove her "point" – that all Muslims are violent.

Islamophobe Pamela Geller had previously been on the fringes of public view until 2010, when she helped lead the "Ground Zero Mosque" controversy. As Deepa Kumar points out in her book *Islamophobia and the Politics of Empire*, Islamophobes moved from their initial campaigns against Muslim community centers and schools in 2003 into the full public sphere with the assistance of more "liberal Islamophobes" who built on the media furor over "homegrown terrorism." Pamela Geller would be assured to gather media attention and confidence that she could easily turn the attention to the ISIS sympathizers in our midst.

Charleston Emanuel AME Church Attack – Christian White Supremacists Don't Exist

Dylann Roof with Apartheid-era South African and White Rule Rhodesia Flags on his jacket.
(Dylann Roof – Facebook)

On June 17, a young white man killed nine people at a prayer service in Charleston, South Carolina. His attack was very methodical as he sat through a Bible study group for an hour before opening fire on all those present. White supremacist photos and material had been found on social media. Why is this incident part of a discussion of Islamophobic attacks? The same conservative spokespeople and media who encouraged the view of Muslims as terrorists were now saying that the church in Charleston was attacked because it was a Christian church. The shooter himself said he was there "to shoot black people," and when one member of the congregation pleaded with him to stop replied, "No, you've raped our women, and you are taking over the country ... I must do what I must do."

This was one of the major events of 2015, demonstrating that there is an element of racism in Islamophobia and a denial that anyone can be a terrorist other than a Muslim.

Paris Attacks and the War on Immigrants (Especially Muslim Ones)

As Americans experienced the shootings in San Bernardino just three weeks ago, it is easy to forget that calls from people like Donald Trump, the leading Republican candidate for President, to halt all Muslim immigration to the U.S. occurred on December 7, two days before the San Bernardino attacks on December 9. In fact, Trump was already making similar statements back in August.

Trump suggested on August 21 that it's easier for Muslim immigrants to enter the U.S. than Christians fleeing ISIS.

"There's a real assault on Christianity when you look at what's going on in Syria and ISIS," the presidential candidate said on the Yellowhammer Radio program Friday. "Do you know that if you're a Christian from Syria, you cannot get into the United States? If you're a Muslim from Syria, it's one of the easiest places to get into the United States from."

The Paris attacks occurred on November 13, when a coordinated attack by Muslim extremists in Paris killed thirteen people. Like the Charlie Hebdo attack earlier in the year, there was no initial threat to the U.S., but the media and politicians responded as if the attacks had occurred on American soil. This was the start of major political figures, including most Republican Presidential candidates and more than half of the state's governors, saying that the U.S. needed to stop admitting any Syrian refugees. (Early on, one of the Paris attackers was reported to have had a Syrian passport and entered Greece with other refugees. It was later reported that the passport was likely to have been a forgery. It was later confirmed that all the Paris attackers were from Europe.)

This was the beginning of another element of the mainstreaming of Islamophobia – i.e., multiple political figures in positions of power, governors, senators, and representatives were saying that a group of refugees should not be admitted to the country because of their religion. Later when it was pointed out that some Syrians were Christians, even "moderate" political figures like Jeb Bush said that only Christian Syrian refugees should be admitted.

It's important to point out that there was a lot of reported criticism of this position from other politicians, including President Obama, but there was no public groundswell of outrage that these individuals should step down or that what they said was so outrageous. The governors of thirty-one states took an Islamophobic, racist position based on little to no evidence, and nothing happened to them. Imagine if thirty-one governors had said we were only going to accept white South African immigrants or only Muslim immigrants from Nigeria (because the mainly Christian Nigerian army was accused of a massacre of Nigerian Muslims). The reaction would assuredly be very different.

It is also easy to dismiss people like Trump as extremists whom most Americans don't take seriously, but after relentless media coverage of Trump and other Republican candidates with similar Islamophobic positions, there is a significant impact on the public. A recent national poll showed six in ten Americans don't want the U.S. to allow Muslim refugees from Syria into the country.

Armed Intimidation to Terrorize Muslims at Prayer

As an American by-product of the post-Paris attacks, on November 21, several armed self-styled "patriots" turned up with guns at various mosques across the country to actively intimidate Muslims as they went to pray. Although this was clearly intended to terrorize Muslims practicing their faith, no one was arrested or charged. As mentioned above, many mosques were physically attacked during 2015, so a comparison to an armed group of KKK members surrounding an African-American church in the 1960s would not be out of line.

American Muslims Become the Presidential Primary Wedge Issue

America has a history of bringing up populist or wedge issues during election cycles, especially during the presidential election period. Earlier, it was abortion, gay rights, and immigrants from Mexico. This year, equating all Muslims as potential, if not actual, terrorists has been a political goldmine for candidates like Trump, Cruz, and Carson. This focus has led to national security being the issue of biggest concern for Americans in recent polls. Instead of healthcare, the economy, gun violence, the political dysfunction in Washington, DC, or more importantly, the institutional racism in the criminal justice system highlighted by the Black Lives Matter movement, national security has been boosted by the media to be the electorate's top issue. Given that the actual number of attacks on the U.S. by Muslim extremists in 2015 has been small – the acceptance of Islamophobia in the mainstream has exacerbated this politics of fear.

Since 9/11 almost twice as many people have died in attacks by right-wing groups in America than have died in attacks by Muslim extremists.

Attack and Discredit Muslim Civil Rights Groups and Demonstrations of Solidarity

The last major trend, and one that may be the most disturbing, is attacking civil rights organizations that are working within the system to fight back against Islamophobia.

There has been a concerted effort for a long time to demonize the Council on American Islamic Relations (CAIR), the largest civil rights organization for Muslims in the country, by suggesting it supports terrorists. During the Holy Land Foundation case in 2008, CAIR, along with 300 other organizations and individuals, were listed unfairly as "unindicted co-conspirators." They were never charged with any crime, but suspicion was thrown over them just the same. Any commentator or politician like Ben Carson (a Republican candidate for President) who wrote that they should be investigated is basing it on this long-ago discredited accusation. So not only are American Muslims victims of multiple acts of Islamophobia, but the largest organization to provide legal protection is being smeared. Again, one can only think of the FBI's charge that Martin Luther King's organization, the Southern Christian Leadership Conference, (SCLC) was made up of Communists.

In November and December, many Muslim women who were wearing a hijab were the victims of the attack. Many Christian women decided to don the hijab in solidarity against this Islamophobic and racist targeting of women based on the clothing they wear.

Wheaton College Professor Larycia Hawkins

The first African-American tenured professor at Wheaton College, Professor Larycia Hawkins, was suspended by the college for a Facebook post that said:

> "I stand in religious solidarity with Muslims because they, like me, a Christian, are people of the book...and as Pope Francis stated last week, we worship the same God."

Many students at the school and elsewhere decided to wear the hijab to show their support for her and for Muslim women under attack.

A much-discussed *Washington Post* article by two Muslim women, Asra Q. Nomani and Hala Arafa was published on December 21 during the height of multiple attacks on women wearing the hijab. The article criticized Christian women who wore the hijab in solidarity with Muslim women by bringing up the old Islamophobia argument that the head covering represents "Islamism" and associated wearing the hijab with being a terrorist. "This modern-day movement spreads an ideology of political Islam, called 'Islamism'.... codified by Iran, Saudi Arabia, Taliban Afghanistan and the Islamic State." As Darakshan Raja notes in her Guest Blog on Muslimgirl.net

> "What Nomani and Arafa also conveniently leave out is that the same root problem of erasing Muslim women's agency is also the driving force behind Islamophobes who terrorize, ban, and police Muslim women for wearing the hijab. These dehumanizing binaries between "oppressed" and "empowered' due to the scarf are felt mainly by most Muslim women. Rather than competing between our various struggles and dangerously arguing that we have "one" valid struggle, the world needs to recognize that Muslim women are resisting against multiple systems of violence."

Nomani and Arafa also set their sights on CAIR. "Staff members at the Council on American-Islamic Relations, which has pressed legal and PR complaints against U.S. companies that have barred employees from wearing hijabs on the job, has even called their organization "the hijab legal defense fund." Instead of being a civil rights organization that fights all forms of discrimination against Muslims, the authors deride CAIR's efforts as limited to defending women wearing a hijab.

The two Muslim authors certainly have a right to their opinion, but they present it as if they are speaking for all Muslim women. It also seems particularly egregious to criticize women of other faiths who are trying to fight this anti-Muslim atmosphere and to also continue the attack on CAIR, one of the organizations attempting to defend the American Muslim community.

Islamophobia Goes Mainstream

With this list of events continuing throughout 2015, what made Islamophobia mainstream this year?

Even with the murders of three young Muslims; armed men threatening Muslims at worship, record number of attacks on Muslims and mosques, most Republican presidential candidates and state governors taking anti-Muslim positions – there has been no major public outcry, no blistering speech by the President condemning this wave of Islamophobia; and no Department of Justice or FBI broad investigation into anti-Muslim attacks.

The American-Arab Anti-Discrimination Committee (ADC) called on Donald Trump to end his presidential campaign. The group argued that Trump's call for a temporary ban on Muslims entering the United States proves he is not fit to lead the country. "With the enormity of the challenges we face as a nation, Trump must end his campaign," ADC

President Samer Khalaf said in a statement. "His words have led to violent acts of hate, and he is not good for the country." But of course, their very reasonable statement was completely ignored by the candidate and the rest of the media.

So why did Islamophobia go mainstream this year?

For those seeking political power in the country, the unique combination of the many facets of Islamophobia – religious, political, cultural, racial, and immigrant bigotry – has all come together in a toxic stew. The political leaders of the country, including the President, have failed to lead against this hatred that violates every American value of equality and freedom of religion. It is no accident that this atmosphere of fear and Islamophobia has taken over the country at a time when activists in the Black Lives Matter movement have forced the country to face institutional racism in the criminal justice system. What better way to refuse to deal with that problem than to just shift to a new target of bigotry and racism – American Muslims.

Reading this examination of the widespread Islamophobia that gripped the country in 2015, encouraged by the Republican candidates for President, and ignored by the leaders of the Democratic Party, was a preview of what the country experienced after Trump was elected and would be repeated again with his reelection in 2024.

Another area that I covered as a journalist for the Chicago Monitor was related to the fight against the CVE Program described earlier, where the goal was to get mosques, schools, and other organizations to profile Muslims who could be terrorists. Another version of this was the profiling that was occurring in the Chicago Police Department (CPD) that allowed the CPD to hand off people they had arrested or just stopped to the local Counter-Terrorism Center. The Chicago Police Department (CPD) racially profiled any Arab or person of color for even minor violations. At the time, the CPD listed very little information on those they arrested and often, some minor detail would lead to the arrest record passed to the local terrorism center. The campaign was successful in raising this issue to the mainstream media and forcing the CPD to turn over their arrest records. The following article describes the campaign led by the Arab American Action Network (AAAN) Youth against this practice.

Chicago Arab and Black Youth Campaign Against Racial Profiling by the FBI

Arab and Muslim youth deliver anti-profiling campaign letters to FBI Headquarters.

Chicago Monitor
By Bill Chambers - August 20, 2016

With 50 supporters from multiple activist groups, members of the Arab American Action Network's (AAAN's) Youth Organizing Program delivered a letter to Michael J. Anderson, Special Agent in Charge of the Chicago Division of the FBI, and held a press conference, on Thursday outside the gates of the FBI Headquarters on Roosevelt Road.

The letter demands an end to the FBI Chicago Division's policies of racial profiling, including the use of Suspicious Activity Reports (SARs) and undercover informants and the unveiling of the Countering Violent Extremism (CVE) program. This was the latest action in the AAAN's four-year Campaign to End Racial Profiling against Arab and Muslim communities in Chicagoland.

"Every minority in America is treated like a problem long before they are treated like a person," began a member of the Arab American Action Network's (AAAN's) Youth Organizing Program at the community launch of the campaign in August 2015.

During the summer of 2012, a small group of youth at the AAAN was determined to begin a community-based campaign to put an end to racial, national, and religious profiling by law enforcement, which saw a sharp increase after the events of 9/11. The youth of the campaign conducted surveys, data analysis, and extensive research and built alliances across racial lines with other organizations, communities, and youth to further their ultimate goal of equality and justice for all.

The group held their first protest in 2013 outside of the Chicago headquarters of Immigration and Customs Enforcement (ICE). The AAAN youth publicly and officially launched the campaign at the community town hall meeting in 2015, which attracted 175 people. At that meeting, the AAAN Youth were joined by a guest panel discussion, including Veronica Morris Moore from Fearless Leading by the Youth (FLY) and Idalia Cervantes from the Illinois Coalition for Immigrant and Refugee Rights (ICIRR). At that time, the surveys had been returned and initial analysis of the data had begun.

Between August of last year and Thursday's delivery of the letter to FBI Headquarters, the AAAN Youth had completed multiple FOIA requests to gather additional information on SARs, and the Obama Administration had introduced the Countering Violent Extremism (CVE) program in December of 2015.

AAAN Youth at Gate of FBI HQ

The demands contained in the letter are based on the results of the community survey of over 450 Arab and Muslim residents within Chicagoland, which detailed their experiences with different levels of law enforcement.

The survey found that 1 the FBI had visited out of 10 community members who responded, and 85% of those visited had been asked questions about their religion, national origin, political beliefs, or immigration status. These and other statistics from the survey results suggest an FBI policy of singling out Arabs and Muslims for hyper-scrutiny through policies and programs like SARs and CVE.

"We have known our whole lives that the FBI especially harasses our people and community," said Sobhiya Salem, a leading youth organizer with the AAAN, "but now we have data from our survey and other research that will strengthen our demand that this racial profiling end immediately."

The letter, reproduced below, was written by members of the AAAN's youth organizing program and signed by several allied organizations, including the American Friends Service Committee, Chicago Alliance Against Racist and Political Repression, Assata's Daughters, Korean American Resource and Cultural Center, Chicago Desi Youth Rising, and others was hand-delivered to the guard at the gate of the fortress-like FBI building. The protesters were told that the letter would be given to Anderson, but they were not allowed into the building.

My Chicago Activist Life

Razan Khalil

The press conference held on the sidewalk just outside of the gate included AAAN youth leaders and members of the Chicago Alliance Against Racist and Political Repression (CAARPR). The Bluest Lie Collaborative, and others. After the delivery of the letter, AAAN youth leader Razan Khalil began the press conference with a statement from the AAAN Youth.

> "For the past four years, the AAAN Youth Program has led the campaign against racial profiling and has been fighting to put an end to police killings, SARs, informants, and CVE within our communities. SARs are used to target specific people that law enforcement considers suspicious. SARs cover innocent acts such as walking into a building and asking about their office hours, buying binoculars, or taking pictures of a train station…Since the FBI decides what is suspicious, it can lead to abuse of authority."

Razan Khalil continued – "In the current climate, it will lead to the targeting of Arabs and Muslims…Countering Violent Extremism is a new program the FBI is unveiling. This program also targets our communities. Why is our community being targeted while violent white nationalists are shooting up churches in South Carolina, KKK violence, and in Chicago police killings of Paul O'Neil, Rekia Boyd, Laquan McDonald, as well as torture at the Homan Square black site? With all these examples of terrorism carried out by police and white nationalists – why doesn't the FBI focus on that?"

Hoda Katebi CAIR-Chicago

Hoda Katebi, Communications Coordinator from CAIR-Chicago, connected the Youth Campaign against Racial Profiling to the wave of Islamophobia in the country.

> "We are at a time of heightened Islamophobia. The time when the amount of clothing a woman chooses to wear is somehow correlated to her level of oppression. Muslims can be kicked off airlines for doing math. Muslims can be killed in Queens, NY, for leaving a mosque. It's the same climate that renders our safety irrelevant. No, we are the security threat. Isn't it strange that law enforcement and media outlets can't quite figure out how Muslims can be shot execution style, but in 24 hours, are able to identify the intentions, motives, and family history of anyone who commits a crime with a Middle Eastern sounding name."

Katebi describes how the targeting of Muslim communities is just part of a system that negatively impacts countries in the Middle East, refugees, as well as Muslims here in Chicago.

"Of course, they are all part of a larger political system whose imperialist and colonialist projects in the Middle East have created a refugee crisis that they won't take responsibility for. Whose prisons and "security measures" hold and torture our Palestinian siblings in jails and cages. Whose militarized police force in the US shoot Black children sixteen times and whose hyper-surveillance of Muslim communities have not only correlated to increased physical and mental health problems among our youth but has created a situation where it's possible that a young Muslim woman Itemid Al-Matar can be tackled by several Chicago Police officers, unprovoked, publicly strip-searched, simply for trying to catch the Red Line [subway] to go home. CAIR-Chicago proudly calls for an end to SARs, CVE, and all forms of discrimination."

Parish Brown from The Bluest Lie Collaborative expressed the group's opposition to the Blue Lives Matter ordinance that is up for consideration in the Public Safety Committee of Chicago's City Council. (The proposed ordinance would categorize offenses committed against police officers, firefighters, and emergency medical technicians as hate crimes. Fines would increase from a range of $25-$500 to $500-$2,500 and allow jail terms of up to six months.)

Parish Brown - The Bluest Lie Collaborative

"The Bluest Lie Collaborative. We are a small rapid response team of young Black organizers whose mission is to kill the Blue Lives Matter hate crime expansion ordinance sponsored by notorious 14th Ward Alderman Ed Burke...In line with the nation-wide wave of reactionary legislation, we understand the emerging Blue Lives Matter trend as a cynical historic power grab to silence, criminalize, to intimidate organizers, protestors, and everyday citizens whom CPD and public servants are supposed to protect."

Brown went on to challenge even the justification for the Blue Lives Matter ordinance itself.

"CPD cannot be trusted to investigate hate incidents. They are already privileged under the law. No legal path exists to charge an on-duty police officer with a hate crime. Law enforcement and Department of Justice data tells us there is no crisis of hate crimes on police...Violence against police is at an all-time low. Deaths by police violence are at an all-time high. Don't buy the bluest lie. Please sign our petition so we can stop these attacks on our communities and work for liberation."

Adrian Harris – CAARPR

Adrian Harris from CAARPR described the solution required to end police crimes against those in the Arab,

Muslim, Black, Latino, and other communities impacted by racial profiling by the Chicago Police, i.e., community control of the police. (An ordinance for a Civilian Police Accountability Councilor CPAC has been introduced into the Chicago City Council.)

> "We see the many ways our city fails to respond to reported misconduct stemming from their departments. A resolution should arise from our very own individual communities. Moving forward, we must find methods of coming together with our neighbors, aldermen, and city officials in demanding an all-Civilian Police Accountability Council (CPAC), elected within the communities that will at last have the people power to say we are not here to be messed over legally. The minority population of this district, this Grand Republic, will not be profiled again. We are unable to remain your humble, docile, and ignorant populace, while being aware that our hometown is slipping further and further into a police state. The CPAC ordinance will be passed, and your department will have to find other avenues for your tyrannical behavior."

The campaign has also started a Facebook page.

The AAAN Youth leaders said that if they don't hear back from Special Agent Michael Anderson, they plan on continuing to protest and demand the end of the use of Suspicious Activity Reports (SARs) by the FBI Chicago Division and that the Chicago office refuse to be part of any Countering Violent Extremism (CVE) programming.

The complete letter and organization endorsements:

To Michael J. Anderson, Special Agent in Charge of the Chicago Division of the FBI:

We, the undersigned, are demanding an end to the FBI Chicago Division's policies of racial profiling. These include Suspicious Activity Reports (SARs), the Countering Violent

Extremism (CVE) national program, and the use of undercover informants targeting our communities. These tactics and policies have a detrimental effect on our families. In fact, according to an Arab American Action Network (AAAN) survey of Chicagoland Arabs and Muslims:

- 1 out of 12 community members surveyed believe an informant has contacted them.
- 1 out of 10 community members surveyed were visited by the FBI, with over 50% of those interactions taking place in their homes.
- 2/3 of community members surveyed do not trust federal law enforcement; and
- 1/3 of community members surveyed believe there are confidential informants within the Arab and Muslim communities of Chicagoland.

The rampant use of informants and the hyper-surveillance of people in our communities have led to the following results:

Arab and Muslim community members surveyed were less likely to discuss their political beliefs, knowing that law enforcement is so prevalent and 17.5% of community members reported experiencing hardship after an interaction with law enforcement (including financial difficulty, needing to move, and even divorce).

We also recognize at the time of writing this letter that the Movement for Black Lives in this country and city is at its peak. The hyper-surveillance of Arab and Muslim communities by the FBI cannot be separated from mass policing, mass incarceration, and killing of Black people by the Chicago Police Department and law enforcement agencies across the country.

We write this letter officially calling for you to publicly declare the end of the use of SARs by the FBI Chicago

Division, and that your office will refuse to partake in any CVE programming.

Signed:

The Youth Organizing Program of the Arab American Action Network
American Friends Service Committee-Chicago
Assata's Daughters
The Bluest Lie Collaborative
Chicago Alliance Against Racism and Political Repression
Chicago Desi Youth Rising
Council on American Islamic Relations (CAIR)-Chicago
Korean American Resource & Cultural Center
Students for Justice in Palestine (SJP)-De Paul University
SJP-Northwestern University.

Once again it is an organization like the AAAN that led the movement to end racial profiling by the CPD of many different communities in Chicago. This campaign was part of the larger Black Lives Matter movement that was targeting police killings of people of color. The campaign shined a bright light on the practice of racial profiling and was able to get much of this halted in the CPD. Once again, there was tight solidarity between the Arab community and the Black community in fighting this repression that was widespread in America at the time.

There were some positive developments during 2015 when an active campaign to make Malcom X birthday a state holiday was surprisingly successful.

Illinois Designates May 19 as Malcolm X Day

Chicago Monitor
By Bill Chambers - May 19, 2015

On this day when Malcolm X would have been 90 years old, the State of Illinois has designated "May 19, 2015, and every May 19 thereafter as "Malcolm X Day." The Senate passed unanimously a resolution proposed by the Council of Islamic Organizations of Greater Chicago (CIOGC) and sponsored by State Senator Jackie Collins (D-Chicago 16th). Malcolm X is being recognized in the words of the resolution as "a singular human rights activist and one of the most influential African-American leaders in history." His birthday on May 19 will be commemorated as a day of service in keeping with the values that Malcolm X represented in his life.

The focus of Malcolm X Day will be for all citizens in Illinois to honor the human rights values that he embodied. The CIOGC had a team of volunteers working on the resolution for more than a month. The CIOGC is a unifying body across multiple Muslim organizations in the Chicagoland area and those that worked on the resolution represented African American, Arab, South Asian, and Eastern European communities among others. The genesis of Malcolm X Day grew out of a CIOGC-sponsored event called "Malcolm X: The Voice That Lives Within Us" that was held at the end of March. As part of Black History Month, this event helped educate the larger Muslim community about the full story of Malcolm X's life.

After multiple requests from members, CIOGC leadership took up the idea and decided to add it to their Illinois legislative agenda for this term. Dr. Bambade Shakoor-Abdullah, a CIOGC Board Member who had also been on the Muslim Advisory Council for former Governor Quinn, was also instrumental in supporting the resolution. Illinois State Senator Jackie Collins of the 16th Senate District agreed to be the sponsor and worked closely with the CIOGC to draft the resolution and help shepherd it through the Illinois Senate.

In the CIOGC press release about the passing of the resolution, CIOGC Chairman Dr. Mohammed Kaiseruddin commented on the values of Malcolm X:

> "Malcolm X was the embodiment of courage with which he stood up for truth and justice. The truth was so important to him that, to embrace it, he showed no hesitation in changing his ways and rhetoric."

State Senator Jackie Collins issued a statement about the newly created Malcolm X Day.

> "Both the city of Chicago, where Malcolm X often spoke and worked, and communities throughout the state need to hear his message of human rights, the equality of all people, and power in the service of justice. I am excited about the potential of Malcolm X Day to inspire more of us to commit to serving our neighbors...During my time in public service, I have stood on the shoulders of the great men and women of the Civil Rights Movement, and it is an honor to continue the struggle for equality and justice today, hand in hand with people of goodwill from many traditions, faiths, and backgrounds. Malcolm X was a powerful voice for the values that should unite all of us – Christian, Muslim, of any other faith, or of no faith. I draw strength from his words of clarity and action."

Malcolm X's birthday has legal status only in the city of Berkley, California. Earlier this year, New York state passed a one-time resolution to "commemorate the 90th birthday of Malcolm X." It has also been proposed as a holiday in Atlanta and Washington, D.C. With today's action, Illinois is the first state to declare May 19 as "Malcolm X Day officially."

The wording of the resolution "encourages the citizens of Illinois to pay tribute to the life and works of Malcolm X through participation in community service projects on this day." All communities in Illinois will be able to honor Malcolm X, "who died to uphold the universal message of human rights for all and that every human being has the right to dignity and rights in the country they live in." Malcolm X encouraged people not only to be involved in community service but also to fight for social justice for all people. In this way, we truly will be following the words inspired by Malcolm X that can be found in the resolution:

Malcolm X's contributions to society [underscore] the value of a truly free and equal populace by demonstrating the great lengths to which human beings will go to secure their freedom; "Power in defense of freedom is greater than power on behalf of tyranny and oppression," he stated, "because power, real power, comes from our conviction which produces action."

CAIR-Chicago and the *Chicago Monitor* got even more active during the Trump presidency as the number of anti-Muslim attacks greatly increased. One impressive protest that CAIR-Chicago sponsored was when Trump announced the "Muslim Ban" – a list of Muslim majority countries from which he would ban all travel and immigrants. This was an attack on the Muslim community around the world. CAIR-Chicago organized a very large protest at Chicago O'Hare Airport and set up tables with lawyers who would answer questions about the ban and help people get in the country.

The following article covers that protest.

Protestors Challenging Trump #MuslimBan Shut Down O'Hare Terminal

Chicagoans Tell DHS Let's Be Clear, Refugees Are Welcome Here!

Chicago Monitor
By Bill Chambers - January 29, 2017

Three thousand protestors of the Trump #MuslimBan of travel from six Muslim-majority countries shut down the operation of the International Terminal at Chicago O'Hare Airport until all detainees were released.

Yesterday evening, a press conference and five-hour protest were held to resist President Trump's Executive Order called "Protection Of The Nation From Foreign Terrorist Entry Into The United States" that placed a 90-day block on entry to the US from citizens from Iran, Iraq, Syria, Yemen, Sudan, Libya and Somalia. It also suspended the admittance of all refugees to the US for a period of 120 days and terminated indefinitely all refugee admissions from Syria. All seven countries on this list are Muslim majority countries.

A total of 16 people were detained under the order for several hours at O'Hare before being released by 10:30 p.m., according to immigration attorneys at the airport. The attorneys, many from the International Refugee Assistance Project, had set up in the terminal all day, waiting for relatives of those detained to seek them out for help.

The release came for the detainees at O'Hare after pressure from lawyers, protestors, and a federal judge issued an emergency order, temporarily barring the U.S.

from deporting people from nations subject to the ban. After the ACLU and other groups petitioned on behalf of two Iraqi men detained at JFK Airport, Judge Ann Donnelly of the federal district court in Brooklyn ordered an emergency stay, blocking the deportation of any individual currently being held in airports across the United States. The stay only applies to those in the air or detained at airports immediately after the executive order was signed. Later there were also similar decisions by judges in Virginia and Washington State.

All the decisions are temporary and only apply so far to people already in airports or on planes to come here yesterday. There are hundreds, thousands more that these decisions do not help.

President Trump's signature on the #MuslimBan executive order has taken the Islamophobia he made mainstream during the presidential campaign and made it into US immigration and refugee policy.

Hatem Abudayyeh

Multiple organizations, including the Arab American Action Network (AAAN), Illinois Coalition for Immigrant and Refugee Rights (ICIRR), CAIR-Chicago, Jewish Voice for Peace – Chicago, Organized Communities Against Deportations, Syrian Action

Network, Black Lives Matter – Chicago, the Council of Islamic Organizations of Greater Chicago and many others held a press conference including members of these organizations, family members of detainees, and local Chicago politicians.

Hatem Abudayyeh of the AAAN emphasized the refusal to allow Muslims and Arabs from the seven countries only makes the communities here even more a target of hate crimes, and the crowd chanted, "all must be immediately released Now!"

Suzanne Akhras Sahloul

Suzanne Akhras Sahloul from the Syrian Community Network and representing ICIRR, questioned where our Illinois politicians were opposing this ban. "Governor Rauner needs to say all refugees are welcome here."

Ahmed Rehab from CAIR-Chicago got one of the biggest cheers from the crowd, reminding them of Trump's failed campaign stop "Welcome to Chicago, the city that banned Trump!" He also indicated that CAIR as a national organization, was filing suit against the executive order on Monday.

Ahmed Rehab

There were multiple local politicians there to show their support, including Cook County Commissioner Bridget Gainer; Chicagoan Martin 'Marty' Castro, the first Latino to head the United States Commission on Civil Rights; Illinois State Senator Daniel Biss; and 35th Ward Alderman Carlos Ramirez-Rosa.

Alderman Carlos Ramirez-Rosa

Ramirez-Rosa said he was proud to represent many of those who were targeted by these attacks on immigrants, including Latinos, Muslims, and Arabs. He declared, "Let my people free!"

The protest occupied the street in front of the terminal and moved inside to continue until all detainees were freed.

Large protests at other US airports were reported yesterday, including Denver, Dallas, Dulles airport in northern Virginia, Boston, Philadelphia, Seattle, New York City, Houston, San Diego, Los Angeles, San Francisco, Minneapolis, and Newark.

A Department of Homeland Security official said the travel ban affected 375 travelers, 173 of whom were denied entry to the U.S. prior to boarding flights headed to the U.S. The official said 109 people who were in transit to the U.S. were denied entry, and 81 people were granted waivers because of their legal permanent resident or special immigrant visa status.

There is no estimate of the number of detainees remaining at US airports.

The same coalition of groups is planning a second day of protests at the International Terminal at O'Hare Airport tonight.

Not only the number of people who turned out for this protest but also the wide range of organizations who stood with the Muslim community to fight this racist and anti-Muslim ban was so encouraging for every Muslim in the city. This was one of the protests that proved to me that Chicago was behind its Muslim community and would not allow its rights to be attacked.

There were also multiple groups working on the issue of police training, either given by Israeli officials on trips to Palestine or by so-called terrorism experts that used anti-Muslim propaganda in their sessions. The following article is about one of the more effective protests against this militarization of the police.

Chicago Youth Protest Police Militarization And Anti-Muslim Training

Chicago Monitor
Bill Chambers - October 10, 2016

Yesterday, Arab, Black, Latino, Asian, and Muslim youth protested the Illinois Tactical Officers Association (ITOA) training conference and weapons expo being held from October 9-13 at the Stonegate Banquet and Conference Centre in Hoffman Estates, just an hour outside of Chicago. The conference provides SWAT and "counter-terrorism" training for local police departments, state police, and Homeland Security agents. The conference's keynote speaker was Sebastian Gorka, whose background includes being an anti-Muslim speaker and author, writer for the far right-wing website Breitbart News Network, and Donald Trump's National Security Advisor.

Youth representatives from multiple faith-based and human rights groups who sponsored the rally and march had already obtained 3,000 signatures on an online petition demanding that the Stonegate Banquet and Conference Center stop hosting the ITOA conference. One of the organizers indicated that attempts had been made to meet with the conference center manager without success. The rally at Millennium Park included speeches from the young organizers behind the #StopITOA campaign.

Skanda Kadirgamar of the War Resisters League

Skanda Kadirgamar of the War Resisters League emphasized the ITOA conference gave police departments access to "more dangerous weapons on the belts of police officers and dangerous ideas into their heads...ITOA supporters capitalize on a culture of fear. This training represents an assault on the security and peace of mind of communities of color."

Skanda put the ITOA conference into the context of military violence across the globe. The tactics they teach are the "night raids used to disrupt the comfort and safety of the people of Pakistan and Iraq. These tactics and technology have been used elsewhere, and now it's coming here...People have been lost. There are always civilian casualties that are remembered by numbers; we never hear their names... Whenever you hear words like 'public safety,' we need to question that. Public safety means more police. The answer is always more violence. Public safety – whose safety is that?"

Melisa Stephen

Melisa Stephen, from For The People Artists Collective, questioned the government's spending priorities. "We need resources for our communities, not the military-police complex. As another teacher strike in Chicago demands resources for our schools and more and more mental health crises and emergencies are responded to with military force and SWAT teams, the federal government pours tens of billion of dollars into militarism and the use of force. Where are our priorities?"

The group marched down the sidewalks of Michigan Avenue ostensibly to protest at the Cook County Department of Homeland Security and Emergency Management (DHSEM) headquarters to "highlight the ways that Chicago taxpayers are subsidizing ITOA's militarization and Islamophobia" but made some unscheduled stops along the way. The protestors stopped traffic at Michigan and Randolph by unfurling an orange plastic fence across the road but continued marching when the police arrived.

Once the march reached Michigan and Lake Street, several protestors sat down across Michigan Avenue and were chained together. The Chicago Police SWAT team arrived, and after about an hour of working on freeing the protestors, they were arrested and taken to the station. Fifteen were arrested, charged with obstructing traffic misdemeanors, and released later that same night.

One of the protestors explained the wider reach of their campaign against police militarization.

In their statement of opposition to the ITOA conference, the #STOPITOA stated: "The Chicago Police Department has a history of collaborating with ITOA for tactical training, and ITOA has a long-standing relationship with the Cook County Department of Homeland Security. ITOA promotes its use of military tactics with toxic racism and Islamophobia...The conference will train local police and EMTs to operate 'like tactical squads in the military' and incorporate 'new data and surveillance technology' in their work, directly contributing to racialized law enforcement violence against communities of color in the Chicagoland area.

While Chicago is still reeling from budget cuts that have resulted in the closure of over 50 public schools mental health clinics, and severe cuts to social services, the city spends over $4 million a day on the Chicago police alone. ITOA is directly involved in training and arming those police, even using empty school buildings as training grounds for Cook County officers. Weapons manufacturers from around the world also use ITOA to sell military-grade equipment to local police forces– equipment that shocked the country when it was deployed against civilians in places like Ferguson, Minneapolis, and Baton Rouge (and is used regularly by repressive governments such as Israel)."

Sebastian Gorka, a speaker at the conference, has been involved in training FBI and Special Forces personnel for several years. He was identified in a report by the Muslim Public Affairs Council as "one of the top 25 pseudo experts on Islam," along with Robert Spencer and Pamela Gellar.

"While he is a noted expert on post-Communist democratization in Eastern Europe, as well as defense and national security issues, he has no training in Islamic studies and has made biased comments about Islam."

For instance, in giving a backhanded compliment to Muslim Americans who helped law enforcement prevent a 2010 terrorist attack in Portland, Oregon, Gorka stated:

"It's those Muslims who are American citizens who take the U.S. Constitution seriously and who believe in the values of the U.S. Constitution, those people who understand the best that shariah, for example, is antithetical to the values of this great nation. So I think absolutely, the local community and those people who are patriotic Americans, but also Muslims, will be one of the most important sources of intelligence for us."

Additionally, he has stated, "You can make the argument that Osama Bin Laden was the Martin Luther of Islam."

Given the statements that Donald Trump has made about Muslims during the Presidential campaign, it is disturbing but not surprising that Gorka is his National Security Advisor.

But the protestors were also demanding that the Cook County Department of Homeland Security and Emergency Management stop providing funding and resources to ITOA training that includes educating local law enforcement on how to be anti-Muslim.

Before the protest, some #STOPITOA organizers reported harassment from individuals associated with the conference. After sharing a statement online about a teach-in on issues of police militarization in Illinois, they described many "trolls" making negative comments directed at one of the hosts of the Facebook event page. Another host began receiving multiple anonymous calls followed by immediate hang-ups at her workplace from a number in Maryland.

But the most disturbing incident was the following:

"Then, on the evening of Sunday, September 18th – less than a week after publicly launching the #StopITOA campaign – my office was broken into overnight, with several locks picked, multiple locked doors damaged, and drawers rummaged through. My laptop and cameras were the only items taken, despite being in a locked cabinet, while numerous other computers and expensive technology sat out in the open. Ironically, even CPD – who were called by the office manager to submit a police report for insurance purposes – acknowledged that I was the presumable target if only my belongings were taken."

The organizers ignored the harassment and attempts at intimidation continuing their planning for the rally and protest.

The #STOPITOA group has also organized a call-in campaign to the Centre's manager, threatening a boycott of the venue until the Stonegate Center stops hosting the ITOA conference.

The protest helped publicize the conference and the biased training that the CPD was getting from these so-called terrorism experts. This was one of the last such conferences that was held in the Chicago area.

Some of the research work I did while I was at CAIR-Chicago was on the history of the FBI attacks on social justice groups in the U.S. This work was particularly relevant at the time (2016) as the FBI was continuing to target the BLM movement as well as Palestine activists.

As part of their orientation process, I gave the following presentation to all the new interns who started work at CAIR. In 2024, for a presentation to Masjid Al-Taqwa, I added slides on the FBI surveillance of the Honorable Elijah Muhammad, Malcolm X, and the Nation of Islam from the 1930s to today, plus updating for new technology.

U.S. Government Repression of Social Activists: Past & Present

Bill Chambers

Definitions

FBI
- Primary federal criminal investigative body and internal intelligence agency representing Department of Justice DOJ) and Department of Homeland Security (DHS)

Other surveillance bodies
- National Security Agency (NSA)
- Operational groups of DHS

Social Activists
- Any group supporting an alternative political system, advocating for human / civil rights, or opposing U.S. foreign policy

Legal Justifications

Specific laws or authorized programs "governed" or been used to justify FBI actions
- 1917 Espionage Act
- 1918 Alien and Sedition Act
- 1940 Smith Act
- 1947 Truman Doctrine
- 1950 McCarran Act
- 1940-1980s COINTELPRO
- 2001 Uniting and Strengthening America by Providing Appropriate Tools Required to Intercept and Obstruct Terrorism Act (USA PATRIOT Act): Portions renewed as USA Freedom Act on June 2, 2015
- 2010 *Holder v Humanitarian Law Project*

Early History: Focus on Labor, Socialist & Communist Groups

WWI Period:

1917 Espionage Act
- seditious talk illegal during war

1918 Alien and Sedition Act
- Expel anarchists from the US
- Greatly expanded FBI
- First target Industrial Workers of the World
  - Started in Chicago
  - Combine immigrants: one union & anti-war
  - 9/17 DOJ raided 488 IWW halls – leaders got 20 years - organization destroyed

More Labor, Socialist & Communist Group Targeting

- **1938 FBI launched investigation into subversion**
  Multiple industries, unions, colleges, black and youth groups

- Smith Act 1940 - crime to advocate overthrowing U.S. govt by force or violence - applying Espionage Act to peacetime - 1943 18 members of Socialist Workers Party got 10 years

- 1947 Truman doctrine – target infiltration of disloyal persons (i.e. Comm) within US govt - list of proscribed orgs

- 1950 McCarran Act required Communist front group members to register - FBI never stopped after McCarthy hearings

FBI and Moorish Science Temple: 1926-1960

- FBI's first interaction with surveillance of an American Muslim group
- Racism plus focus on "non-mainstream" religions

FBI and Moorish Science Temple: 1926-1960

- Marcus Garvey file as spokesman for black nationalism, social protest and separatist movements.
- FBI marked Muslim groups for surveillance campaigns, rounding up and arresting Muslims on segregation laws, refusing to serve in draft, and "acts of sedition" from 1942 on.

FBI and Moorish Science Temple: 1926-1960

- Marcus Garvey file as spokesman for black nationalism, social protest and separatist movements.
- FBI marked Muslim groups for surveillance campaigns, rounding up and arresting Muslims on segregation laws, refusing to serve in draft, and "acts of sedition" from 1942 on.

NOI, Civil Rights, MLK, Black Liberation: 40s to Early 70s

Nation of Islam and Malcolm X

- Surveillance started of Master Fard in 1942
- Refusal to serve brought FBI attention to NOI
- In 1950s, discontent with govt. = Communists
- Hon Elijah Muhammad & Family under constant surveillance with informers, wiretaps, etc.

Nation of Islam and Malcolm X

-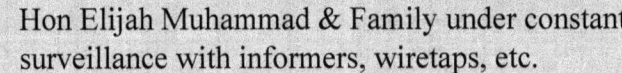
  https://vault.fbi.gov/Nation of Islam/Nation of Islam Part 1 of 3/view
- **NOI Report 6/25/55**

  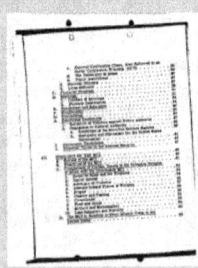

Nation of Islam and Malcolm X

- J. Edgar Hoover signed off on operation anonymously distributed leaflets critical of NOI leadership
- FBI opened file on Malcolm X in 1953 and continued surveillance until assassination in 1965 - 9K pages
- Continuing with organizations he founded:
  – Muslim Mosque, Inc. and Organization of Afro-American Unity (OAAU)

Nation of Islam and Malcolm X

Upon Death of Hon. Elijah Muhammad
- From FBI COINTELPRO memo 1/7/69
- FBI plan to "change philosophy" of NOI
- Influence contenders for leadership with informants
- Split NOI into factions or destroy organization

NOI, Civil Rights, MLK, Black Liberation: 40s to Early 70s

MLK and Civil Rights

- Extensive surveillance from late 1950s under FBI Racial Matters Program (individuals and organizations involved in racial politics)

- Until death in 1968, MLK target of campaign to neutralize him as effective civil rights leader

- Investigation of MLK and Southern Christian Leadership Conference (SCLC) under Communist Infiltration Program (COMINFIL)

NOI, Civil Rights, MLK, Black Liberation: 40s to Early 70s

MLK: "It would be encouraging for us if Mr. Hoover and the FBI would be as diligent in apprehending those responsible for bombing churches and killing little children as they are in seeking out alleged communist infiltration in human rights movement."

Black Liberation – Late 60s to Early 70s

COINTELPRO (Domestic Counterintelligence Program) targeting "Black Nationalist Hate Groups" - 1967

- SCLC, Student Non-Violent Coordinating Committee (SNCC), Revolutionary Action Movement (RAM), Congress of Racial Equality (CORE), and NOI
- Ramsey Clark - LBJ atty general, started "community surveillance program" targeted black urban centers – coordinated DOJ, military intelligence & FBI for preventive action against riots
- FBI Rabble Rouser Index: threat to "domestic security"

Black Liberation - Late 60s to Early 70s

Black Panther Party (BPP) - 1968-1971
- Fred Hampton, Jr. - deputy chairman IL
- Bodyguard/Director Chapter Security an informant
- Threatening letters - Jeff Fort, Blackstone Rangers head, Hampton had put hit on him
- Undermined SDS ties by racist cartoons
- 12/4/69 raid on Chicago HQ by State's Attorney's Office, Chicago Police Department, and FBI - Hampton killed sleeping

American Indian Movement - 70s

- 1969 Pine Ridge Reservation: 69 AIM members & supporters killed by FBI and BIA police
- Few convictions against AIM members but lengthy trials

Norman Zigrossi ASAC of Bureaus Rapid City office - "They [Indians] are a conquered nation, and when you are conquered, the people you are conquered by dictate your future. This is a basic philosophy of mine. If I'm part of the conquered nation, I've got to yield to authority. [The FBI must function as] a colonial police force."

Sanctuary and Latin American Solidarity – 80s

- Chicago Sanctuary movement hub (churches defied INS and protected Central Americans)
- CCR and NLG list 215 cases of counterintelligence activities 1984-1988
  - Accused of being terrorist controlled
  - Visited financial supporters
  - Committee in Solidarity with the People of El Salvador (CISPES), Maryknoll Sisters, Muslim Students Association, Amnesty Int., Clergy and Laity Concerned, US Catholic Conference, National Association of Women Religious

Churches offer santuary to Salvadorean refugees

Puerto Rican Independence Movement Late 70s to 80s

- Centered in Chicago and NYC
- Young Lords – Puerto Rican street gang in Lincoln Park
- Young Lords Party 1968 focused on self-determination, gentrification, and displacement
- From 1936 to 1995, FBI COINTELPRO targeted organizations and individuals advocating independence
- Collected information on independence leaders' "weaknesses, morals, criminal records, spouses, children, family life" to "disrupt their activities and compromise their effectiveness."

Puerto Rican Independence Movement - Late 70s to 80s

- 1977 - New tactic - grand jury subpoena.
- Refused to comply with more than 20 subpoenas, 7200 pro-independence activists spent 4 to 18 months in jail
- Oscar Lopez Rivera was in prison after 30 years on "seditious conspiracy" charges until freed by Obama 2017

Palestinian Activists - Late 80s to Present

LA 8 - 1987
- 7 Palestinians and Kenyan arrested for organizing support of a PLO faction
- 20 years of prosecution and deportation proceedings

Dr. Ashqar and Muhammad Salah – 1995-1997
- Acquitted of conspiracy and terrorism-related charges of supporting Hamas. Salah convicted of obstruction of justice and served 21 months
- Ashqar in federal prison in Petersburg, VA for 13 years for refusing to testify to grand jury and inform on activities of other activists – release in 2017

Palestinian Activists - Late 80s to Present

Ghassan Elashi and the Holy Land Foundation – 2002
- HLF shut down under Patriot Act.
- Using the Material Support Law provision, five founders accused of providing "assistance" to designated "terrorist groups" (Hamas) in Palestine
- Ghassan Elashi, Palestinian-American cofounder, sentenced to 65 years in a Communications Management Unit (CMU) prison facility in Marion, Illinois, nicknamed "little Guantanamo" due to the overwhelming majority of Muslims and persons of Arab and Middle Eastern descent

Palestinian Activists - Late 80s to Present

Sami al-Arian – 2003

- Former professor and activist, charged with supporting designated terrorist organization in Palestine
- Case based on FBI wiretaps and fax transmissions
- Acquitted on 8 of 17 counts, deadlocked in favor of acquittal on the remaining 9
- House arrest since 2008 for criminal contempt
- Federal prosecutors dropped charges and deported to Turkey February 2015

FBI Raid & Grand Jury Against Anti-War & Palestine Activists - 2010

Sept. 2010: FBI raid homes and subpoena antiwar and international solidarity activists (Minneapolis, Chgo)

We Remember the Dirty FBI Campaign Against Dr. King

Stop the FBI Attack Against the Anti-War Movement

- Seize documents, computers, cell phones, passports, family photos, children's artwork
- 14 subpoenas to Chicago federal grand jury
- Looking for evidence on "material support of terrorism".
- Activists with groups, including the Palestine Solidarity Group - Chicago, Students for a Democratic Society, Twin Cities Anti-War Committee, Colombia Action Network, Freedom Road Socialist Organization

FBI Raid & Grand Jury Against Anti-War & Palestine Activists - 2010

Dec. 2010: Subpoenas focus on Palestine Solidarity

- 9 more activists subpoenaed (all from Chicago: 6 Arab-Americans and 3 Palestine solidarity activists who travelled to Palestine).
- All refused to testify
- Asst. U.S. Attorney Barry Jonas, HLF prosecutor, lead investigation
- Materials returned to those whose homes were raided and no more case activity

Rasmea Odeh Case

- Rasmea Odeh, Chicago Palestinian community leader, arrested 10/13
- Indictment claims she didn't disclose on immigration application arrest and conviction by Israeli military court 45 years ago
- Associate Director and Community Adult Women Organizer - Arab American Action Network (AAAN)
- Convicted on "unlawful procurement of naturalization" and sentenced to 18 months in prison and deportation

FBI & NSA Spying on American Muslims

- Edward Snowden NSA documents showed 7,485 email addresses listed as monitored between 2002 and 2008
- Nihad Awad, the Executive Director of CAIR, the largest Muslim civil rights organization in the country.
- Faisal Gill worked as a consultant for the American Muslim Council, founded to encourage participation by American Muslims in the political process.
- Agha Saeed founded the American Muslim Alliance, NYT described in 10/01 as "the main organization devoted to the political assimilation of the nations seven million Arab-Americans."

DHS Surveillance of #BlackLivesMatter Movement

- Began after Ferguson protests
- DHS Office of Operations Coordination collects information, including location data, on Black Lives Matter activities from public social media accounts, including Facebook, Twitter.
- Social media surveillance of protests in Ferguson, Baltimore, Washington, DC, and New York.
- DHS produced minute-by-minute reports on protesters' movements in demonstrations, silent vigils, a funk music parade and a walk to end breast cancer.

Countering Violent Extremism (CVE) Program - 2019

- COINTEL-PRO like program that the Department of Homeland Security seeking Muslim community cooperation
- Given resistance from Muslims nationwide, CVE Program ended up a miserable failure.

Palestine Activism - 2024

Student encampments at 80 colleges
- Use local police to disrupt
- Call them antisemitic

DNC Protests
- Monitor groups and leaders

Conclusions

- "Preventive intelligence" - get around investigating protected free speech activity
- Attack groups/movements showing success (growth, coalitions)
- Consistent set of tactics – label a movement; broad surveillance; informants; prevent popular support; undermine financial support; prevent coalitions; grand jury investigations; set up local law enforcement groups (Counterterrorism Centers or "fusion centers")

Conclusions

- Use of new technologies: hack phones, facial recognition, social media (for evidence, misinformation, and monitoring - WhatsApp)
- Independent of the party in power – Democrat or Republican
- Ignore White Supremacist groups
- Current focus – Palestine activists & Muslims

The presentation used historical facts to demonstrate the FBIs long history of trying to destroy social justice groups and any activists who challenged U.S. foreign policy. Under the new Trump Administration in 2025, the FBI will continue to be used to attack Palestine activists, participate with ICE in the mass deportation campaign, and surveil anyone who opposes Trump's policies.

As part of my anti-racism work as a Muslim, I joined the Muslim Anti-Racism Collaborative and am still a supporter of their work. The Muslim Anti-Racism Collaborative (MuslimARC) was launched in February 2014 to provide anti-racism education and resources to advance racial justice. Their Facebook page describes the work that they do.

> MuslimARC is a faith-based racial justice education organization. Our vision is Education for Liberation. We work to create spaces for learning and developing racial equity, connect people across multi-ethnic networks, and cultivate solutions for racial equity.

MuslimARC focuses primarily on education to fight racism within the Muslim community but has also established solidarity formations with other groups to work on specific campaigns. "MuslimARC has reached nearly 10,000 people on the ground and hundreds of thousands online since launching in 2014." (Facebook page) MuslimARC is a human rights education organization. Their work involves raising awareness and training Muslim communities on issues of racial justice. To uproot racism, they focus on developing and delivering education on internalized, interpersonal, and institutional racism. In trainings and workshops, MuslimARC addresses both personal and systemic racism. In the Appendix, "MuslimARC Releases Guide for White Muslims by White Muslims," is an example of the training materials they publish that I helped write with another member.

Much of MuslimARC's work involved running training sessions for people to do anti-racism work, but more importantly, organizing anti-racism programs for various Muslim communities. The organization was started by Muslim sisters of color, mainly African American, who were protesting their treatment by other Muslim communities. African American Muslims were often not considered "real" Muslims, discriminated against when they went to other mosques that were mainly Arab or South Asian, or were called "abeed" on social media, which is Arabic for "slave". This level of racism in the Muslim community was understandable, given that mosques in large cities like Chicago were very segregated for the most part.

Through the leadership of the CIOGC in Chicago, MuslimARC was welcomed into planning sessions to hold anti-racism workshops in the Muslim communities in the area. The only thing that held that work up was the start of the COVID epidemic, which shut down many of the mosques in the area, forcing them to be exclusively online for a long period of time. MuslimARC continues to hold training sessions and anti-racism workshops and has often given presentations at national Muslim conferences.

Working at CAIR-Chicago and getting my Master's Degree in Islamic Studies inspired me to write my first book, *The Muslim American Fight for Social Justice: From Civil Rights to Black Lives Matter*. The book grew out of my reading about the Civil Rights and BLM movements and not hearing about Muslims being involved. When they certainly were. The book started as my Master's Thesis for the American Islamic College. I began a PhD program in Religious Studies at the Chicago Theological Seminary (CTS) and intended to expand the thesis into a full book. Unfortunately, the day my classes started at CTS was when everything shut down because of the beginning of the COVID epidemic. I decided I could not complete a PhD and do the research I needed to do online and left the program to expand the book and publish it myself. This is an excerpt from the Introduction that explains the focus of the book.

> The history of the Civil Rights Movement is full of references to Dr. Martin Luther King Jr. and the Southern Christian Leadership Conference that led the fight against institutional racism within American society. Most Americans and historians of the period considered Malcolm X an influential "Black Nationalist" leader during that period. Discussions of the Civil Rights movement emphasize the contributions of Christians, both Black and white and Jewish activists, who were an integral part of this struggle for social justice. But where were the Muslim Americans?
>
> They were there the whole time as the Nation of Islam (NOI), a key part of the movement fighting racism based upon Islamic principles of social justice. Most Americans did not consider members of the NOI as Muslims or part of any religion, even if they knew about the NOI. Malcolm X was a Muslim and was praised for his "evolution" to orthodox Islam only after his hajj to Mecca near the end of his life. Muslim Americans were also fighting another part of American racism in the 1950s and 1960s, the denial of their religion.

The book tells the history of Muslims in America who were the first to fight for social justice, the Nation of Islam (NOI), and how that fight evolved into diverse groups like the Imam W. Deen Mohammed Community of Al-Islam (of which I am a member), Inner-City Muslim Action Network, Muslims for Social Justice, Muslims for Ferguson, and the Muslim Anti-Racism Collaborative. For the book, I interviewed the leaders of many of these groups as well as their members. It was clear in the research I did for the book that the African American Muslims in the NOI not only had to contend with the racism of Jim Crow in America but also the anti-Muslim sentiment that the NOI was not a religion, and they were not Muslims.

The section below reproduces my conclusion to the book and helps explain the primary thesis.

The Muslim American social justice groups formed after 9/11 all believe their anti-racism practice is a direct expression of their Muslim identity. Groups like Muslims for Social Justice may express that belief less in Islamic terms than political ones, but even they wanted an expression of their faith outside of the masjid and the community center. One frustration they all had in common was that masjids were not organizing or supporting work in anti-racism. They were contributing to the problem by being segregated enclaves. The negative impact of 9/11 had activated the members of these groups about their identity being Muslims in America. They had grown up with the Black Lives Matter movement and the solidarity that existed between Christian, Jewish, socialist, Palestinian, Latinx, and immigrants—all organizing against police violence in their own neighborhoods or in places like Ferguson, Philadelphia, and Chicago.

Islamophobia after 9/11 had increased, as well as hate crimes against Muslims, Jews, Latinx, and immigrants. These were all the communities under attack, with the institutional racism of America encouraging those attacks. Muslim American activists already knew they had an identity different from the American identity offered to their parents and then quickly withdrawn after 9/11. These Muslim activists had an American history full of communities fighting for social justice and had no qualms about expressing nasiha to their government through protests. They were involved in 'asabiya, nation, and community building, developing a national social media, and local community ummah based upon the core social justice principles expressed in the Qur'an and by Prophet Muhammad. They would continue to struggle against the racism in their own Muslim American community, knowing that there can be no true social justice, no united Muslim American ummah without all Muslims being treated as brothers and sisters, no matter their race or ethnicity.

But how did the post-9/11 Muslim American social justice groups get to this activist place? They got here by the example, the struggle, and the model of African American Muslims. The Nation of Islam under Elijah Muhammad built an Islamic community based upon the racist conditions of America in the 1930s and beyond. They were the first Muslim Americans to develop their own Muslim identity and to refuse the white, Christian American identity thrust upon them. For their efforts, they were denied their religion; their social justice practices were called Black Nationalism, and the FBI targeted them. Even as some of their members became famous and respected in American popular culture, like Malcolm X and Muhammad Ali, the media, through reporting and film, denied that they were Muslims. Even in recent history (2022), *Beyond Bilal: Black History in Islam*, the author has a very brief section on the NOI and says, "The Nation of Islam can be described as a black nationalist movement" (Briggs 162) agreeing with the FBIs assessment. There is also no mention of Imam W. Deen Mohammed establishing Al-Islam as a unique manifestation of Sunni Islam within the Muslim American context. There is still work to be done to advocate an accurate representation of Muslim American history.

The American rejection of the Nation of Islam, whether under Elijah Muhammad or Minister Louis Farrakhan, as being Muslim or even a legitimate religious expression continued into the transition to the WDM community. The broader Muslim American community ignored even

Imam W. Deen Muhammad as an important Muslim leader. African American masjids would remain within segregated African American communities in Chicago, Detroit, Philadelphia, New York, Los Angeles, and Atlanta. But African American Muslims would continue to fight for social justice, support the Black Lives Matter movement as individuals and organizations, to speak out against the government's racist domestic and foreign policies, and practice an Islam adapted to their community's needs since the first Muslim slaves came to America.

The post-9/11 Muslim American social justice groups not only had a civil rights movement to emulate, they had a long tradition of Muslim Americans fighting for social justice not only for their own community but also for all Americans of every race, ethnicity, and religion.

By doing presentations of the book, I was able to reach multiple Muslim communities and hopefully make some impact.

Black Lives Matter and Community Control of the Police (2013-2016)

The Black Lives Matter (BLM) began in 2013 to protest a number of Black people who had been unjustifiably killed by police across the country in questionable circumstances. An unarmed Michael Brown was the first person killed in Ferguson, Missouri, that started the national uprising against police racism and violence. The BLM movement was active in Chicago and had close ties to the goal of community control over the police. I participated in multiple BLM protests in Chicago and the suburbs. It was so surprising to see BLM signs not only in front of our house but in front of many houses, even in the more conservative Western suburbs. Multiple mass protests in Chicago only intensified after the Chicago Police killed Laquan McDonald and then attempted to cover it up with the help of Mayor Rahm Emmanuel. The Mayor had attempted to put an official band aid on the problem of police violence by appointing a Chicago Police Board headed by Lori Lightfoot, who would later become mayor herself. But this board had few enforcement powers over the Chicago Police Department (CPD) and being appointed by the mayor had no credibility.

Typically, the Muslim community in Chicago would only come out for Palestine protests, but this time, the main umbrella organization, the Council of Islamic Organizations of Greater Chicago (CIOGC), sponsored a protest that turned out thousands, as the article below describes. It is also important to note that the goal of this protest was to demand community control of the police. The mainstream media reporting ignored the very specific goal of this march and treated it as a typical "goalless, leaderless" BLM march attacking the police.

Chicago Muslims Mobilize to Support Community Control of the Police

By Bill Chambers
Chicago Monitor - August 18, 2015

As a logical follow-on to its successful initiative to pass a resolution designating May 19 as "Malcolm X Day" in the State of Illinois, the Council of Islamic Organizations of Greater Chicago (CIOGC) is supporting and mobilizing for the August 29 mass march for community control of the police. The march was started by the Chicago Alliance Against Racist and Political Repression

(CAARPR), who have been fighting for a Civilian Police Accountability Council (CPAC) for many years. Now, with the momentum built by CAARPR, the Black Lives Matter Movement, We Change Genocide, Fearless Leading by the Youth (F.L.Y.), and many other organizations—the demand for civilian control over the Chicago Police has grown into a mass movement of solidarity between community organizations in the city. With the CIOGC being a federation of over 60 greater Chicagoland Islamic organizations representing over 400,000 Muslim Americans, the Chicago Muslim community is actively helping to mobilize for this march.

Frank Chapman from the Chicago Alliance Against Racist and Political Repression (CAARPR) describes the campaign his group is leading for an elected Civilian Police Accountability Council (CPAC).

> "This is not a 'review' board, but an 'accountability' council to be sure that victims of police crimes receive justice... It's not only controlling how the police are policed but also how our own communities are policed."

Together with representatives from multiple community organizations, CAARPR has drafted a CPAC ordinance for the City Council that includes the responsibility for investigating all police shootings and allegations of police misconduct. The group is calling for a mass march to Chicago City Hall on August 29 to demand an all-elected Civilian Police Accountability Council. The last planning meeting for the march had representatives from over 65 organizations, including the CIOGC.

The draft resolution for the Civilian Police Accountability Council (CPAC) has the following important components.

Establish an elected CPAC over the Chicago Police Department. It shall have the authority to:

- Appoint the Superintendent of Police.
- Re-write the police rule book, including all use of force guidelines, Standard Operating Procedures, Rules, and General Orders.
- Investigate police misconduct.
- Investigate all police shootings, including all police involved shootings that kill unarmed people.
- Provide increased transparency of all investigations, including police involved shootings, and greater statistical analysis of demographic information of complaints by type and victim.
- Increase rates at which complaints are sustained are based on thorough investigations of all allegations of police misconduct and violations of the U.S. Constitution and Human Rights law.
- Be the ultimate authority regarding discipline in the Chicago Police Department.
- Indict police officers for crimes they commit.
- Establish its own budget.
- CPAC will replace the current rubber-stamp Chicago Police Board. (The nine members of the Board are not elected and are "private citizens appointed by the Mayor with the advice and consent of the City Council.")
- CPAC will take over the job of the Independent Police Review Authority (IPRA) and eliminate it.
- CPAC will reduce bias and guarantee fair treatment of victims of police misconduct.
- The primary goal of the CPAC resolution is to make a systematic change in how Chicago's communities

are policed. The Council, comprising elected community members from all the police districts, would be empowered to hold police accountable for the crimes they commit and to control and decide how Chicago communities are policed.

The resolution is a response to a history of unjustified police shootings; the torture of over 200 suspects under former Chicago Police Department (CPD) detective and commander Jon Burge, and the over 3,500 suspects, 82% of which are black, interrogated at the CPD's Homan Square facility. In its statement of support for the march, the CIOGC explains further some reasons it is encouraging all Chicagoland area Muslims to take part.

"CIOGC encourages the Muslim community to join a mass protest on Saturday, August 29th, at 12 noon for a march from Chicago's Federal Building to City Hall to demand that the City Council enact legislation to create an elected, civilian police accountability council... This march coincides with the #BlackLivesMatter movement and the teachings of the Prophet Muhammad (peace be upon him), who used coalition building as a major strategy in his efforts for peace.

"The Chicago Police Department (CPD) has shot 400 people in the past eight years, but city officials have declared that only one of those shootings was unjustified. More recently, the Chicago Police Department and City Hall have come under scrutiny for detainment and acts of torture at the Homan Square police warehouse interrogation facility. Chicago has ranked at the top of the list for fatal police shootings in major U.S. cities."

Representatives from the CIOGC have made announcements about the march and handed out fliers at area mosques and community centers over the last few weeks. The organization also created this video appealing to the Muslim community to "March together in solidarity with Black Lives Matter for a historic march. Just doing two things: standing together in solidarity and asking the City Council to pass a law to establish civilian oversight over the Chicago Police."

Tabassum Haleem, Executive Director of the CIOGC, reminds those in the Chicago Muslim community that protecting the oppressed in society is a central component of Islam and a way to act in solidarity with all people of faith.

> "As with all great religions, Islam calls upon its followers to not only acknowledge one's relationship with God but also with fellow human beings. Similarly, prayer and remembrance of God are only a small part of worship, while the calls to action are numerous, firm, and inclusive of all of humanity. Protecting individuals against oppression in all its forms is one of those clear mandates, whether it's economic, political, social, or legal. Like many cities in the U.S., Chicago faces challenges of inequities and inequality that affect too many of our brothers and sisters. Therefore, it is incumbent upon all Muslims to initiate, participate in, and collaborate with any effort that removes oppression and creates an environment that allows all of us to reach our highest potential and live with the dignity bestowed upon us by our Creator."

As the unified voice of Chicago Muslims, CIOGC found in the Black Lives Matter Rally and March an opportunity to partner with people of faith to act against oppression and injustice. As the Qur'an reminds us: "You who believe, uphold justice and bear witness to God, even if it is against yourselves, your parents, or your close relatives. Whether the person is rich or poor, God can best take care of both. Refrain from following your own desire so that you can act justly—if you distort or neglect justice, God is fully aware of what you do." Qur'an 4:135 Surat An-Nisā' (The Women)

The March for Community Control of the Police is a significant event in Chicago's history. Multiple communities in the city, led by grass-roots organizations and by youth of color, are demanding an end to police injustice by calling for the communities themselves to manage law enforcement.

As Imam Abdul Malik Mujahid, Volunteer Chairman, Justice for All, said:

> "Stand in Solidarity. Civilian oversight for the Chicago Police. Is it too much to ask? Everyone is coming. Churches are coming, mosques are coming, temples are coming. Labor unions are coming. Are you coming?"

Once again, the March for Community Control of the Chicago Police will be on Saturday, August 29, at 12:00 PM. The march will start at Federal Plaza, Adams and Dearborn, and end at Chicago City Hall.

This was truly a historic march for the Muslim community in Chicago to act in solidarity with the Black community's call for an end to police violence and establishing community control of the police. BLM was one of the most important civil rights movements since the days of Martin Luther King, Jr. and Malcolm X. As the article says, "As the unified voice of Chicago Muslims, CIOGC found in the Black Lives Matter Rally and March an opportunity to partner with people of faith to act against oppression and injustice."

I was very involved in the fight for community control of the police, attending many of the rallies and press conferences in front of city hall. I saw this effort closely aligned with my beliefs in social justice, anti-racism, and stopping the repression by law enforcement. At the time, I wrote multiple articles for the *Chicago Monitor* on the progress of the campaign. The following one was early in the campaign. The Chicago Alliance Against Racist and Political Repression (CAARPR) was the lead organization demanding what they called an elected civilian police accountability council (CPAC). Other organizations and unions, like the Chicago Teachers Union, were also supporters. The early marches were ignored by the city government and were portrayed, like the large march above, as having only very vague demands about police accountability. The response from the city was usually, "We already have a Police Review Board in place for handling these 'bad apples' issues, and in any case, it is not a widespread problem for the CPD." This response ignored the fact that the city had been paying out millions of dollars a year to settle cases of police misconduct and the Board members were all appointed by the mayor with no community input. This was the same mayor who tried to cover up the case of the unjustified killing of Laquan McDonald. In his case, there was an actual video of the police conduct that under pressure, the city finally released. This next article expresses my frustration with the Mayor and the CPD dragging their feet on this obvious problem.

Why is the Demand for Community Control of the Chicago Police Being Ignored?

Chicago Monitor
By Bill Chambers - December 11, 2015

Chicago protest police crimes.

On December 10, 2015, International Human Rights Day, over 500 people rallied and marched in Chicago, demanding an elected Civilian Police Accountability Council (CPAC) – meaning true community control of the Chicago Police Department (CPD). But as has been true every time Chicagoans in the hundreds have made this very specific demand, the Chicago local media, as well as the Mayor's office and City Council have completely ignored it.

Sister of Heribito Gobinez

The protest was initiated by the Chicago Alliance Against Racist and Political Repression (CAARPR) and included organizations such as the Black Lives Matter Movement, We Change Genocide, Fearless Leading by the Youth (F.L.Y.), and the Black Youth Project 100 (BYP 100). It began in Federal Plaza with the crowd listening to the stories of the family members of the many victims of police violence. They heard from relatives who spoke of the killing of Laquan McDonald, Ronald Johnson, Flint Farmer, and many others. The CPD victims were from both the Black and Latino communities of the city. The sister of Herbito Gobinez, who died in CPD custody in July, demanded the release of the police video and a federal investigation of his death. The Gobinez family made this same demand last summer and were told, "The investigation is ongoing and will take time." The Gobinez case was just one more example of a victim of CPD violence who had been put off by the claim that the mayor-appointed "Independent" Police Review Board (IPRB) was taking its time to investigate the case. As we learned from the Laquan McDonald case, it took ongoing protests to make the IPRB act.

The CAARPR and the survivors/victims of police crimes of murder and torture also delivered a letter/complaint to the U.S. Department of Justice (DOJ). This letter offered detailed, factual allegations made by over fifty signatories to the letter who were and are victims of police crimes and torture. The survivors/victims also filed formal complaints individually to further demonstrate to the DOJ that there is a pattern and practice of racial discrimination when it comes to law enforcement in the City of Chicago.

With chants of "16 shots and a cover-up," the marchers continued through the Loop and onto City Hall. At one point, the marchers surrounded City Hall with a police tape that contained all the victims of CPD violence. There were, of course, chants for Mayor Rahm Emanuel and Cook County State's Attorney Anita Alvarez to resign, but the focus was "no peace, no justice, no racist police."

CPAC has been written up in a draft ordinance for over a year. There was a protest in August with over 3,000 Chicagoans from the Black, Latino, Arab, Muslim, and many more communities demanding the implementation of CPAC even before the Laquan McDonald video was released and before the Department of Justice investigation into the CPD was announced. The city administration and city aldermen met that very clear demand last August with a deafening silence.

The CPAC resolution has the primary goal of making a systematic change in how Chicago's communities are policed. The Council, consisting of elected community members from all the police districts, would be empowered to hold police accountable for the crimes they commit and to control and decide how Chicago communities are policed. And this is the control that the Mayor and the CPD do not want to give up.

Now, the demand for community control of the police has been made once again. This is the one concrete change that can be accomplished by the City Council right now that will prevent CPD crimes from going on for months or years without any action. The DOJ investigation will likely take months like it did for Ferguson (six months) and Cleveland (21 months). People like Herbito Gobinez deserve justice now, not even more months from now.

In his speech to the City Council, Mayor Rahm Emanuel said

"We are here today because Chicago is facing a defining moment on the issues of crime and policing, and the even larger issues of truth, justice and race...We can either be defined by what we have failed to do — or what we choose to do."

If the Mayor is serious about that, his administration can choose to introduce the CPAC resolution to the City Council tomorrow. Mayor – it's already written down for you – just implement it.

It was clear to everyone who was involved in this campaign that Mayor Rahm Emanuel was doing everything he could to not act on any proposal for community control of the police. At the time when this article was written, a large number of community organizations were demanding that some form of community involvement be implemented to review these cases of police misconduct. The current Police Review Board created by the Mayor was ineffectual at stopping these killings, and most often, the policeperson involved had no consequences.

This next article is further along in the campaign and goes into detail about the obstacles the city was putting in the way of any type of reform of the CPD. Even the Obama Administration had put the CPD under Federal investigation by the DOJ after the murder of Laquan McDonald by CPD officer Jason Van Dyke. When the Trump Administration came to power in 2016, all federal investigations into police departments across the country were halted.

Times Up for Community Control of the Chicago Police

Muslim Journal
By Bill Chambers
06/21/20

Chicago is the only large city in America with a police force with a history of racism, surveillance of activists, torture, murder, and other forms of police violence that has never been reformed. Let that fact sink in.

From surveillance and attacks on anti-war activists, civil rights marchers with Martin Luther King, Jr.; rioting at the Democratic National Convention in 1968; helping murder Fred Hampton Jr. of the Black Panther Party; the torture of over 200 suspects under former Chicago Police Department (CPD) detective and commander Jon Burge; and the over 3,500 suspects, 82% of which are Black, secretly interrogated at the CPD's Homan Square facility; killing and cover-up of Black men like Laquan McDonald; and most recently the Chicago Police Department (CPD) missing 70% of the deadlines for reform in the First Year of the Department of Justice (DOJ) Consent Decree. On June 19 of this year, "a new report from the independent monitor overseeing the federal consent decree to reform the CPD shows...the city missed 89 deadlines and met just 35 in the first year of the decree." (NBC News Chicago).

The CPD had been under Federal investigation by the DOJ during the Obama Administration after the murder of Laquan McDonald by CPD officer Jason Van Dyke. When the Trump Administration came to power in 2016, Attorney General Sessions scuttled all the police department investigations, including the one in Chicago. The State Attorney General Lisa Madigan filed a lawsuit in August 2017 to keep the five-year court-ordered consent decree in place. Mayor Lori Lightfoot and CPD Superintendent Brown's joint response to this lack of progress was to say the report "illustrates how the level of transformational change and reform that we are working towards cannot be achieved overnight." Their response reflects a long history of resistance to CPD reform and a refusal to put structural changes in place that make this reform happen. Just remember there is a reason why the CPD was put under a court-ordered consent decree by the Obama Administration to force reform.

If the global movement for #BlackLivesMatter teaches us anything, it's that "reform" is not enough and that structural changes in how America, and especially cities like Chicago, do policing must be implemented. Thus far, Mayor Lightfoot's only response has been to start a new "Use of Force Working Group" that includes community members such as Arewa Karen Winters, great aunt of Pierre Loury, killed by Chicago police in 2016 and leader of Justice for Families. During the press conference, Winters called officers "psychopaths with guns." This is not implementing structural change in policing; this is not even making reforms.

Chicago has a recent history of demanding community control of the CPD that came way before the demands of activists for that control in the last month.

In August of 2015, when Rahm Emanuel was mayor, as a logical follow-on to its successful initiative to pass a resolution designating May 19 as "Malcolm X Day" in the State of Illinois, the Council of Islamic Organizations of Greater Chicago (CIOGC) supported and mobilized for an August 29 mass march for community control of the police. The march was initiated by the National Alliance Against Racist and Political Repression (NAARPR), which has been fighting for a Civilian Police Accountability Council (CPAC) for many years. With the momentum built by NAARPR, the Black Lives Matter Movement, We Change Genocide, Fearless Leading by the Youth (F.L.Y.), and many other organizations – the demand for civilian control over the Chicago Police had grown into a mass movement of solidarity between community organizations in the city. With the CIOGC being a federation at the time of over 60 greater Chicagoland Islamic organizations representing over 400,000 Muslim Americans, the Chicago Muslim community actively helped to mobilize for this march. The August 29 march included over 3,000 Chicagoans from every community in the city demanding community control over the police.

The Civilian Police Accountability Council (CPAC) ordinance that was introduced into the City Council was defeated by then Mayor Rahm Emmanuel, the FOP Union, and the mayor's allies in the City Council.

On June 12, hundreds marched through Chicago's Washington Park neighborhood, demanding the defunding of the CPD and the creation of CPAC. The march and rally were organized by the National Alliance Against Racist and Political Repression, Black Lives

Matter Chicago, Southsiders Organized for Unity and Liberation, and many other organizations.

Now Chicago has another movement for community control of the police, with many of the same organizations, such as BLMChicago and the NAARPR, once again demanding that there be a structural change in the CPD and community control of the police become a reality. The Civilian Police Accountability Council (CPAC) ordinance has been improved. In addition to appointing the Police Superintendent, having its own budget, and making the final decisions on police disciplinary action, there have been three significant changes.

1) Originally there were elected representatives from each of the city's 22 police districts. Now, they have been collapsed into 11 equally sized districts.

2) Now, there are requirements for anyone running for the Council to have a two-year history of activism in civil rights or human rights organizations.

3) The current Police Board (handles final review of cases of misconduct) and the Civilian Office for Police Accountability or COPA (investigates cases and recommends discipline) will remain in place, but instead of the director of each group being appointed by the Mayor (e.g., Rahm Emmanuel created COPA), CPAC will appoint the directors.

Across the country, there have been demands to #DefundthePolice. It is important to remember that the ability to shift funding from the police to other social services in the city will never be effective without true community control of the police. Right now, it's on the whim of whoever the current major is, and our mayor has not indicated any desire to shift any funds.

The current "police reform" bill supported by Mayor Lightfoot and many Chicago community organizations is called Grassroots Alliance for Police Accountability or GAPA. GAPA allows the mayor, whoever that is at the time, to still appoint its members, appoint the Police Superintendent and the director of COPA, and essentially maintain control over all police investigations and decisions regarding police crimes. This is not community control of the police – it's a community advisory board appointed by the mayor with no real power. There are efforts right now to get the new CPAC ordinance passed in the new City Counsel, and there still is resistance.

Times Up for the Chicago Police Department to reform itself or to be half-heartedly reformed by the Mayor. There is a movement once again for true community control of the Chicago Police. Muslims from across Chicagoland supported it in 2015. It's time for us to not only support it, but to demand that it be implemented.

This last article about Community Control of the Police indicates the delaying tactics the city used to avoid passing the ordinance. Eventually, an ordinance did get passed that was a combination of CPAC from the Chicago Alliance Against Racist and Political Repression (CAARPR) and the Grassroots Alliance for Police Accountability or GAPA, a version that other grass roots community organizations created. The most important thing that happened was that there are community leaders being elected to serve on the police review board and while I write this there are elections going on for those seats.

Genocide in Gaza (2024-2025)

"Refugees from Gaza" by Elaine Fleming 2023

The war on Gaza by Apartheid Israel began on October 7, 2023, when Hamas forces overran the small outposts of the Israeli army, killing 1,140 soldiers and settlers. Hamas also took 240 hostages with them back to Gaza. Apartheid Israel's extensive bombing campaign began quickly, and an invasion of all of Gaza by Israeli troops continued after that. As of October 2023, Gaza had been under a brutal blockade for 18 years in conditions many reported as looking like "an open-air prison." I preferred the term "concentration camp" since the Palestinians living there were not guilty of anything other than wanting their homes and land back.

While I am writing this memoir, the Israeli genocide in Gaza has been going on for sixteen months. A very tenuous ceasefire has taken effect with prisoner exchanges on both sides. Almost no one believes it will last to phase two (which includes Israeli troop withdrawals).

"Ramadan in Gaza" by Elaine Fleming 2024

At the start of the war in October 2023, the Chicago Coalition for Peace in Palestine held almost daily protests that were attended by thousands. As the war wore on, protests were usually held weekly or if the Israelis had committed some major atrocity. I personally attended some of these protests and found it hard to shake the feeling they had no effect, reminding me of all the huge protests against the war in Iraq and that the war still went ahead. Over 18 college campuses, including DePaul University in Chicago, had encampments to protest the war but were met by police violence and university administration intransigence.

Gaza protest in Chicago

But over time, it did seem like these protests did have an impact on the Biden Administration, especially during primaries in states like Michigan that organized over 100,000 people to write "uncommitted" on their ballot. There were efforts to try to negotiate a ceasefire (that was undermined every time by Netanyahu's end goal of destroying Hamas) and to find ways of getting by the Israelis' purposeful starving the Palestinians by limiting humanitarian aid.

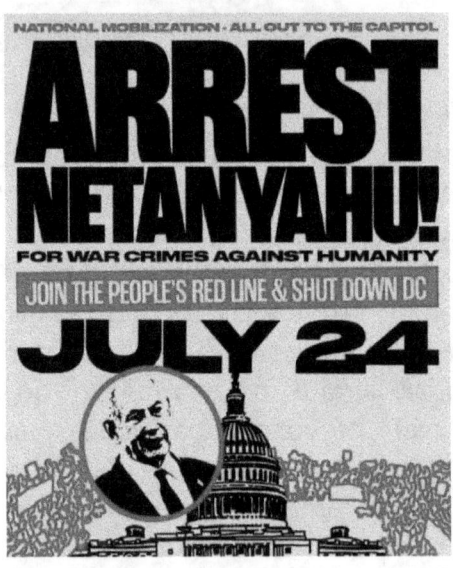

The Biden Administration's unwavering support for the Netanyahoo government during this period led to the International Court of Justice (ICJ) to take up a case for genocide put forth by the South African government. The result was the court warned the Israelis to stop doing actions that would constitute genocide. The Israeli government ignored the warning. In May 2024, the ICJ's prosecutor requested arrest warrants for Israeli Prime Minister Benjamin Netanyahu, his defense chief, and three Hamas leaders over alleged war crimes. Even with all this happening, Netanyahoo was still invited to speak to Congress by the Republican House Speaker Representative Mike Johnson. There was a movement by about half of the Democrats not to attend his speech and there were thousands of protestors in DC when he did come on 7/24/24. VP Kamala Harris said she had "another campaign engagement" so she wouldn't have to stand in the back of him while he gave his speech. Netanyahoo's speech was horrible, as my continual Facebook post will attend to:

Scumbag war criminal beginning speech after standing ovation for genocide.

"It's civilization against barbarism."

Netanyahoo is repeating all Apartheid Israel propaganda about rapes, babies being burned alive, etc. He talked about all the hostages he helped rescue, but the truth is that the number was about 3, and one was in the audience. He bragged that he had good meetings with hostage families, which was actually reported to go badly because they were so angry that he had not worked hard enough to free their loved ones.

He went so far as to make a claim about Biden, saying, "He's a proud Irish American Zionist." We were supposed to think that this was a compliment. It isn't, and it is also false because real Irish support Palestinians. Then Netanyahoo spent the last ten minutes praising Israel Occupation Forces soldiers who were in the audience. Saying that they "Rose up like lions." Lions who murder women and children?

Now, he is saying many Jews stand with terrorists. "They should be ashamed of themselves." Saying that Iran is funding American protests against Israel. "For all we know, Iran funds the protesters outside- you are becoming Iran's useful idiots."

Now, he is attacking college presidents "who couldn't bring themselves to condemn genocide against Jews...the attacks on Israel are attacks on Jews everywhere." Using every Zionist trope criticizing "blood libel against the Jewish state." I watched as the courageous Rep. Rashida held up a sign "stop genocide". A lone voice in the overwhelming welcome of this cruel racist.

Netanyahoo: "IDF should be commended for what they did...ICC is trying to shackle Israel's hands from defending itself...soon it will come for other democracies like America...Iran wants to impose radical Islam on the rest of world...Only my country stands in their way...We are not just protecting ourselves. We are protecting you. Our victory will be your victory."

Throughout all this time, there was a continual undervaluing of Palestinian lives. In order to remember that this attitude has been happening a very long time, the following article was from the last large loss of Palestinian life in the Gaza war in 2014. At that time, the world was shocked at the level of civilian casualties. At that time, the count was 2,000. The article describes one of the protests in Chicago that was replicated around the world. Reading this now, it seems hard to believe that only ten years later, there would be a full genocide of the Palestinian people happening in Gaza. This protest in Chicago was 8,000 people, one of the largest ever held in the city in support of Palestine.

Chicago Protests Media Silence On Palestinian Deaths In Gaza

Chicago Monitor
Bill Chambers - August 12, 2014

Last Sunday, an estimated 8,000 people protested in Chicago against the media silence on the over 2,000 deaths in Gaza during the current conflict. Proving the point, the protest was barely covered by the local media.

With a ceasefire ending the day before and fighting resumed, the Chicago protestors had reason to believe that the large number of civilian deaths in Gaza would be still newsworthy. But surveying the local Chicago news media, only one TV news channel, ABC Channel 7, and one Chicago newspaper, the Sun-Times, even bothered to report on the protest.

The main themes of the march and rally were the condemnation of Israel's killing of civilians and bombing of hospitals, schools, and mosques and a demand for an end to the seven-year siege of Gaza. The protesters stressed the magnitude of the assault on Gaza reflected in the latest statistics published by the Palestinian Centre for Human Rights.

2,008 Palestinians, 1,670 Civilians, Including 471 Children and 252 Women, Killed.

8,150 Palestinians, Mostly Civilians, Including 2,171 Children and 1,449 Women, Wounded.

As Hatem Abudayyeh, one representative of the Chicago Coalition for Justice in Palestine, stated, "The Palestinians in Gaza are living in an open-air prison. So what the Palestinians are saying is that you must end the siege and killing of the Palestinian people; you must end the occupation." From the meager coverage in the local media, those messages repeated by multiple speakers were ignored. In the ABC News Channel 7 report, the message was reduced to "They criticized the United States and Israel". The *Chicago Sun-Times* ran a piece that focused vaguely on only one of the messages of the march – "Palestinian flags fluttered through the streets of Chicago on Sunday as protesters descended on the Loop to demand an end to U.S. support for Israel."

The other distinguishing characteristic of this protest compared to previous marches for Gaza over the last month was the emphasis on world support for the Palestinians. This included marchers carrying flags from over 15 countries, including Brazil, Venezuela, Bolivia, Ireland, Spain, Iran, Iraq, Syria, Libya, and South Africa. Multiple speakers represented people from countries in solidarity with the Palestinians. Jorge Mujica, a long time Mexican labor activist who is running for alderman in Chicago this year, stressed that "I'm not here because I am running for alderman, but because I have always been here for the Palestinian community." He went on to stress Latin America's strong support for the Palestinian people. Zanoni Cuesta, an Ecuadoran activist in Chicago, spoke about the support of the people of Ecuador for Palestine and President Correa pulling the ambassador to Israel because of the attack on Gaza. Maria Pizarro, a Chilean activist in Chicago who was exiled from her country after the coup against Allende in 1973, also spoke of the broad support the Palestinians have across Chile and the Chilean government suspending its existing free trade agreements with Israel.

Me participating in the protest.

These speakers at the rally represented the broad support the Palestinian position has in other countries, but if you follow the local media in Chicago (and often the national media) you would believe the U.S. government's position of supporting Israel diplomatically and financially is the dominant world view. In addition, if you were aware that thousands of Chicagoans continue to march in support of the Palestinians in Gaza, you would still get no answers from the local media about why they were even protesting.

By the time my memoir is published, I can add a postscript that a ceasefire has been implemented, but only in phase one with prisoner swaps. We don't know if this ceasefire will hold. No matter what happens, nothing can erase the over 48,000 Palestinians killed by the Israelis in their political war of revenge. There was a movement to replace President Biden with another candidate (that I wholly supported) that gathered steam every time he debated or gave an interview but never materialized because of the resistance of the Democratic Party. The Party continued to claim Biden had no real problem. While I was working on this section of the memoir, the Republican National Convention (RNC) was going on in Milwaukee. Only a few days before, there was an assassination attempt on Trump. He was only grazed, but it added more concern that he would continue to rise in the polls over President Biden. I did not attend the RNC protest, but below is an article published by the Coalition to March on the RNC.

Thousands march against the Republicans on the first day of the RNC

Fight Back! News
By Ryan Hamann
July 17, 2024

More than 3500 march on the opening day of the Republican National Convention in Milwaukee.| Brad Sigal/Sigal Photos

Milwaukee, WI – After two years of work, the Coalition to March on the RNC culminated its efforts with a 3500-person rally and march on the opening day of the 2024 Republican National Convention. The Coalition was truly national in character, composed of more than 120 organizations representing all manner of social movements. The principle rallying cry of the broad united front was to fight against the racist and reactionary Republican agenda.

"The most visible figurehead of the Republican Party right now is Donald Trump, but we want to be clear: we are marching on the Republicans' entire agenda. Our speakers today represent a broad movement against the entire Republican platform," said Omar Flores, one of the co-chairs of the Coalition. "We are marching on every Republican state slashing funding for DEI initiatives in education, every Republican governor putting up more razor wire to militarize the Southwest border, every Republican voting for right-to-work bills, and every Republican signing bombs they are sending to Gaza."

"For decades Republicans have been on a mission to deprive the majority of people in this country of their basic human rights. Their attacks on Black and brown people, on women, on immigrants, on the LGBTQ community, and on the working class have destroyed the lives and livelihoods of millions of people. Defeating the Republican agenda is a matter of life and death for working and oppressed people," said Kobi Guillory, a leader with the Freedom Road Socialist Organization.

Guillory continued, "We have to protect ourselves in this country, and we have to stand in solidarity with oppressed people around the world. Our government is committing genocide in Palestine and reinforcing deadly militarism and fascism around the world. We live in the belly of the beast, the headquarters of the imperialist system. It is our responsibility to destroy this system so that people here and internationally can live their lives in peace, justice, and equality."

As is commonplace in Milwaukee and in other cities and on campuses all across the country, particularly since October 7, some of the loudest chants of the day were in support of Palestine. "Free, free Palestine!" "From the river to the sea, Palestine will be free!" and "From the sea to the river, Palestine will live forever!" were just a few examples.

"In the debate, we heard Trump say that Israel must be allowed 'to finish the job.' We know what that means, that Trump not only supports the genocide, but he also wants to intensify it, kill more and more Palestinians," said Hatem Abudayyeh, the national chair of the U.S. Palestinian Community Network.

"But Trump in Milwaukee this week and Genocide Joe Biden in Chicago next month shouldn't forget that the vast majority of the world stands with Palestine and its right to self-defense and resistance in Gaza, that the Palestinians and the Lebanese and the Yemenis and hundreds of millions of other Arabs in the region will continue to resist and ultimately defeat the U.S. and Israeli war machines, and that people in the U.S. want money for healthcare and childcare and jobs and immigration and education, not occupation."

One of the main goals over the two years of organizing the Coalition was to take their demonstration within sight and sound of the Fiserv Forum in downtown Milwaukee, where the RNC was being hosted. It was a pitched battle with the city of Milwaukee, the police, and the Secret Service, but ultimately, they won. At the point in the march where Fiserv was only a block away, Carly Klein from Reproductive Justice Action Milwaukee spoke.

"Wisconsin was one of ten states with pre-existing laws that banned legal abortion, and when Roe fell a law written in 1849 was immediately reinstated. Suddenly, anyone performing, assisting, or receiving an abortion could receive a felony charge and up to ten years in prison," Klein said. "We refused to sit quietly in the face of adversity, and, in September of 2023, abortion services resumed in the state of Wisconsin due to the pressure applied by militant grassroots organizations. Because when we fight, we win!"

Chants of "Fight, fight, fight! Abortion is a human right!" helped to drown out a handful of pro-lifers who'd climbed up onto the barricade surrounded by the marchers. From the onset, the Coalition had "Defend women's and reproductive rights" as one of its points of unity. It was expanded to also include LGBTQ rights in light of the stepped-up attacks by the GOP against those communities.

Many more people representing various groups from around the country spoke and gave greetings both before and after the march. Despite constant hand-wringing from the city about violence from protests, the actions organized by the Coalition were seamlessly executed, and everyone was kept safe, achieving their aim of hosting a "family-friendly mass demonstration".

With the mobilization against the RNC come and gone, most of the member groups of the Coalition to March on the RNC will now be pivoting their attention to the Democrats and their national convention in Chicago next month, with many of those groups belonging to the sister grouping that is the Coalition to March on the DNC.

"As those who stand against the war machine and for the rights of working and oppressed people, we invite you to join us in Chicago in August and support the buildup of what we aim to be the largest march on the DNC in history!" said Zhenya Polozova, a member of the Chicago Anti-war Committee and a representative of the Coalition to March on the DNC.

Polozova declared, "The ruling class will never independently grow a conscience and rescind their support for Israel's genocide or any of their repressive policies against the working class and oppressed people. We all have a role to play in ending this genocide and weakening the imperialist system. I'll see you all in the streets of Chicago on August 19th! Long live Palestine!"

This was the same Coalition that organized to march on the DNC. The turnout would be far larger, but there was more of an emphasis on pressuring the Biden Administration and Kamala Harris to take some action against the genocide of Gaza.

In another nod to Democratic President Johnson dropping out of the running for reelection in 1968 because of the very unpopular Vietnam War in 1968, on 7/21/24 Democratic President Biden dropped out of the presidential race. There had been a month of questioning his ability to govern after a disastrous first debate with Trump. He looked every year of his age by rambling, saying incomprehensible statements, and generally looking like everyone's failing grandfather. There was also a lot of concern among the electorate, especially among Arabs, Muslims, and young people, that he was doing nothing to stop the genocide in Gaza. (It would continue for another six months.) He also endorsed/anointed VP Kamala Harris and the news assumed she would be the candidate of the Democratic Party. Some Democrats suggested that there should be some form of short primary to test her popularity, but they were ignored. The Democratic Party was thrilled that they were out of the losing shadow of Biden and that they didn't want to chance to mess with this new "momentum". For the next few weeks, there was a love-fest about Kamala Harris among the Democrats especially given she might be the first woman President. (One of my good older female friends from Masjid Al-Taqwa said, "There is no way they are going to elect a Black woman President.")

For the most part, her campaign strategists did a good job of having her spend a lot of time in all the swing states and even some red states, but they failed to give her a message that distinguished her from the very unpopular Biden. Twice during interviews, when she was asked what she would do differently than Biden, her answer was, "I can't think of anything."

She also ignored the growing disgust with the war on Gaza and the impact that would have on swing state voters in states like Michigan. Rather than even saying the vaguest condemnation on supplying weapons to the Israelis for genocide, she actually doubled down on her support for Israel and parroted some of the Israeli propaganda (as did Biden) on sexual assaults by Hamas on Israeli settlers. That was proven untrue.

Two days before the first March on the Democratic Nation Convention (DNC) in August 2023, this brief listing of the casualties in Gaza from the *Mondoweiss* daily report gives a snapshot of one day in this ten-month war. It will give you some idea of what had been going on in Gaza the ten months before the DNC was held. It gives you an idea of the scale of destruction the Democratic Party was ignoring.

'Operation al-Aqsa Flood' Day 307: At least 56 Palestinians killed across Gaza as Israel bombs two more schools in latest massacres

By Qassam Muaddi August 8, 2024

Casualties

- 39,699 + killed* and at least 91,722 wounded in the Gaza Strip. The identities of 32,280 of the killed have been identified, including 10,627 children and 5,956 women, representing 60% of the killed, and 2,770 elderly, as of August 6, 2024. Some 10,000 more are estimated to be under the rubble*
- 620+ Palestinians have been killed in the occupied West Bank, including East Jerusalem. This includes 140 children.**
- Israel revised its estimated October 7 death toll down from 1,400 to 1,140.

- 690 Israeli soldiers and officers have been recognized as killed, and 4096 as wounded by the Israeli army since October 7.***

* Gaza's branch of the Palestinian Ministry of Health confirmed this figure in its daily report, published through its WhatsApp channel on August 8, 2024. Rights groups and public health experts estimate the death toll to be much higher.

** The death toll in the West Bank and Jerusalem is not updated regularly. This is the latest figure according to the Palestinian Ministry of Health as of August 8.

*** These figures are released by the Israeli military, showing the soldiers whose names "were allowed to be published." Israeli daily Yediot Ahranot reported on August 4, 2024, that some 10,000 Israeli soldiers and officers have been either killed or wounded since October 7. The head of the Israeli army's wounded association told Israel's Channel 12 the number of wounded Israeli soldiers exceeds 20,000, including at least 8,000 permanently handicapped as of June 1. Israel's Channel 7 reported that according to the Israeli war ministry's rehabilitation service numbers, 8,663 new wounded joined the army's handicap rehabilitation system since October 7, as of June 18.

To provide some context, the current number of Palestinians killed in Gaza when my memoir was completed in February 2025 is over 48,000. It is very likely much higher as no systematic attempt to recover bodies from the rubble has even begun. The majority of Gaza has been damaged or destroyed, including all schools, mosques, general infrastructure, and hospitals. Sixty percent of all buildings have been damaged.

There had been numerous protests in the U.S. and around the world against President Biden and Vice President Harris to stop sending billions of dollars in military aid to Israel. All of the protests were ignored. Very few Democratic politicians said anything about Palestine or would use the word "genocide" that the International Criminal Court (ICC), the UN International Court of Justice (ICJ), and human rights organizations had begun to use. None of this pressure had any effect on the policies of the Biden Administration or the Presidential campaign of Kamala Harris. There was great expectation that a large protest at the DNC and the growth of the "Uncommitted" movement, especially in Michigan, home to the largest Arab population in the country, to refuse to vote for Kamala Harris unless she changed her position on Gaza. Just in Michigan alone the Uncommitted were up to 100,000 people.

A few days before the DNC of August 2024, there was an effort to allow the leader of the Uncommitted movement or a Palestinian speaker to have some time to speak during the weeklong convention. The request was refused. Instead, they allowed an American family of one of the Israeli hostages to speak. The protestors coming to the convention clearly got the message that the genocide of 39,000 men, women, and children, including the destruction of all of Gaza, was not important.

The Coalition to March on the DNC, made up of over 270 groups, applied for permits in November of 2023. The City of Chicago delayed even discussing the permit until about a month before the DNC. This approach was typical for the city to delay permits as long as they can. The route the City offered was about three miles east of the United Center, where the convention was being held. The law allows demonstrators to be within "sight and sound" of the event. The Coalition took the City to federal court and eventually allowed only a one-mile march from Union Park where the rally was, to the United Center.

The Coalition rightly countered that if the expected 20,000 people showed up, many protestors would never be able to leave the park, and they would be "kettled" in that one-mile stretch. An alternate longer march was proposed and rejected. Five days before the first demonstration on the first day of the convention, the City finally provided a permit to use Union Park, but the Coalition could not use their own stage, sound equipment, and porta potties. Vendors were ready to have contracts signed for all this equipment, but now they could not get them signed. The Coalition went back to court for an emergency injunction to allow for this equipment. The request for an injunction was withdrawn when the constitutionality of denying the request for equipment was based on an illegal "content-based decision." There was no issue of "safety and security" so the City finally agreed to issue the permit only three days before the protest.

Meanwhile, the mainstream news media was fear mongering by running a film from the 1968 DNC and wondering, "Will there be violence again in the streets of Chicago?" They never mention that in 1968, it was later proven what happened was a police riot and that the protestors were given no permits to stay in Grant Park (a major Chicago park) after curfew. In similar fashion, when the current Chicago Police Superintendent Larry Snelling was asked what he will do with protestors who don't follow the approved route, he simply said, "They will be arrested."

The following is my article for the *Muslim Journal* on the Coalition to March on the DNC on the first day of the convention. It covers my experiences at the DNC protest. At least a memoir that began with me trying to figure out a reason to give to my parents to go to the DNC in Chicago in 1968 would include a DNC protest in 2024 when I was actually there.

Thousands March on the DNC to Demand an End to the War in Gaza

Muslim Journal
9/20/24
By Bill Chambers

Over 17,000 protesters from 270 different groups joined the Coalition to March on the DNC on Monday, the first day of the Democratic National Convention (DNC) in Chicago. The Coalition was very well organized, with security and legal support during the entire day. The lead organizers for the Coalition were the U.S. Palestine Community Network (USPCN) and the National Alliance Against Racist and Political Repression (NAARPR), drawing attendees from across the country. The protesters gathered in Union Park, about a mile and a half from the United Center where the convention was being held. After listening to a number of speakers, the protesters marched without incident the one and half mile march to a park about three blocks away from the convention center.

But this successful non-violent protest almost was not permitted. The Coalition to March on the DNC applied for permits in November. The City of Chicago delayed even discussing the permits until about a month before the DNC. The route the City offered was about three miles east of the United Center. The law allows demonstrators to be within "sight and sound" of the event. The Coalition took the City to a federal court that eventually allowed only a one-mile march from Union Park, where the rally was, to the United Center.

The Coalition rightly countered that if the expected 20,000 people showed up, many protestors would never be able to leave the park, and they would be "kettled" in that one-mile stretch. An alternate longer march was proposed and rejected. Five days before the first demonstration on the first day of the convention, the City finally provided a permit to use Union Park, but the Coalition could not use their own stage, sound equipment, and porta potties. Vendors were ready to have contracts for all this equipment but now could not get them signed. The Coalition went back to court for an emergency injunction to allow for this equipment. The request for an injunction was withdrawn when the Constitutionality of denying the request for equipment based on a "content-based decision" which is illegal. There was no issue of "safety and security" so the City agreed to provide the permit. But even this was three days before the protest.

Meanwhile, the mainstream news media was fear mongering by running a film from the 1968 DNC and wondering "Will there be violence again in the streets of Chicago?" They never mentioned that the protests in 1968 were proven to be a police riot, and the protestors were given no permits to stay in Grant Park (a major Chicago park) after curfew. In similar fashion, when Chicago's Police Superintendent Larry Snelling was asked what he will do with protestors who don't follow the approved route, he simply said, "They will be arrested."

Thankfully for all concerned, the "violence" was limited to 100 protestors from some unknown group who remained behind, trying to break through the police barriers after the march left the park. Only 14 people out of thousands were arrested. The fear that there might be a large number of counter-protesters ended up being ten people holding Israeli flags surrounded by double that number of police and press.

The line-up of speakers focused on the central issue of ending US arms to Israel while they were committing genocide on the Palestinian people. The organizers' strategy was to put the same pressure on Vice President Kamala Harris to change her policy on continuing supplying Israel with arms that were placed on President Joe Biden which was a major factor in his dropping out of the race. People were hopeful because VP Kamala Harris had made more comments about being concerned about civilian deaths in Gaza, but they also felt it was time for her to act. There were a large number of Palestinians and Muslims in the crowd, many indicating they would not vote for her without some change in policy.

Some of the major speakers included Hatem Abudayyeh from the USPCN and Tarek Khalil from the American Muslims for Palestine (AMP).

Dr. Cornel West, who was also running for President at the time, made a surprise appearance, speaking briefly about his support for the goals of the march, and was surrounded by press on his way out. This reporter was lucky to have shaken his hand before he spoke.

Hatem Abudayyeh (USPCN)

Hatem of the USPCN said,

"We are not going to let the top Democrats get a pass.... This mass of people is what they are afraid of. They are afraid of the unity between Black people and Palestinians in this country, between the Palestinian people and the undocumented immigrants in this country, and between the working class and the Palestinians in this country. I want to thank you for all that you are doing for our families and our people."

Tarek Khalil (AMP)

Tarek Khalil of AMP helped represent the large numbers of Muslims at the protest:

"Kamala Harris, we need justice for the Palestinian people, and I'm speaking! While you're speaking, Palestinians are dying. While you're speaking, hospitals in Gaza have been bombed and destroyed. While you're speaking, women, children, teachers, students, scientists, doctors, and nurses have been killed all with our tax dollars and US-made weapons. We are here at the DNC to tell Genocide Joe and Kamala Harris, not in our name!"

There were also a number of short interviews I did with some of the groups attending the march, including Jewish Voice for Peace, Organized Labor for Palestine (OLP), Students for a Democratic Society (SDS), and the American Friends Service Committee (AFSC).

Audrey and Malkeh (JVP)

"We are here because we believe in freedom and safety for everyone, no matter what race, how much money is in their bank account, or where they were born. We need to get this message across to the Democratic party that the best way to keep those people safe is to end the shipment of arms to Israel. We are here to join the call by the Palestinians to support a full arms embargo and the message to everyone attending the DNC that we demand, with the Palestinian people, an end to the genocide and to stop sending weapons and aid to Israel."

Organized Labor for Palestine

Richard Berg (OLP)

"I'm recently retired as an organizer for charter schools for the Chicago Teachers' Union. It's important for organized labor to be here to protest the genocide in Palestine. What's happening in Gaza right now is unconscionable. They've destroyed every school and every university with weapons and money supplied by the U.S. Here we are in Chicago where they say we can't fund our schools because COVID money is drying up, and instead, that tax money is going to kill women, and children in Gaza."

Daniel Wancher (AFSC)

"The top demand of this march is to tell the DNC that we stand with Palestine and want to stop the U.S. aid to Israel. The Israeli apartheid regime is using U.S. funding and U.S. weapons to continue its genocide in the Gaza strip. AFSC has long supported the cause of Palestinian rights. We have supported the Palestinians ever since their displacement during the Nakba. There are other demands of this march for immigrant rights, reproductive justice, and LGBTQ+ rights. We are supportive of all of those things because it's the way to build just peace in the world."

Fae Hodges (SDS)

"I'm from the University of Minnesota chapter, and we are here to say end aid to Israel and to agitate for a free Palestine. That means an end to genocide and apartheid and to have a free Palestine for all peoples. The Democratic Party and the people who represent us need to be accountable for immigrant rights, workers' rights, LGBTQ rights, and a free Palestine."

The next day, there was a video report circulated on social media of some of the 30 "uncommitted" convention delegates, mostly from Michigan, holding up a banner saying "Stop Arming Israel" during President Biden's speech. The "Uncommitted Movement" was made up of 100,000 primary voters who entered "uncommitted" on the ballot instead of voting for

President Biden because of his Gaza policy. Those holding up the banner were harassed, and blocked with "I Love Joe" signs, and one Muslim woman was assaulted by someone holding those signs. CAIR-Chicago published a press release on Tuesday morning:

The Chicago Office of the Council on American-Islamic Relations (CAIR-Chicago), the nation's largest Muslim civil rights and advocacy organization, today condemned DNC members for assaulting a Muslim woman and other delegates who were silently holding a banner that said, "Stop arming Israel."

Video from the Democratic convention last night appears to show a DNC attendee hitting a Muslim woman over the head with a sign for holding up a sign that said, "Stop arming Israel." Other individuals attempt to rip the banner out of their hands.

CAIR-Chicago Executive Director Ahmed Rehab said:

"The American people have every right to make this reasonable, humanitarian, and patriotic demand. If not in the people's arena of politics, then where? The violent censorship that seems always to meet this message to silence it only underscores its veracity and urgency, as well as the oligarchic stranglehold plaguing our politics."

The goal of the Coalition to March on the DNC and the Uncommitted delegates inside the convention is to put the maximum pressure possible on VP Kamala Harris to act on stop arming Israel so that she can still receive all the votes from the Palestinian, Arab, and Muslim communities.

Irish Americans for Palestine in front of the James Connolly Statue

The very first group I met at the march was, ironically, a new group called Irish Americans for Palestine. Some of them had never heard of Irish Northern Aid, so I was able to give them a short history of Irish Republican activism in Chicago. I joined the group, and we have been busy organizing events supporting Palestine and joining up with other groups to protest the Trump Administration's attack on the Federal Government and criminalizing immigrants, Muslims, and pro-Palestine supporters, among many others. But that is the next section, the nationwide resistance to Trump.

Resistance to Trump (2025-)

After running a campaign without a message differentiating herself from President Biden and ignoring the genocide in Gaza, Vice President Kamal Harris lost to Donald Trump on November 5, 2024, by 1.5% of the popular vote and decisively in the Electoral College, 312 to 226 votes. Kamala Harris lost in every swing state. Immediately, Trump claimed a mandate from the American people. I thought there was a possibility that Kamala Harris would lose, but I was surprised by the definitiveness of her loss. Everyone around me, including my wife Elaine, was crushed that the positivity engendered by Harris' nomination was brutally crushed. What I found especially frustrating is that even a minimal comment from Harris about the genocide in Gaza could have won her the election. This was confirmed by a poll that was done in early January comparing voters who voted for Biden in 2020 and did not vote in 2025. As reported by Dropsite News,

> "Twenty-nine percent of non-voters who supported Biden in 2020 said U.S. support for the genocide was the top reason they sat out the 2024 election, according to a survey by YouGov."
>
> --"Kamala Harris Paid the Price for Not Breaking With Biden on Gaza, New Poll Shows" by Ryan Grim 1/5/25

Many of the polls showed that the Democrats lost votes not only in Arab and Muslim areas but also in the African American and Latinx communities who normally vote Democratic. Even with this evidence, the Democrats have done little to examine why they lost and have been scrambling to stop President Trump's avalanche of Executive Orders destroying the federal government. I have yet to hear any mention of the genocide in Gaza from any Democratic leader. There has been great disillusionment about the Democratic Party which has failed to protect the most vulnerable communities and programs in this country.

The day before President Trump's inauguration there was a great deal of speculation about Executive Orders he would sign on day one. The one that was clearly planned was the mass deportation of undocumented immigrants. When I started to think about this, it seemed to me that America has a long history of deporting immigrants, so this was not anything new. I taught a class on the history of U.S. immigration law when I was at American Islamic College and this seemed like a good opportunity to update that presentation to include ways of fighting back. Trump's plans have been tried before in American history, as well as in his first term. It is important to know how people resisted these efforts in the past. Some of these plans, especially regarding immigration, Trump tried to implement during his first term and cities like Chicago had effective approaches for blocking these efforts that just need to be reactivated. On the next few pages is a presentation I gave to my masjid's Sunday Taleem (educational session) about the religious and racial history of U.S. Immigration.

The Religious and Racial History of U.S. Immigration

Bill Chambers

Masjid al-Taqwa Taleem
January 19, 2025

Social Justice is a Core Islamic Principle

- Quran directs us that Muslims have a responsibility to fight for social justice:
  - All "tribes" and "races" equality reaffirmed
    - "People, We created you all from a single man and a single woman and made you into races and tribes so that you should get to know one another." (Qur'an: 49: 13)
- Providing every person with "dignity, equality and justice"

Immigration Scope

- Voluntary and Involuntary
  - "Voluntary:" Chose freely to come
  - "Involuntary:" Slave, indentured servant, fleeing from oppression/violence
- Legally and Undocumented
- Path to citizenship?
- Temporary, revokable status: student or work visa

Immigration Law Determined by Religion, "Race", and Usefulness

- Religion
  - Name the top two religions that came here.
  - Religion long been used as a limit.
- "Race"
  - "White" always preferred, but who is considered "white" changes.
- Usefulness
  - Provides useful work function and can trump religion and race

Legal and Social Construction of Citizenship

- Legal citizenship changed over time
  - From state control to federal government control
  - Changing acceptance of race, religion, country of origin, or birth right
  - Ability for citizenship to be revoked

Legal and Social Construction of Citizenship

- Social citizenship changed over time
  - "You may be invited to the table, but that doesn't mean you are welcome."
  - Citizen without full rights of free movement, voting, running for office.
  - Born citizen (Native Americans, African Americans, Mexicans) but no full rights
  - Polarized racial hierarchy: Asians join Europeans at top; Caribbean, Latin American, (and Africans) at bottom

Legal and Social Construction of Citizenship

- Post-WWII "American Civic Religion" (Kambiz GhaneaBassiri - *A History of Islam in America*)
  - White and Christian preferred
  - Amorphous concept of loyalty to American democratic values.
- Post-9/11
  - Gap between legal citizenship and social citizenship (Zareena Grewal *Islam is a Foreign Country*)
  - "In Dearborn, everyone understands citizenship is more than legal status, that national belonging is fragile and can be withheld from those deemed foreign and different even if they are technically legal citizens."

Legal and Social Construction of Citizenship

- Making of Foreigners
  - Immigrants from outside the country as well as groups within the country
  - Designated "foreigners" as a political strategy
  - Native Americans, Women, the Poor, African Americans, Mexicans Americans, Latinx, Asian Americans, and political minorities (Socialists, Communists)

History: Unregulated Immigration and Its Opponents

- Colonial America to mid 19th Century
  - Free born white persons
  - Loyal to U.S.
  - Increasing categorizations through race

Unregulated Immigration and Its Opponents

- Colonial America to mid 19th Century
  - In phases, voluntary immigration.
  - Few restrictions for first 100 years.
  - Need for labor.
  - Fear that some immigrants wouldn't fit into vision of liberty: language, subversive, competition for labor, us and them, capacity for citizenship.

Unregulated Immigration and Its Opponents

- 1795 first immigration act
  - Five years of resident
  - No dual citizenship
  - Two-year advance notice
  - Denounce loyalty to other countries
  - Convince allegiance to Constitution
  - Free born white persons

Unregulated Immigration and Its Opponents

- Alien Enemies Act 1798 – Trump considering use
- 1864-1917: laws became very strict
- 1866 -14th Amendment – born here except for Japanese and Chinese
- Only 1% of Europeans denied

Regulation, Exclusion, and Racism

- 1870s to 1920s
- 35-50m Europeans and 1m Asia, Mexico, Canada from 1820-1920
  - Cheap labor in transition from rural, agrarian society to urban, industrial one.
- Movement to stop Chinese immigration
- 1882 Chinese immigration stopped for 10 years; extended 10 years when expired
- Growing racial superiority 1892 – law added more to restricted list. Wanted skilled immigrants.

Regulation, Exclusion, and Racism

- Immigration Act of 1924 banned all Asian immigrants became the only group prohibited from entering the United States by race
- Racism, religion, and poverty major factors in structuring immigration (e.g. quotas)
- Law change in 1965 provided "equal" regulated immigration from non-European world
- Three massive waves of voluntary immigration: 1840s & 1850s; late 1890s to WWI; and 1965 change in immigration law

Muslim Americans and Racism in American Society

In the aftermath of 9/11, there is a temptation among many immigrant Muslims to seek acceptance by mainstream American culture in exchange for a domesticated Islam that can only support the state and the dominant culture and never challenge these. (Jackson, *Islam and the Blackamerican*)

- As Sherman Jackson says that after 9/11, immigrant Muslims became a "suspect class" and now their chances of penetrating white supremacy in the US were "nil."

Trends in American Immigration

- History of Widespread deportations
  - In 1882, Congress passed Chinese Exclusion Act stopped immigration and deported Chinese laborers (skilled or unskilled) for a period of 10 years. First in American history to place broad restrictions on immigration.
  - Government formally deported around 82,000 Mexicans from 1929 to 1935.
  - 2001 after 9-11 govt deported thousands of Arabs, South Asians, and Muslims.

Trends in American Immigration

- Current time (2011-2025)
  - Large number enter illegally
  - Immigrants mostly non-white
  - Less opportunity: less jobs in industry propelling earlier immigrants to middle class; lower paying service jobs
  - Post-9/11 immigration laws increasingly more restrictive especially toward Muslims
  - 2024 increased public rejection of immigrants: used politically by Trump

Trends in American Immigration

- Myths and Realities About Acceptance
  - Ellis Island and the success of European immigrants
  - Angel Island and the "success" of Asian immigrants
  - Redefinition of "white" over time
  - Cycle of open and closed borders

Trump's Plans

- Large scale deportations
- Target "criminals" (even misdemeanors) & anyone around them
- Sanctuary Cities targeted first – Chicago on Tuesday ICE sending 100-200 to arrest 300 (Guardian 1/18/25)
- Red State law enforcement cooperation with ICE

Trump's Plans

- Restrict 14th Amendment (birthright citizenship) by using 1798 Alien Enemies Act
- Declare emergency to add Pentagon resources to border
- Travel bans
- Student visas cancelled from certain countries

Trump's Plans

Sanctuary City Chicago Raid – 1/21/25

- Likely target individuals going to work or coming back from work from 5AM-9AM
- Looking for individuals with outstanding warrants.
- CPD not participate and not interfere
- ICE agents often in plain clothes and may try to identify you by calling your name on the street.

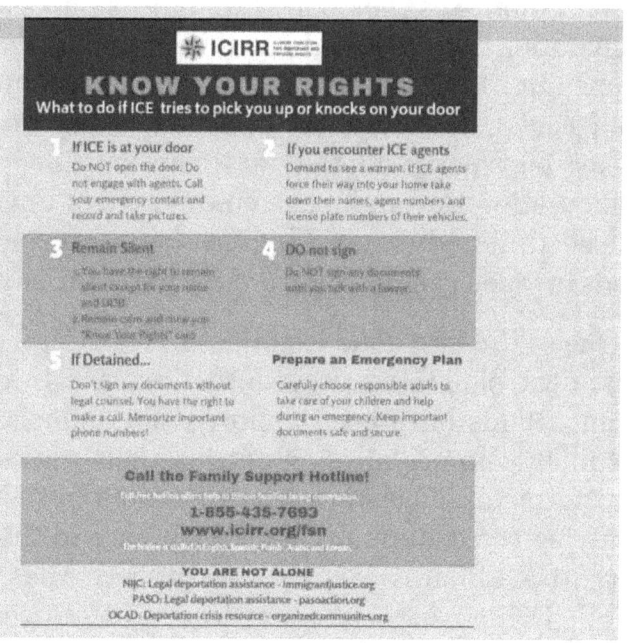

Stopping Trump's Plans

- Sanctuary Cities refusal to work with ICE
- Immigration groups and allies warning system for ICE
- Protests blocking detention centers
- ACLU and CAIR already organizing for legal challenges
- Turn out at airports for travel bans (CAIR-Chicago provided lawyers last time)
- Protect immigrants in your communities

The Sanctuary City raid in Chicago, as stated in the presentation, was "postponed". This was a good example of how preparation for raids like this can prevent them from happening. The Trump Administration said since the plan had been leaked, they could not go ahead with it. Trump planned to make a big splash with the start of his mass deportation plan on Inauguration Day and make an example of Chicago. But it was cancelled more because Chicago was ready and had extensive plans in place to stop ICE from invading the city.

One of the first good examples of resisting Trump is to have your own plans and procedures in place to deal with these agents. Raids have been approved for schools, churches, and hospitals who are all now putting their procedures together. Two forms of effective resistance are to not let agents in and notifying the community that agents are in the area. It is also not just ICE that is participating in these raids. It is also DEA, ATF, DHS, and ATF officers "deputized" to deport undocumented immigrants. Recently, Trump has started to send deportees to Guantanamo Bay.

Protests were organized around the country on Inauguration Day. The article below describes one in Chicago, even though the temperature that day was below zero.

Chicago: 2500 march in negative wind chill to stop the Trump agenda

Fight Back! News
By Faayani Aboma
January 21, 2025

Chicago marches against Trump.| Photo: Alec Ozawa/Fight Back! News

Chicago, IL – Negative wind chill could not keep the Coalition to Stop the Trump Agenda from mobilizing 2500 people to Federal Plaza in downtown Chicago to protest the inauguration of Donald Trump.

In the cold midday sun, protesters rallied at the Plaza, marched to Trump Tower, and then rallied a second time there – all to mark a new phase of struggle that will see the social justice movement face grave dangers in the agenda of Donald Trump and his fellow Republicans.

Over 80 organizations are members of the Coalition to Stop the Trump Agenda. They are united around the demands to fight the racist and reactionary Republican agenda, defend and expand immigrant rights, stand with Palestine; defend the right to unionize and strike; stop police crimes; defend women's LGBTQ and reproductive rights; and defend education and academic freedom.

A number of the forces organizing today's action led last year's March on the DNC, including the Chicago Alliance Against Racist and Political Repression (CAARPR), U.S. Palestinian Community Network (USPCN), Students for a Democratic Society (SDS), and Anti-War Committee. As in the case of the March on the DNC, the coalition is broad, containing forces from across the movement, including those in immigrant rights, Palestinian rights, Black liberation, labor, and more.

A plurality of march attendees were Latino immigrants, including three busloads of immigrant workers from the suburban DuPage County organization Worker Center of Immigrant Solidarity.

The involvement of immigrant rights groups like Illinois Coalition for Immigrant and Refugee Rights (ICIRR) and Mijente is important, especially since the Trump administration's very first attacks in the U.S. will likely be directed against immigrants.

"We came here in spite of everything; we have paid our taxes, we've built our families here, our kids were born here, and we're not going anywhere!" said Martín Unzueta, executive director and founder of Chicago Community & Worker's Rights and spokesperson for Mijente.

Other immigrant organizations mobilized as well, including the HANA Center, a Korean American immigrant justice organization, and Anakbayan, a youth organization fighting for Filipino rights and liberation.

In addition to immigrant rights groups, some of the Palestinian rights organizations that led 16 months' worth of protests against the Israeli/U.S. genocide in Gaza, including USPCN and Students for Justice in Palestine (SJP) – Chicago, took part in the march.

With a ceasefire in Gaza reached just last week, Palestinian rights groups have emphasized that such a victory was only the result of fierce resistance on the part of the Palestinian people and their allies across the world and not the benevolence of Trump, Biden, Blinken, or any other figure in Washington.

"This achievement only belongs to the steadfast Palestinian resistance and the people of Gaza," said Noura Ebrahim, USPCN member and co-founder of Boycott Divestment Sanctions – Chicago.

Also protesting Trump were Black liberation organizations like CAARPR, Black Lives Matter Chicago, GoodKids MadCity, Chicago Torture Justice Center, and more.

The involvement of Black liberation organizations is also important, given that Trump's previous presidency saw Black people in the U.S. experience further economic degradation, the intensification of police repression (such as the killings of George Floyd and Breonna Taylor), and more mass incarceration of Black communities. Trump will seek to continue that trend in his second term, though the resistance, as last time, will be fierce.

"We cannot allow Trump to carry out mass deportations of immigrants. If they come after them today, they'll come after the rest of us tomorrow," said Frank Chapman, field director of CAARPR and executive director of the National Alliance.

To mark Martin Luther King Jr. Day, Daryle Brown, a minister at the historic Trinity United Church of Christ, greeted the rally with a prayer.

Organized labor is also an essential element of the coalition, with the Chicago Teachers Union (CTU) and CTU's Black Caucus, United Auto Workers Local 2320, and United Electrical Workers – Western Region among the endorsers of the rally. Many of their rank-and-file members were in attendance.

"Fighting for the rights of oppressed people is not new in Chicago! We stand united here," said Dr. Diane Castro of CTU.

Other organizations in the Coalition to Stop the Trump Agenda include the Anti-War Action Network, Community Renewal Society, Arab American Action Network, United Working Families 50th Ward, and others.

You will notice that the 80 groups that were part of the Coalition to Stop the Trump Agenda are some of the same groups that have been part of anti-Iraq War, Pro-Palestine, BLM, and Community Control of the Police protests that you have already read about in this book. This Coalition demonstrates the long-held solidarity between all communities and social justice groups in Chicago. This is why Trump doesn't like Chicago. We are organized and we fight back.

Protests like this have continued across the country, often focused on immigrant rights. As far as tactics go, I think the time for large marches is over. They are helpful to get solidarity between the groups that are working together to oppose Trump and his policies. Trump has made it difficult to organize, given his "Shock and Awe" approach, issuing Executive Orders covering so many areas of basic rights at the same time. Trump is doing this intentionally to please his base but also to overwhelm the opposition, whether it is the Democrats in Congress or the social justice groups in the streets.

In three weeks, Trump has issued more than 53 Executive Orders covering policies including ending affirmative action for Federal contractors; declaring an emergency on the southern border to add more troops; gender references in the Federal government only men and women; establishing the Department of Government Efficiency (DOGE) headed by Elon Musk; a federal hiring freeze; pausing all federal financial assistance; eliminating all Diversity, Equality, Inclusion (DEI) programs and departments; withdrawing from the Paris Climate Accords; regulatory freeze pending review; withdrawal from the World Health Organization; and many others. These are only the ones he signed on Inauguration Day. Since then, he has paused all foreign aid and issued orders concerning K-12 education.

Given the broad swath of these orders that affect almost every area of American life, it is hard to put together a resistance plan for all of these. In the next section, I outline some of the resistance tactics I learned in a life of activism. The vast majority of these I learned from the young people who led many of the actions I participated in. I am sure there are many more ideas in the current younger generation and it is their time to lead. To make the point clear, all of these tactics are non-violent and have been used many times in the past.

Resistance Tactics

Prioritize – As I described above, the Trump Administration is attacking many areas at once. It is important to prioritize the efforts that are putting the most people in danger.

Right now, it would be the undocumented. They are in danger of being torn from their families, put in detention centers, sent back to their country where their lives may be in danger, or actually sent to Guantanamo Bay. The Sanctuary Cities are on the front line of this onslaught and are already making plans. Whatever setting you are in, a school, hospital, clinic, church, mosque, business, or targeted neighborhood, make sure everyone is not only educated about their rights but also know what to do when ICE and company invade their space. Flyers and online seminars of "Know Your Rights" information is critical. You don't need to even answer the door unless ICE has a judicial warrant and usually they do not. It should not be only the immigrant rights groups doing this pushback. It should be the coalition of multiple groups with a common goal that has worked in Chicago so well in the past.

Disruption- I recommend using disruptive tactics like targeting individuals from the Administration when they come to town, give a speech, or even go out to eat. Disrupting speakers from Apartheid Israel, whether they are political officials, IDF members, or dance groups, was a very effective tactic when the Palestine Solidarity Group – Chicago existed. These Israelis stopped coming to Chicago. The Trump Administration is like the Apartheid Israel government, i.e., racist, religious supremacist, undemocratic, supports genocide, doesn't care about international law, and does not believe all citizens deserve equal rights. I'm sure that people can think of many more disruptive tactics than those I have listed here.

Boycotts - Boycott companies and their products who were out front supporters of Trump, like Tesla and Metaor removed their Diversity Equality Inclusion (DEI) departments now that Trump has rolled them back in Federal agencies. Some of the companies that rolled back or eliminated their DEI policies were Walmart, Target, Amazon, GM, Pepsi, Chipotle, McDonalds, Disney, Comcast, PBS, and Google. Companies who defended their DEI program include Cosco and Apple. For successful boycotts, it is important to pick one or two targets that are possible for people to give up easily or move to another option. For example, buying a different electric car instead of a Tesla or not eating at McDonalds. For social media companies like Meta and Google, do not buy anything advertised or sponsored on Facebook, Instagram, or Google. That is how they make their money. If you can find an effective alternative platform, then switch. If you choose a single target, it is easier to see the real impact of the boycott. Coalition groups with experienced organizers should be the ones setting this strategy. One person or single group declaring a "national boycott" will not be effective and only makes people discouraged when it fails. Be patient. As I described elsewhere, boycotts can be very effective but they also can take a long time to work.

Boycott and Divestment Against Apartheid Israel - There is also a greater opportunity to start effective BDS campaigns in the U.S., where so far they have been marginally effective before. This year, Starbucks announced losses between $6-7 billion from the boycott of their products. Apartheid Israel's image has collapsed in the minds of many Americans, especially young people and an increasing number of Jews. BDS needs to step up its targets to include any Israeli product. Before, the focus was on products produced in the illegal settlements. Even in this approach, take the lead from the Palestinian-led BDS campaign to ensure these are global actions. The Palestinian civil society's call in July 2005 for Boycott, Divestment, and Sanctions against Israel was issued until it complies with International Law and Universal Principles of Human Rights (BDSmovement.net). This call includes multiple areas of boycott, not just products. For example, in the arts, an Israeli Dance Group's performance in Chicago was so disrupted by a protest they never came back. In education, an action could be not participating in exchange programs or attending conferences in Apartheid Israel. In sports there is currently a campaign to kick the Israelis out of FIFA. There are many more areas where Israelis can be boycotted.

Lawsuits - In the last year, there has been ramped-up repression against students who are pro-Palestine and getting expelled from school. Groups like Palestine Legal, ACLU, and CAIR have started lawsuits against the offending universities.

While these lawsuits play out, students can restart divestment campaigns against any university investment in companies that support the occupation in Palestine. Especially public universities need to have trustee meetings open to the public so showing up to those meetings, not being disruptive but continuing to pressure school officials. It is also important to give money to groups like Palestine Legal, who are fighting for free speech.

Congressperson Pressure - The best tactic is to contact your Democrat Congressperson to pressure them to use disruptive tactics against their Republican colleagues. Encourage them to walk out to prevent a quorum on voting. You can also demand that they enter threatened agencies like the Department of Education and force their way in. If they are a Republican, contact them about how Trump's policies are destroying your business, your ability to get an education and healthcare, or have stopped sorely needed infrastructure projects in your city.

Support Local Services – So far it looks like many local services for health, education, housing, and food will have their federal funding cut. Many of these local agencies will need your money, food, and volunteer services to keep going while these cut backs are being resisted.

Most importantly, take care of yourself and your community while you are resisting. These are all tactics by a group of like-minded people. Keep yourself and your community safe. These are difficult times. Remember to always take the long view like the Irish Republicans who have been waiting 800 years for a free and united Ireland. The African Americans who have triumphed over slavery and Jim Crow and are still fighting racism. Or finally, the Palestinians who will never give up their land and their culture even after genocide.

Conclusion

Over my life as an activist I learned many things. As Spike Lee said, "Do the Right Thing" was a motto that I lived by. In most situations, if I was on the side of the people who were being oppressed and being denied their dignity, self-determination, and human rights, I was on the right side. It was not that complicated. As in the cases of Ireland and Palestine, there was an injustice done to a group of people many years ago that continues to deny people their rights. The media and the occupiers would always try to obfuscate the truth and talk about "good people on both sides" or that the colonizers/settlers have rights now too, "given the facts on the ground." Colonizers and settlers do not have rights, especially when they continue to deny rights to the colonized or the indigenous people.

In all the groups I joined and the protests I was part of, I worked hard to be aware of my own white privilege and be sure the groups or protests were being led by the Irish of the North or the Palestinians themselves. My role was to be supportive, and if I can use my white privilege in a way that supports the rights of others, all the better. These principles also apply to the anti-racism work I did over the years. That was one of the reasons I admired PAR so much, as they saw their role as fighting racism in the white community and being supportive of the Black community when called upon. I also never forgot the lesson I learned from PAR that the central contradiction in American society is racism. The laws, institutions, and foreign policy of this so-called democracy were all built upon racism and continue to prop up a racist system. The last fourteen months of the U.S. supporting a genocidal war against a people of color, i.e., Palestinians, with no one in power batting an eye, copper-fasted my belief of the racism inherent in U.S. foreign policy. If the same thing was happening in any white country as it is in Ukraine, the U.S. would be eagerly sending them armaments to stop the invader.

My activism in Ireland did seem to make a difference even if it has not yet led to its final goal, i.e., a united Ireland. The fight in Ireland has been going on for 800 years and soon with the popularity of Sinn Fein across the country and a new Labour government in power in the UK, it is possible to envision a united Ireland. What's made the difference in Ireland? Having real leaders on both sides who have been able to lead their people in the right direction and a U.S. that for once took the right side.

My activism in Palestine is a much cloudier picture. Arguably, Palestine is worse off than any time in the last 75 years. The Israelis are continuing to steal land in the West Bank, and Gaza has been all but destroyed. For Palestine, there have been no strong leaders on either side, and the U.S. has actively taken the wrong side, for which it will be judged harshly in the future. The only sign of hope is the steadfastness of the Palestinian people and the increasing isolation of Israel from all other nations.

My anti-racism activism has also had questionable results. There have certainly been advancements in the rights of African Americans over the years, except we are in a period where those rights are being actively rolled back. It is hard to believe that we were given a choice for President between a racist, immoral, xenophobic, fascist and a representative of an administration that presided over one of the worst genocides in history. Our choice in that election sums up where the U.S. is: a rapidly declining empire. The election of Trump is even more an indicator of that escalating decline. My biggest regret is that I couldn't play even a small part in changing the decline of this country in morals and beliefs to become a true democracy. I still plan on being an activist and am excited to join Chicago Irish for Palestine, but I want to pass on my activist role to my children and all the young people who are still refusing to be part of an unjust America.

Appendix

Palestine Support and Solidarity in Chicago: 2000-2016

From Palestine in America - 2016

Chicago has a long history of demonstrating support for Palestinian national rights, beginning with chapters of the General Union of Palestinian Students (GUPS) at local colleges during the student movements of the 1970s and 1980s and grass-roots, community-based organizations established at around the same time—all supporting the foundation and ongoing resistance of the Palestine Liberation Organization. The fifth regional conference of GUPS was held in Chicago in 1986. This article will focus on the period from 2000 to the present when there was tremendous growth of both Palestine solidarity organizations as well as Palestinian-led organizations that continued the fight for self-determination and the right of return for all Palestinians.

Founding of Palestine Solidarity and Palestinian-led Groups

In the early 2000s, the focus of Palestine support work in Chicago was the education of the public on the military occupation of Palestine as well as continued protests in reaction to the Israeli attacks on the West Bank and Gaza during the first and second intifadas. During this time, one of the main groups in Chicago was Al-Awda Chicago, which organized several hundred people to support Palestine in Federal Plaza in 2002 with the theme "Palestinians for Life,

Refugees Until Return."Al-Awda Chicago also emphasized showing solidarity with other people resisting oppression, like the Zapatistas, and ran programs, including movies at local churches and community centers in Pilsen, about the Palestinian resistance and Zapatista organizing in Chiapas, Mexico.

During this same period, the Palestine Solidarity Group (PSG) – Chicago was also formed. PSG organized protests, conducted delegations to Palestine for activists, and produced events like the Café Intifada held annually at the Southwest Youth Collaborative (SWYC). The "Café Intifada" was co-founded by SWYC and PSG as a multi-cultural, spoken word event in support of Palestine and other progressive causes; many local universities, starting with DePaul in the mid-2000s, began organizing their own Cafés Intifada, and they continue to the present day.

A constant theme of this work from the 1970s to today is that solidarity with Palestine in Chicago always means solidarity with other oppressed groups in the city as well.PSG often focused on Palestinian political prisoners during this period, working closely with Addameer Prisoner Support and Human Rights Association in Ramallah to advocate here in Chicago for an end to administrative detention and torture of Palestinian prisoners in Israeli jails. The Director of Addameer, Sahar Francis, did multiple tours of the Chicago area (and nationally). In Chicago, these tours were organized with the Boricua Human Rights Network to provide mutual support for Palestinian as well as Puerto Rican political prisoners like Oscar López Rivera.

From 2005 on, there was the formation of multiple other Palestine support and solidarity groups, many of which would show continued growth. Although originally founded in 1996, Jewish Voice for Peace began to become actively involved in supporting other groups during this period. The US Palestinian Community Network (USPCN), a Palestinian community-based organization, was founded in 2006 with chapters across the country and held important Palestinian Popular Conferences in Chicago in 2008 and 2010. The American Muslims for Palestine (AMP) became active in participating in citywide protests and running workshops at local colleges. Chicago was AMP's most active chapter, and recently, they have branched into lobbying in Washington DC on Palestine issues. Suburban groups such as the Committee for a Just Peace in Israel and Palestine in Oak Park were founded and ran educational programs on Palestine. The small local chapter of the International Solidarity Movement (ISM) was also involved in supporting protests and became one of the local drivers for the Boats to Gaza campaign that also occurred during this time.

Impact of the BDS Movement

During the period before the foundation of the BDS movement in 2005 and the full launch of that global campaign, much of the organizing work in the city was to oppose the appearance of Israeli government officials, such as Ehud Olmert, whose speech at the University of Chicago in 2009 was shouted down by protesters for his being the architect of the assault on Gaza that year. Protests of Israeli government officials were also common in the UK and other countries around the world, with the added threat of possible arrests for war crimes. This is the reason that top Israeli government officials do not make appearances on college campuses or outside of Washington DC and AIPAC conferences anymore.

Chicago participated in the Academic and Cultural Boycott of Israel by multiple groups protesting performances of Israeli government sponsored groups like the Batsheva Dance Company (who no longer tours in the U.S. after 2012 when most of their performances were disrupted by protests). The Israeli Film Festival was also an annual protest target.

Chicago has a long tradition of protesting the Friends of the IDF and the Jewish National Fund (JNF) fundraisers held annually at various Loop hotels.

The Caterpillar shareholders meeting held at Northern Trust Bank in the Loop was a target of protests for six years until the corporation finally moved it to Joliet to escape the protests. Every year starting in 2004, a group of shareholders would try to pass a resolution to end the sale of militarized bulldozers to Israel that were used to destroy Palestinian homes, olive trees and build the Apartheid Wall. In 2010, the last year before the meeting was moved to Joliet, fourteen different protestors disrupted the shareholders' meeting.

PSG conducted a two-year campaign in 2009-2010 to end Chicago's sister city relationship with Petach Tikva – a city founded upon stolen Palestinian land and the site of what was called "Israel's Guantanamo" – the largest detention center for Palestinian prisoners. The city did not end the relationship, but representatives from Petach Tikva were forced to stop participating in the Sister City festivals and having their meetings in public for fear of protests.

There were two other major BDS campaigns conducted in the city led by organizations such as Jewish Voice for Peace and the American Friends Service Committee Chicago. One was directed at SodaStream who made their products in a plant in the West Bank. There were multiple protests at Target and Macy's to get the retailers to stop selling SodaStream products. That campaign eventually ended when SodaStream pulled out of their factory in the West Bank and their financial situation had declined propitiously because of the nationwide boycott activity. TIAA-CREF Financial Services was another campaign target to push the retirement funds company to divest from corporations that profited from the occupation, such as Hewlett-Packard, Caterpillar, and Motorola Solutions. That campaign also ended in success, as TIAA-CREF indicated in their financial reports that they had dropped investments in Caterpillar and SodaStream.

Chicago Protests the Assaults on Gaza

The growth of the Palestine support and solidarity movement in Chicago was accelerated by the two Israeli assaults on Gaza in 2008-2009 and again in 2014 when thousands of Chicagoans turned out for protests that continued for days. During the 2014 protests, the Coalition for Justice in Palestine was convened by many Palestinian, Arab, Muslim, and student organizations in the city. The

Coalition organized all the citywide protests at that time and continues in that role today.

The 2014 Gaza protests also led to Jewish Voice for Peace turning from a very small, often marginalized group within the American Jewish community to one of the fastest growing Palestine solidarity groups organizing their own protests and campaigns.

Chicago's Palestine Solidarity Movement Under Attack

In 2010, there was a concerted attack on the Palestine support and solidarity movement in Chicago and the Midwest by the FBI and the Department of Justice (DOJ) when 23 individuals, the great majority of Palestinians or Palestine supporters, were subpoenaed by a grand jury investigating "material support for terrorism." Several had their homes raided and ransacked by the FBI looking for evidence to support the investigation. All of those subpoenaed refused to testify and for some period, Palestine solidarity activists had to divert some of their energies to defending these individuals. The defense campaign was very successful, gathering support from faith-based groups, human rights organizations, unions, and multiple congressional representatives. None of the individuals was ever charged with a crime. This DOJ attack eventually focused on Rasmea Odeh, a leader in the Chicago Palestinian community, charging her with "unlawful procurement of naturalization," which has led to a multi-year defense campaign to stop her from losing her citizenship and being deported. Currently, an appeals court in Cincinnati has sent her case back to the court in Detroit for another hearing on admitting expert testimony in her case.

Dominance of the Students for Justice in Palestine Movement

But after this period of the movement is under attack, arguably the most significant development for Palestine support and solidarity in Chicago was the rapid growth of Students for Justice in Palestine (SJP) chapters at every university and college in the Chicago area. This was also a nationwide phenomenon, but nowhere was it more active than here in Chicago. Where a few years ago, developing a divestment campaign on a college campus was a non-starter, beginning with a very hard-fought campaign at DePaul University involving outside pro-Israel groups like StandWithUs and the Israeli Consult General of the Midwest – multiple student governments across Chicago were successful in passing BDS resolutions including Loyola, University of Illinois at Chicago, Northwestern, and the University of Chicago.

Just as the FBI and DOJ attacked a well-organized and successful Palestine solidarity movement in 2010, now, in 2016, the students at Chicago universities (and elsewhere across the country) are seeing attacks by groups accusing them of anti-Semitism and denying other students' freedom of speech. But this time, the attacks are from pro-Israel groups well-funded by an Israeli government feeling the financial impact of the global BDS movement. As these groups are trying to manipulate the law to undermine the SJP work on campus, there are also new organizations like Palestine Legal Support that are fighting back.

Solidarity with Palestine Means Solidarity with All Oppressed People

Following a Chicago tradition of solidarity with other oppressed groups begun long ago, Chicago Palestine activists were in Ferguson supporting the beginning of the Black Lives Matter movement. Organizations like the USPCN continue to march with the Chicago Alliance Against Racist and Political Repression, Black Lives Matter – Chicago, BYP 100, We Charge Genocide, and others to demand justice for police crimes and for community control of the Chicago police.

It is easy to forget that Chicago has a very long tradition of being a leading city in supporting Palestinian resistance to the occupation. Many of these activities chronicled here were not reported in the corporate media, and when they were, the numbers of protestors, the significance of the protest, and the solidarity with other oppressed people were always under-reported. That's why it's fitting to end on one more note of recognition for Palestine solidarity in Chicago – the publication here of the first U.S. Palestinian-led news service – Palestine in America.

Bill Chambers was a member of Al-Awda Chicago and the Palestine Solidarity Group – Chicago. He currently is Editor-in-Chief of The Chicago Monitor.

MuslimARC Releases Guide for White Muslims by White Muslims

The author of the MuslimARC Guide writes an introduction:

By Bill Chambers
Muslim Matters April 19, 2019

As people who are both white and Muslim, we straddle two identities -one privileged in society and the other not. We experience Islamophobia to varying degrees, sometimes more overtly depending on how we physically present ourselves, and we have been socialized as white people in a society where white people hold more social power than People of Color (POC). The focus of the toolkit is to provide resources and information that will help guide us toward good practices and behaviors, and away from harmful ones, as we challenge racism within the Muslim community (ummah) and in society at large." MuslimARC Guide

As part of our mission to provide education and resources to advance racial justice within the Muslim community, the Muslim Anti-Racism Collaborative (MuslimARC) is producing a series of community-specific guides to be a resource for those who want to engage in anti-racism work within Muslim communities.

The first in this series, the Anti-Racism Guide for White Muslims, has been written specifically for white Muslims by white Muslims under the guidance of the anti-racist principles of MuslimARC. While white Muslims know that Islamically we are required to stand for justice, growing up in a society that is so racially unequal has meant that unless we seek to educate ourselves, we rarely have the tools to address racism effectively.

The Anti-Racism Guide for White Muslims is a tool and resource that speaks to the specific needs of white Muslims who are navigating deepening their understanding of racism and looking for concrete examples of how, from their specific social location, they can contribute to advancing anti-racism in Muslim communities. The Guide also addresses views and practices that inadvertently maintain the status quo of racial injustice or can reproduce harm, which we must tackle in ourselves and in our community to uproot racism.

The Guide was developed by two white Muslim members of MuslimARC, me (Bill Chambers) and Lindsay Angelow. The experiences, approaches, recommendations, and resources are based upon our own experiences, those of other white Muslims we have encountered or spoken to, and research and analysis by others cited in the Guide.

As white people, we are not always aware when we say or write something that reflects our often-narrow analysis of racism and need to be open to feedback from Muslims of Color. My personal process of helping to develop this Guide made me aware of the many times I was in discussions with Muslims of Color, especially women when I had reflected better upon the privilege I experience as a white person and the white male privilege that comes with it. It is difficult not to feel defensive when you realize you may have said too much and listened too little on a topic that is not about you.

Talking about racism is a hard topic, and we expect that for many white Muslims reading the Guide, there may be a feeling of defensiveness and difficulty learning from the examples given because they feel the examples don't apply to them. You may feel the need to call to attention the various forms of injustice you feel you have experienced in your life, for example, where you felt like an outsider as a convert in a Muslim community. Our advice is to recognize that those reactions are related to living in a society where we are very much shielded from having to understand racism deeply and examine our role in it. In the spirit of knowledge seeking, critical thinking, and the call to justice communicated to us in the Qur'an as expectations that Allah has of Muslims, we must push past those reactions and approach the subject in the spirit of knowledge, skill-seeking, and growth.

"People, We have created you all from a single man and a single woman and made you into races and tribes so that you should get to know one another (49:13)." One of our most important purposes is to really "get to know" one another, build just and loving communities together, all the time knowing we all come from the same source and will return together. If this Guide does anything, let it inspire a deeper understanding of our unique identity as white Muslims and how to use it to advance a more just society.

You can find the #AntiRacismGuide for White Muslims at http://www.muslimarc.org/whitemuslimguide

Acknowledgments

There are so many people who have intersected with my activist life it will be difficult to name them all. But some of the biggest influences on me have been Hatem Abudayyeh, Joe Iosbaker, Maureen Murphy, Lamis Deek, Shirien Damra, Debbie Southern, Margari Hill, Imam Tariq Al-Amin, Dr. Aminah Al-Deen, Nesreen Hasan, Rasmea Odeh, Jim Fennerty, Jerry Boyle, Jeff Pickert, Muhammad Sankari, Hoda Katebi, Deepa Kumar, Tom Burke, Andy Thayer, Jennifer Bing, Brant Rosen, Frank Chapman, Lindsay Angelow, John McHale, Sarah Simmons, Kevin Clark, Dick Reilly, Bekah Wolf, Ali Abunimah, Sahar Francis, Ali Jaradat, Newland Smith, Colin Fagan, Conor McGrady, Davy Rasmussen, Alex Rezvan, Vince Casey, and Paul O'Connor.

I also want to thank all the past and present staff of organizations I was honored to play a part in their actions including People Against Racism, Irish Northern Aid, Clan na Gael, Pat Finucane Centre, Coiste, Palestine Solidarity Group - Chicago, the Arab American Action Network (AAAN), United States Palestinian Community Network (USPCN), Addameer, American Friends Service Committee (AFSC) – Chicago, Jewish Voice for Peace (JVP)-Chicago, Students for Justice in Palestine, Chicago Alliance Against Racist and Political Repression (CAARPR), Freedom Road Socialist Organization (FRSO), Code Pink, CAIR-Chicago, American Muslims for Palestine, Masjid Al-Taqwa, HEART Women and Girls, and the Muslim Anti-Racism Collaborative. I have nothing but admiration for the great work you've done in the past and, for some, the great work you continue to do. The legal monitors from the National Lawyers Guild offered strong support for all of our actions both during and afterward.

The one person who supported her activist husband with great love no matter what, was my lovely wife, Elaine Fleming.

About the Author

Bill Chambers is a full-time activist with a long history of civil rights, anti-racism, anti-war, Irish Republican, and Palestine solidarity work. As part of his activist work, Bill has traveled extensively to Ireland and Palestine to meet and work with community organizations. He has published multiple articles for the *Electronic Intifada, Palestine in America, Muslim Journal, Muslim Matters,* and the *Chicago Monitor* on Islamophobia, surveillance of Muslims and social justice groups, Palestine solidarity campaigns, Black Lives Matter, and the movement for community control of the police. He currently is a member of: Masjid Al-Taqwa Chicago (part of the Imam W. Deen Mohammed Community); the Muslim Anti-Racism Collaborative and the Chicago Irish for Palestine.

He has had a varied work career as a Student Support Services Coordinator and Counselor at the American Islamic College; worked in the Communication Department at CAIR-Chicago, Editor-in-Chief of the *Chicago Monitor*; a Mental

Health Unit Coordinator of an Adolescent Program, and a Technology Strategy Consultant for state and county governments including LA County and the District of Columbia. As a technology strategy consultant, Bill published multiple articles in technology journals and presented at numerous industry conferences for over ten years.

Bill has a BA in English from Northwestern University; a MA in English from Tufts University; a MA in Islamic Studies from the American Islamic College in Chicago; Professional Certification in Family Therapy from the Family Institute of Chicago; a diploma from the University of Galway in Irish Studies; and has begun a Master's program in Gaelic Literature and Culture at University College Cork. His previous books are *Huwarra Watercolors* (poetry and photos about his trips to Palestine) and *The Muslim American Fight for Social Justice: From Civil Rights to Black Lives Matter*.

Bill grew up in Detroit and now lives in the Chicago area with his wife, Elaine Fleming.

www.ingramcontent.com/pod-product-compliance
Lightning Source LLC
LaVergne TN
LVHW021754060526
838201LV00058B/3092